Effective Learning and Teaching in Modern Languages

How should you be teaching language to your students?
What techniques do the best teachers use?
Tailored to meet the needs of teachers, lecturers and tutors of Modern Languages, this comprehensive guide will help you to improve your understanding of the subject and will also enhance your practice in the classroom.

Effective Learning and Teaching in Modern Languages offers insights from the latest research into learning and teaching within the discipline, and also outlines innovative teaching techniques, covering all the subjects critical to a lecturer of Modern Languages, including:

- the demands made of students and staff in Modern Languages;
- the 'four skills', assessment, grammar, vocabulary and translation;
- technology-enhanced learning;
- residence abroad;
- subdisciplines such as linguistics and business, area, cultural and literary studies;
- professional development.

Providing both a clear overview of the discipline and a wealth of techniques, practical advice and useful resources, this book will be welcomed by lecturers or tutors new to the profession and experienced lecturers wanting to keep up with the latest developments and improve their students' learning.

James A. Coleman is Professor of Language Learning and Teaching at the Open University. A leading figure in European language education, he has published widely on language learning in the university context, including individual differences, audio-visual media and new technologies, residence abroad, and language testing.

John Klapper is Professor of Foreign Language Pedagogy and Director of the Centre for Modern Languages, University of Birmingham. He is a National Teaching Fellow and has published on various aspects of language learning and teaching, including immersion, teacher education, methodology and materials development.

D1145632

Effective Learning and Teaching in Higher Education series

Each book in the Effective Learning and Teaching in Higher Education series is packed with advice, guidance and expert opinion on teaching key subjects in higher education.

Current titles in the series include:

Effective Learning and Teaching in Business and Management
Edited by Bruce Macfarlane and Roger Ottewill

Effective Learning and Teaching in Computing
Edited by Alastair Irons and Sylvia Alexander

Effective Learning and Teaching in Engineering
Edited by Caroline Baillie and Ivan Moore

Effective Learning and Teaching in Law
Edited by Roger Burridge, Karen Hinett, Abdul Paliwala and Tracey Varnava

Effective Learning and Teaching in Mathematics and its Applications
Edited by Peter Kahn and Joseph Kyle

Effective Learning and Teaching in Medical, Dental and Veterinary Education
Edited by John Sweet, Sharon Huttly and Ian Taylor

Effective Learning and Teaching in Modern Languages
Edited by James A. Coleman and John Klapper

Effective Learning and Teaching in Social Policy and Social Work
Edited by Hilary Burgess and Imogen Taylor

Effective Learning and Teaching in Modern Languages

Edited by
James A. Coleman and John Klapper

Routledge
Taylor & Francis Group

LONDON AND NEW YORK

First published 2005 by Routledge
2 Park Square, Milton Park, Abingdon, Oxon OX14 4RN

Simultaneously published in the USA and Canada
by Routledge
270 Madison Ave, New York, NY 10016

Routledge is an imprint of the Taylor & Francis Group

Typeset in Bembo by
Florence Production Ltd, Stoodleigh, Devon
Printed and bound in Great Britain by
TJ International Ltd, Padstow, Cornwall

British Library Cataloguing in Publication Data
A catalogue record for this book is available from the British
Library

Library of Congress Cataloging in Publication Data
A catalog record for this book has been requested

ISBN 0–415–34663–0 (hbk)
ISBN 0–415–34664–9 (pbk)

Contents

Contributors

Elspeth Broady is Head of the School of Languages, University of Brighton

James A. Coleman is Professor of Language Learning and Teaching, Department of Languages, The Open University

Derrik Ferney is Associate Dean of the School of Law, Languages and Social Sciences, Anglia Polytechnic University

Agnès Gower is Language Coordinator in the Department of French Studies, University of Birmingham

Elizabeth Hauge is Senior Language Teaching Fellow in English, Centre for Language Study, University of Southampton

David Head is Professor of International Business Communication and Director of the Plymouth Business School, University of Plymouth

Diana Holmes is Professor of French in the Department of French, University of Leeds

Stella Hurd is Senior Lecturer in French, Department of Languages, The Open University

Sophie Ioannou-Georgiou is Adjunct Lecturer, Department of Foreign Languages and Literatures, University of Cyprus

Michael Kelly is Professor of French, University of Southampton and Director of the Higher Education Academy's Subject Centre for Languages, Linguistics and Area Studies

Marie-Madeleine Kenning is Senior Lecturer in the School of Language, Linguistics and Translation Studies, University of East Anglia

John Klapper is Professor of Foreign Language Pedagogy and Director of the Centre for Modern Languages, University of Birmingham

Tim Lewis is Lecturer in French, Department of Languages, The Open University

Paul Meara is Professor and Head of the Research Group, Centre for Applied Language Studies, University of Wales Swansea

Norbert Pachler is Assistant Dean of Continuing Professional Development and Deputy Head of the School of Culture, Language and Communication, the Institute of Education, University of London

Isabelle Perez is Senior Teaching Fellow in French, School of Management and Languages, Heriot-Watt University

Alison Phipps is Director of the Graduate School for Arts and Humanities, University of Glasgow

David Platten is Senior Lecturer, Department of French, University of Leeds

Rosalind Temple is Lecturer in French Language and Linguistics, Department of Language and Linguistic Science, University of York

June Thompson is co-editor of *ReCALL*, based at The Language Institute, University of Hull

Vicky Wright is Director of the Centre for Language Study, University of Southampton, and Senior Academic Coordinator for Strategy at the Higher Education Academy's Subject Centre for Languages, Linguistics and Area Studies

Foreword

Within Modern Languages, there is a long tradition of attention to the needs of learners, and of innovation in curriculum matters. This tradition springs partly from an awareness that language learners will always fall short of the skills routinely deployed by native speakers. It is also partly due to the inherent inter-disciplinarity, which demands additional support for learning while inhibiting the teacher from settling into a comfortable disciplinary pattern. And in more recent times, innovation has been spurred by the need to attract students who now enjoy a vast choice of university subjects. This book brings together the fruits of that tradition to provide practical assistance for anyone teaching in Modern Languages in higher education.

The editors have rightly identified language learning as their core concern. A growing proportion of students of Modern Languages are concerned primarily with language learning, especially where language forms only one part of their degree programme, and where they wish to develop a language competence in support of their studies in another discipline. But however focused a learner is on mastering the language, they continually encounter the embeddedness of language in culture and society. This is a challenge, since language is always *about* something beyond the immediate task of under-standing or producing sentences. It is also an enrichment, since the language learner comes to see the world in a more complex way, articulated in a language other than their own.

Language learning provides the context within which students of Modern Languages approach the associated disciplinary areas of linguistics, area studies, literature, cultural studies and business studies. This broad domain stretches over a substantial part of the remit of the UK Subject Centre for Languages, Linguistics and Area Studies, within the Higher Education Academy. Signifi-cant parts of this remit go beyond the common concern of language students, and would take them into more specialized areas of study. But readers of this book will find much to help them in the activities and information resources of the Subject Centre. A particularly valuable resource is the *Good Practice Guide*, a collection of commissioned articles by recognized authorities in the field. There are frequent references to it in the chapters of this book, and it is available on the Subject Centre website (www.lang.ltsn.ac.uk), along with a rich collection of teaching materials, extensive information, news and links related to learning and teaching in the three subject areas.

Modern Languages is one of the most interdisciplinary fields of study. The core activity of language learning leads away into almost every other field of study. Students and teachers are constantly presented with the opportunity to immerse themselves in a neighbouring discipline. The resulting itineraries are a source of renewal for the subject, and I am sure that this book will assist teachers in Modern Languages to navigate the diverse landscape as it changes around them.

Michael Kelly
Director, the Higher Education Academy's Subject Centre
for Languages, Linguistics and Area Studies

Introduction

James A. Coleman and John Klapper

The scope of this book matches the remit of the UK's Subject Centre for Languages, Linguistics and Area Studies, and thus extends from language learning itself into the domains most often linked to foreign language learning in university curricula. The principal focus is nonetheless on language pedagogy, since language learning is unique in many ways.

Coleman (2004: 148–49) has recently tried to summarize what sets university Modern Language study apart from other subjects. If the cultural and linguistic knowledge acquired is comparable to other disciplines, the development of a sophisticated mastery of one or more foreign languages entails some quite distinctive features that experienced language teachers will recognize.

First, there is the need for extensive practice to build the psycho-motor skills that underpin native-like fluency, pronunciation and intonation.

Then, there is the unique combination of conscious and unconscious learning. Some features are initially acquired deductively, as rules or language 'chunks', and are gradually internalized and automatized, while other features are acquired inductively, through extensive and meaningful use of the target language. This requires tutors to complement explicit teaching with plenty of structured opportunities for students to *use* the language in spoken and written interactions, and to help them acquire the techniques or strategies that will make them more autonomous and more successful language learners.

Individual and social psychology also plays a unique role in language learning. Everybody's personal and social identity has been built up through language and remains intimately tied to their native tongue, but language students have to be open to new identities that will inevitably follow from engagement with foreign languages and cultures. Moreover, they are being asked willingly to abandon that intuitive, confident control over their environment and over relations with other people which native-speaker proficiency guarantees.

Further, they will need to go beyond sociolinguistic and sociocultural know-ledge in order to acquire and demonstrate intercultural competence, an amal-gam of new values, attitudes and behaviours shown in adaptability and openness to otherness. Small wonder, then, that the role played by learner motivation, attitudes and anxiety is more crucial for foreign languages than in any other discipline.

To this list could be added the different role that new technologies play in language learning, facilitating repetitive practice tasks, providing access to written and spoken texts of the target country and to language corpora, and promoting interaction with other target-language speakers via discussion fora and e-mail.

This comprehensive manual for teachers of Modern Languages covers all the above areas as well as the principal 'non-language' domains. Part I takes a close look at the discipline as a whole and the people involved in it. The pro-file of students embraces what they bring from secondary education, and what they do once they graduate. The portrait of staff extends to the opportunities that exist for them to develop themselves as teachers.

Part II first provides an introduction to the theoretical bases of foreign language learning and an overview of research findings relevant to the teaching of languages. It then explores, in turn, the practical aspects of teaching, the 'nuts and bolts' of the discipline, as it were, including designing the language curriculum, the four skills of speaking, listening, reading and writing, grammar, vocabulary, translation and assessment, as well as best practice in using language assistants.

In Part III the focus shifts to different contexts for studying Modern Languages and to broader issues that inform all language study. Following a review of institution-wide, or non-specialist, language learning and the key role of residence abroad for language learners, successive chapters explore aspects of independent or autonomous language learning: in traditional face-to-face provision, in distance learning (which has started to make a significant contribution in terms of student numbers and methodology), and in 'tandem' partnerships. The growth of tandem learning exemplifies the major impact that technology is having on the way languages are learnt. The remaining chapters in this section consider the use of computerized learning packages, the internet and computer-mediated communication, and corpora.

Part IV deals with the different subject areas that make up the complex dis-cipline of Modern Languages. Overviews of linguistics, cultural, business, area and literary studies explain the nature of each subject domain and its role within the discipline, at the same time exploring links with language learning itself.

Each chapter in the volume refers the reader to useful sources of further information and includes reference to key texts on the particular topic.

Effective Learning and Teaching in Modern Languages is aimed at all those with an interest in university Modern Language teaching, but specifically addresses the needs of:

- new entrants to the profession;
- existing academics whose expertise is in literary/media/cultural/area studies but who are also required to teach language;
- foreign language assistants;
- postgraduates undertaking teaching alongside their research.

It aims to be useful and relevant to all academic staff, whether they are located in departments or schools of Modern Languages or in language centres.

While the principal focus is on practices within the UK, authors have consciously sought to address those issues that are common to Modern Languages wherever in the world they are taught.

Many of the chapters are equally applicable to any target language, but we recognize that we have not been able to deal adequately with English as a Foreign Language (EFL). English is the most widely taught language in British universities, with student numbers rising as they fall across other languages. Yet, several factors typically distinguish EFL from other language teaching:

- students have no shared native language, so classes are conducted in the target language, translation as a learning activity is excluded, and integrated independent learning is required to address the heterogeneous grammar and pronunciation needs;
- tutors are virtually all native speakers;
- there may well be no conversation classes, but since students are already undertaking residence abroad, the whole social and media context is a potential classroom, and so they need guidance to gain maximum linguistic and cultural insights;
- EFL is a year-round activity;
- specific purposes teaching is far more widespread than in other languages, particularly as EAP (English for Academic Purposes);
- accreditation and quality assurance depend on a different external agency.

EFL is such a valuable market that it is already well served with 'how-to-teach' books. Nevertheless, we trust EFL teachers too will be able to supplement their professional development by taking from this book whatever serves their needs.

Finally, the editors would like to thank not only the contributors to the book, but also Professor Sally Brown, who originated the project, and all those in Modern Languages whose innovative ideas and whose commitment to effective teaching and learning find echoes in the pages that follow, and have characterized Modern Languages as among the most dynamic of university disciplines.

Part I

University Modern Languages: students and staff

1

Modern Languages as a university discipline

James A. Coleman

Academics working in 'Modern Languages' are perhaps the most disparate disciplinary group in the whole of higher education. 'The study of languages and related studies is essentially multifaceted; few other subject areas combine in such an integrated way the intellectual, the vocational and the transferable' (QAA 2002: 1). So runs the Quality Assurance Agency benchmarking statement which we, in the UK, have developed as a reference point for ourselves. The professional identities of Modern Languages academics and students are so varied that an ethnographic study memorably portrayed them as rival 'tribes' (Evans 1988: 175–77).

As the conventional label implies, *Modern* Languages were established in European universities in contradistinction to *Classical* Languages, whose curriculum and teaching methods they initially adopted a century or more ago. For as long as university entrance was reserved for fewer than one in twenty of the age cohort, it could be assumed that entrants were already highly proficient in manipulating the written systems and rules of the target language. Language classes could therefore focus on the historical evolution of the language and on mastering its stylistic richness through grammar and translation (see Chapter 13), while the majority of study hours were given over to literature. In the canon, Chrestien de Troyes and Corneille, or Goethe and Schiller, replaced Euripides and Virgil, but the underlying assumptions remained unchallenged for decades: my father's French Finals papers of 1932 are interchangeable with my own from 40 years later. Successive centuries of literary output were considered to be the finest embodiment of a nation's culture and its highest linguistic achievement, study of which would bring intellectual and moral improvement.

Language teaching focused exclusively on formal written registers. Practical mastery of the *spoken* language was so little regarded that even into the 1960s the oldest universities actively discouraged students from spending a year abroad, lest the acquisition of merely linguistic skills interrupt the intellectual intensity of a Modern Languages degree.

But towards the end of the 1960s, the hegemony of Single Honours began to be challenged, initially by Joint or Combined Honours courses linking two languages, and soon, especially in the new universities and polytechnics created in that decade, by courses concentrating less on artistic creation and more on contemporary society.

By the 1970s, it was becoming increasingly evident that UK language students' proficiency no longer equipped them to write fluently and accurately or to tackle even modern target-language texts. Comprehensivization of secondary education and the adoption of communicative competence as the goal of language learning (see Chapter 2) meant that schools now concentrated on providing worthwhile but partial competence across the ability range, rather than helping future university entrants to approach native-speaker proficiency (see Chapter 2). While traditionalist language academics have for half a century put the blame on the secondary sector for no longer providing suitably proficient linguists, other responses have been more positive and appropriate. *Le Français en Faculté* (Adamson *et al.* 1980) based teaching on what surveys identified as the areas of weakness for university entrants, and since then university language teaching has increasingly built upon scientific data (see Chapter 5) and demonstrably effective techniques rather than merely traditional approaches.

The content of Modern Language degrees has evolved too. Literature teaching is no longer defined unproblematically as a set of great texts, but rather as a critical questioning of creative processes and of the nature of cultures and identities. Film and other media have acquired the status, the theoretical underpinnings and the methodological approaches once reserved for the written word. The natural alliance between foreign language learning and international commerce has been recognized in a multiplicity of Business Studies courses. Area Studies has expanded its domain from sociocultural knowledge of nation states and imperially based language groups to questions of borders, communities and critical approaches. Linguistic content has grown from dry History of the Language to a range of sub-disciplines exploring language systems, their uses and their roles in society. Chapters 22 to 26 of the present volume address these developments in more detail, while Phipps and Gonzalez (2004) provide a challenging, contemporary take on the evolution of the discipline.

In curriculum terms, the acquisition of foreign language proficiency is, today, allied to a multitude of 'content' domains, from the literary, cultural, linguistic, sociological, historical and political study of the country or countries where the target language is spoken, through cognate areas such as other foreign languages and cultures, to widely different specialisms from Economics to Mechanical Engineering. The typical language student is also different.

Alongside the specialist student profiled ethnographically by Evans (1988) and quantitatively by Coleman (1996), specialists in other disciplines were also following language courses. To the Combined Honours programmes with Law or Chemistry pioneered by the technological universities in the late 1960s and 1970s were added, through the modularization of curricula that typified the late 1980s and 1990s, a wide range of subject combinations. Modularization also saw the birth in the late 1980s of the Languages for All or Institution-Wide Languages Programmes (IWLP) movement (see Chapter 14). For a time, openness to other cultures was fashionable, and students from across all disciplines opted for timetabled, certificated language courses to complement their subject specialism. By 1992 (Thomas 1993), such students outnumbered specialist linguists, a position that continued until the turn of the century (Pilkington 1997, Marshall 2001). A concise but detailed history and bibliography of the IWLP movement is in Ferney (2000). Currently, market forces are painting a mixed picture with regard to non-specialist linguists. A decline in accredited courses – partly due to the refusal of other disciplines to release credits and related funding, as centrally funded schemes are replaced by devolved budgets – is matched by a continuing increase in the numbers of specialists in other disciplines opting for independent language study (see Chapter 14). Meanwhile, the loss of impetus within the IWLP movement is countered by the inexorable rise of university language centres, both in the UK with the Association of University Language Centres (AULC) and across Europe with the Confédération Européenne des Centres de Langues dans l'Enseignement Supérieur (CercleS).

In the specialist domain, since admissions peaked in 1992, a sustained fall in recruitment to Modern Languages degrees has led to the progressive closure of language departments in the UK. There are parallel developments across the English-speaking world, in North America, Australia and Ireland. And despite local variations, and in contradiction of the European Union's explicit policy of multilingualism, across the whole of Europe the rise of English and the decline of other languages is inescapable. The widely used acronym 'EFL' has become a misnomer, as in many countries English is less like a foreign than a second language, whose acquisition is a social and economic necessity, akin to ICT skills and a driving licence. To participate in student exchanges, and above all to share in the globalized higher education market, universities teach through the medium of English. And the ugly term LOTE – Languages Other Than English – is acquiring wider currency, defining by negation just as 'non-white' did in Apartheid South Africa, and with not dissimilar power implications.

The response of Britain's threatened Modern Languages departments has been to unite for self-protection, either voluntarily or more frequently by diktat from above. Single-language departments have typically been collapsed into Schools of Modern Languages, and frequently into broader conglomerates. There is some irony in the fact that many depend on income from English language courses and from international students to sustain the viability of LOTE programmes.

The universities that now teach the majority of specialist language students have managed to retain the link between studying the language and studying the culture(s) of relevant nation states. But in some institutions, Modern Languages have been split, with language teaching separated from 'content', and delivered by the university's specialist language centre. Meanwhile, thanks to the modularization of the curriculum, which allows students from different programmes to share individual modules, combined with financial pressures to maximize attendance within each module, the 'content' traditionally associated with Modern Languages departments is taught through English (McBride 2000). It may well be located in a Department of Cultural Studies, Humanities, Media Studies or European Studies to which, in the most extreme cases, language academics have been transferred en masse: the tribe members' primary allegiance is thus no longer necessarily defined by the foreign language they speak, and the common factor of shared language teaching has gone. In such cases, specialist students lose the horizontal integration of language and content (Parkes 1992) which has been central to both traditional and communicative approaches to language learning.

In at least one leading university, all essays, tutorials and examinations, other than those specifically examining language skills, are in English. The avoidance of target-language use in academic contexts is justified by several arguments:

- intellectually challenging material is beyond learners' competence in the target language;
- the aim is simultaneously to develop students' skills in English;
- a degree from the university is internationally recognized as demonstrating a high-level command of English;
- 'We would be swamped by native speakers.'

The last argument is palpably false since recruitment procedures rely on far more than just language proficiency. However, given the importance for developing high-level proficiency of using the target language in all settings, including the most intellectually demanding, the separation of target-language use and content teaching through English must tend to devalue the former. The split will inevitably be accentuated when content is delivered by departments and language by the language centre. Some of the implications of structural changes on staffing policies are spelled out in Chapter 4.

The progressive collapse of recruitment to specialist language degrees can be traced through three successive Nuffield Foundation reports (Moys 1998,

The Nuffield Languages Inquiry 2000, Kelly and Jones 2003). Single Honours has imploded faster than Combined Honours, but both are increasingly restricted to a dozen or so universities, and specialist provision of other than French, German and Spanish is now geographically limited too. One unintended result has been to make language students more of an elite than ever: the high proportion from independent schools, the low proportion from disadvantaged postcode areas or schools providing a high percentage of free school meals, and the high proportion with exceptionally good advanced level grades mark out language students from all other disciplines bar Medicine and Veterinary Science. At least this implies that they will be capable of benefiting from traditional literary courses or the more exciting type of curriculum delineated in Chapter 26.

An unsuccessful and perhaps misguided attempt to halt the decline in applications by stressing the marketability of foreign language proficiency in the employment marketplace is reported in Chapter 3. An example of a more enlightened approach to mapping the true benefits of a language degree is the Criticality Project (www.critical.soton.ac.uk/index.htm).

Meanwhile, at school level, 60 per cent of state comprehensive schools have already made languages optional a year before the legislation becomes statutory (CILT, ALL and UCML 2003), and the proportion is even higher in disadvantaged areas. The change has resulted in more than half of 14-year-olds dropping languages, in a reduction in vocational and short-course options, and in an apparent loss of interest in languages among younger pupils. Chapter 2 expands on the further shock in store once the marginalization of languages at GCSE cuts by more than half the numbers of pupils eligible even to consider A level, at a time when A level numbers are already in steep decline.

The pattern of departmental closures is disappointing to those who believe in innovation and diversity. Because they are located in the most prestigious universities, it is the most traditional courses, in departments and institutions where most importance is attached to literary research, which have the best survival rates, although students increasingly opt out of literary courses (Coleman 2004, Rodgers et al. 2002). An Oxbridge admissions officer asserts in 2004 that it would be 'perverse' to apply there for other than a predominantly literary student experience. Thus, as Modern Languages tribes face dwindling numbers or even extinction, it is sometimes those who have remained aloof from engagement with contemporary society who appear best protected – although it must also be recognized that many traditional departments have followed the pioneers into more flexible and diversified course offerings which embrace media, film, cultural studies and politics alongside literary specialisms.

The relationship between surviving Modern Languages departments and language centres can be a tense one. The former tend to cling to language teaching even if they are untrained for it and even if they resent the time and effort involved, lest transfer of all language modules to specialist language centres might induce management to phase out costly academic departments. This division of tasks also tends to perpetuate the inferior status of language centres, whose applied language work is perceived as subordinate to research into literary and cultural topics. Research assessment, and the prestige and income linked to successive iterations of the Research Assessment Exercise (RAE), have skewed the functioning of university Modern Languages in many ways that fall outside the scope of the present volume (but see Coleman 2004, Kelly and Jones 2003).

A period of unprecedented decline is not the preferred context for a major disciplinary initiative, but following the national Quality Assessment process of 1995/96, no fewer than ten projects in Modern Languages were awarded more than £2.5 million under the Funding Councils' FDTL (Fund for the Development of Teaching and Learning) initiative to spread good practices and address quality problems identified by the process. Although they had a measurable impact on teaching across the sector (Coleman 2001a) and some of their 'outputs' or 'deliverables' remain available, projects have a limited shelf-life, and it is fortunate that the quality enhancement agenda has been taken up by the Subject Centre for Languages, Linguistics and Area Studies at Southampton University, to which reference will be made throughout this volume, and by the projects of successive National Teaching Fellows.

Support for the discipline comes also from major professional associations, whether language-specific bodies such as the AUPHF (Association of University Professors and Heads of French) or the CUTG (the Conference of University Teachers of German), discipline-specific such as LAGB (Linguistics Association of Great Britain) or BAAL (British Association for Applied Linguistics), the traditionally management-oriented SCHML (Standing Conference of Heads of Modern Languages in Universities), or the over-arching UCML (University Council of Modern Languages).

No doubt Modern Languages at university level will continue to have to respond to major changes: developments in the primary and secondary sectors; evolving internal structures; quality assessment of teaching and research; the pressures of student choice in an increasingly marketized higher education sector; the Bologna process and internationalization of higher education; the inexorable rise of English as a world language and particularly as the language of higher education, allied to the widespread misperception, in anglophone countries, that English is and will remain *the* world language.

But it was Modern Languages that pioneered the integration of personal transferable skills (Coleman and Parker 1992), and which has often been at the forefront of theoretical innovation in cultural and literary studies as well as in education. The flexibility, adaptability and integrity that the profession has demonstrated in the recent past will inevitably be called upon again. Together, the qualities presage not just survival but continued renewal.

Sources of information

FDTL projects: summary of outputs. Online. Available at: www.cilt.org.uk/infos/rtf/51to75/InformationSheet51.rtf (accessed 4 June 2004).

Subject Centre for Languages, Linguistics and Area Studies. Online. Available at: www.lang.ltsn.ac.uk (accessed 19 June 2004).

National Teaching Fellowship Projects

Byrne, N. (2002) *Communitec, National Teaching Fellowship Project*. Online. Available at: www.lse.ac.uk/Depts/language/Communitec/HTML/frame.htm (accessed 19 June 2004).

Klapper, J. (2002) *DELPHI (Developing Language Professionals in Higher Education Institutions) National Teaching Fellowship Project*. Online. Available at: www.delphi.bham.ac.uk/ (accessed 19 June 2004).

Mozzon-McPherson, M. (2004) *CLAIM (Certification of Language Abilities for International Mobility) National Teaching Fellowship Project*. Online. Available at: www.hull.ac.uk/languages (accessed 25 June 2004).

Wyburd, J. (2002) *PORTAL, National Teaching Fellowship Project*. Online. Available at: www.langcent.man.ac.uk/staff/portal.htm (accessed 5 February 2004).

Associations

AULC. Online. Available at: www.aulc.org (accessed 19 June 2004).

AUPHF. Online. Available at: www.bris.ac.uk/auphf (accessed 19 June 2004).

BAAL. Online. Available at: www.baal.org.uk (accessed 19 June 2004).

CercleS. Online. Available at: www.cercles.org (accessed 19 June 2004).

CUTG. Online. Available at: www.cutg.ac.uk (accessed 23 June 2004).

LAGB. Online. Available at: www.lagb.org (accessed 19 June 2004).

SCHML. Online. Available at: www.schml.ac.uk (accessed 19 June 2004).

UCML. Online. Available at: www.ucml.org.uk (accessed 19 June 2004).

2

Who are our students and what do they bring from previous experience?

Norbert Pachler

Introduction

In the wake of the introduction of comprehensive schools from the mid-1960s to the late 1990s, the UK saw a considerable expansion in the number of young people studying at least one foreign language as part of their compulsory secondary education. The 'Languages for All' movement of the late 1980s led to the study of one foreign language becoming an entitlement for pupils of all abilities aged 11–16 in the 1990s. The Programme of Study and Attainment Targets to be covered were set out in the various versions of the National Curriculum Modern Foreign Languages Order (NC MFL Order – see www.nc.uk.net). The number of pupils entered for a GCSE (General Certificate of Secondary Education, the national school-leaving qualification for pupils aged 16) in the three main foreign languages, French, German and Spanish, can be seen in Table 2.1. This can be celebrated as a considerable success in equal opportunity terms with an increasing number of pupils from all social groupings leaving school with a qualification in at least one foreign language. However, a closer examination reveals that for the main foreign languages the peak occurred in the mid-1990s. This reversal of the trend towards expansion is causing significant anxiety among foreign language teaching professionals and major agencies alike.

Table 2.1 Selected examination entries at age 16, 1965–2002 (peak years in bold)

Year	French	German	Spanish
1965	171,996	33,723	10,011
1975	265,440	62,383	16,375
1985	310,983	74,471	17,769
1995	350,027	129,386	40,762
1996	**353,570**	**136,433**	43,754
1997	337,993	135,466	44,703
1998	341,169	135,717	48,364
1999	335,816	135,158	47,969
2000	341,011	133,662	49,981
2001	347,007	135,133	54,236
2002	338,468	126,216	**57,983**

Source: Mitchell 2003: 121–22

Developments at 11–16

Despite the seemingly encouraging statistics, too few pupils – it can be argued – 'get to an acceptable standard in terms both of performance and of a *permanently* learnt and retrievable stock of knowledge and understanding' (NALA 1999: 2).

The introduction of the GCSE examination in 1988, which built on the work of so-called Graded Objectives initiatives in the 1980s, aimed at enhancing access to foreign language learning as well as learners' motivation and their sense of achievement. It did this by setting, and assessing at regular intervals, short-term, achievable learning targets mainly centred around language skills required for practical communication across a range of topics such as 'In the restaurant', 'At the campsite', 'Booking a hotel', etc., in seemingly authentic situations in the target country, based on the needs of adult tourists. However, infrequent exposure to the target language in curriculum time necessitates a considerable amount of revision each lesson, and such repetitions tend to lead to a lack of curriculum progression and linguistic progress. Also, pupils often do not learn 'about the *principles* of pronunciation, or accents, or verb inflexions, or how and why words change their forms, or how to avoid the word-for-word syndrome' (NALA 1999: 3). This is due to the considerable pressure of complying with examination specifications (formerly syllabuses) that are overloaded with topics and over-prescriptive in terms of lexical items and phrases as well as linguistic structures.

The methodology implicit in the NC MFL Order is largely based on the tenets of Communicative Language Teaching, with an emphasis on:

- opportunities for target-language use for meaningful purposes;
- expressing meaning rather than accuracy of form;

- the ability to use language rather than knowledge about language;
- the use of (seemingly) authentic material, contexts and tasks.

Despite the prominence of cultural awareness in the NC MFL Order, an overemphasis in league tables on restrictive, output-oriented success indicators can be seen to have led to a narrowly transactional approach, a lack of creativity and imagination as well as teaching to the test, in particular at Key Stage 4 (pupils aged 14–16) – exactly at a time when pupils are required to make choices about their educational futures. Work at Key Stage 4 can be seen to be characterized by a 'heavy emphasis on recall of often random lexical items and phrases derived from narrowly defined, idealized interactions and exchanges at the cost of transfer of knowledge, structures and skills across topics' (Pachler 2000: 535). The main reason for this can be found in the strictly limited fitness for purpose of the GCSE examination for testing the NC MFL Order and the limited time available for foreign language learning in secondary education, at best approximately only 10–12.5 per cent of curriculum time. It leads to restricted linguistic proficiency among pupils, with learners often able to do little more than take part in basic transactions and rehearse (scripted) conversations in a strictly limited range of contexts characterized by simple and familiar language. Pronunciation often remains approximate, as does pupils' knowledge of language forms, which tends to remain largely implicit.

Trends at advanced level

Systemic weaknesses are placing considerable constraints on the work of foreign language teachers in schools and tend to force them into a preoccupation with grades and percentages of examination passes rather than the development of innovative practice. This can be seen to have a bearing not only on teacher recruitment (see Pachler 2001) but also, worryingly, on the uptake of foreign languages at advanced level. Given the healthy numbers of pupils taking GCSE, the evident lack of interest at A level is perturbing. While, clearly, not all those entered for GCSE are necessarily suited for advanced level study, for a decade or so now the percentage of pupils gaining A*–C has nevertheless consistently been around 50 per cent for French and slightly higher for other foreign languages. Whereas more than 9 per cent of those gaining a GCSE in 1990 went on to complete an A level (General Certificate of Education Advanced Level) in a foreign language in 1993, fewer than 6 per cent did in 1997. This decrease from an already very low baseline is an extremely serious issue which rightly attracts increasing attention from commentators and researchers (see, for example, Fisher 2001). Table 2.2 vividly demonstrates the decline in uptake of foreign languages at 16–18.

One reason for this decline is often said to be a gap between GCSE and advanced level study with the former not really providing a sound foundation

Table 2.2 A level entries 1990–2002 (peak years in bold)

Year	French	German	Spanish
1990	27,245	9,476	3,832
1991	30,794	10,583	4,230
1992	**31,261**	10,338	4,720
1993	29,862	**10,857**	4,850
1994	28,942	10,832	4,740
1995	27,563	10,634	4,837
1996	27,728	10,810	5,331
1997	26,488	10,708	5,748
1998	23,625	10,189	5,649
1999	21,072	9,551	**5,782**
2000	18,228	8,694	5,636
2001	17,939	8,466	5,530
2002	15,614	7,013	5,572

Source: Mitchell 2003: 123

for the latter. The considerably higher demands on students in terms of language generation and productive skills, such as essay writing and presentations, as well as receptive skills, such as reading extensively, presuppose much greater implicit and explicit knowledge of grammar and knowledge about register and vocabulary. At advanced level, students are expected to produce discursive texts on social, political and economic topics for which they require much greater general knowledge and knowledge of the target culture(s). There are also considerably more demands on students to work independently and autonomously. They are required to reflect continuously and systematically upon the learning process and skill development. Lexical items, while still broadly topic-related, are much less closely prescribed at advanced level. Topic work requires a much higher level of general and world knowledge. For example, a concern at GCSE with house and home gives way at advanced level to a concern with economic and social conditions. Or, phrases to do with shopping for food, gifts and clothes are replaced from one academic year to the next by questions concerning consumerism and commercialism. There is a tacit assumption that pupils grow into adults in a matter of a few summer months between their GCSE examinations at the end of Year 11 and the start of their advanced level course in Year 12. Grammar, which is prescribed in detail for both GCSE and advanced level (see QCA 2000 and QCA *et al.* 1999), tends to be taught as lexical items and implicitly at GCSE. The focus is on recognition and there is scope for the learning of paradigms and set phrases. Quite quickly, however, grammar knowledge needs to become active and explicit at advanced level leading to the ability to generate and manipulate language forms independently.

Students who opt for foreign languages at post-16 can be seen to have become more diverse in ability and interests. They no longer necessarily study foreign languages with a view to going on to read the subject at university but often for more pragmatic and short-term reasons such as in order to acquire vocationally useful and transferable skills subsidiary to their main programme of study. (For a detailed examination of foreign language teaching at advanced level see Pachler 1999.)

The critical examination of foreign language study at 11–18 above is not intended as an extension of recent criticisms by some higher education (HE) foreign language tutors bemoaning a seeming decline in standards in advanced level learning and teaching (for a summary of the so-called 'grammar debate' see Pachler *et al.* 1999). Such attacks on foreign language teaching (and teachers) at 11–18 often fail to consider the substantial systemic constraints colleagues face. These criticisms also tend not to acknowledge the many changes to the 11–18 curriculum in recent years that have resulted in students, for example, being much more readily able to communicate meaning orally and give presentations in a wide range of contexts. Instead, they tend to focus on how students are no longer prepared by post-16 level study for seemingly outmoded grammar-translation approaches in some HE courses (see, for example, Olk 2001). While it is acknowledged that prevailing policies and practice are not without various problems and are informed by certain orthodoxies, they are underpinned by a fundamental belief in the importance of exposure to foreign languages as a most valuable endeavour for all students in compulsory education and beyond, and by the realization that this presupposes a broad range of methodological approaches.

Recent policy developments

The Nuffield Languages Inquiry (2000) documented the foreign language 'crisis' and showed that although speaking English is not enough, the Government did not have a coherent approach to foreign languages and that the UK desperately needed more foreign language teachers. The Government's response (see Pachler 2002), a Green Paper which led to the National Language Strategy for England (see www.dfes.gov.uk/languagesstrategy), was disappointing in that it decided to take little note of some key Nuffield recommendations. The strategy is not visibly based on research and introduces an 'entitlement' to primary foreign language study only from 2010. Furthermore, the removal of a modern foreign language from the core curriculum at Key Stage 4 is already reducing motivation at earlier stages.

Most significantly – and worryingly – the strategy puts paid to the 'Languages for All' policy by reducing to Key Stage 3 (pupils aged 11–14) the entitlement to learn at least one foreign language and develop cultural understanding.

A 2002 survey by the Centre for Information on Language Teaching and Research (now CILT, The National Centre for Languages), in collaboration with the *Times Educational Supplement*, into future provision in foreign languages for Key Stage 4 (CILT/TES 2002, sample size: 4,000 Heads of Languages in England of whom 393 (12.6 per cent) returned the questionnaire) does not bode well. For example, the proportion of schools providing a foreign language for all has declined from 73 per cent in 2000–01 to 50 per cent in 2002–03 and the proportion of schools with disapplication rates of over 15 per cent (i.e. schools allowing 15 per cent or more of pupils aged 14–16 to drop foreign languages) has increased in the same period from 8 per cent to 25 per cent. When asked whether their school would be likely to make foreign languages optional if the law allowed it, 29 per cent said their schools would (or had) and in a further 25 per cent of schools this was 'under consideration'. The survey also reported a correlation between both social background and general educational attainment and the likelihood of the ability to drop a foreign language. CILT, the Association for Language Learning and the University Council of Modern Languages (CILT *et al.* 2003) note a disproportionate effect of the policy of redesignating the status of foreign languages on lower ability pupils and that schools with a high percentage of free school meals and low GCSE pass rates were more likely to make languages optional. Another worrying observation relates to the effect of the policy on the decline not only in GCSE examination entries but also in alternative, mostly vocational pre-16 courses. Pupil attitudes, government policies, and teacher supply were considered to be the main obstacles to greater provision by respondents to the 2002 CILT/TES survey. From these results it seems fair to surmise that significant change is likely in relation to who the students that go on to HE level study are and what linguistic experiences and expertise they bring with them.

Problems with provision at 16–19 are also recognized by policy makers who introduced a new structure for advanced level study in the late 1990s which ostensibly makes courses modular. Students follow three units in the first year of advanced level study leading to the GCE Advanced Subsidiary, followed by three further units at A2 level in the second year of study leading to the GCE Advanced Level. The intention behind these changes was to allow students to make more diverse curriculum choices at post-16 and to gain certification for advanced-level work even if the study of a particular subject is not pursued after one year. The changes have, however, led to reduced teaching time and an increased amount of teaching to the test, or at least preparation for examination.

Apprehensive outlook

Taken together, all these policy initiatives and developments will – and are already starting to – have a significant impact on foreign language study in HE and pose considerable challenges for foreign language teachers and their students alike. Kelly and Jones (2003: 2), for example, draw our attention to the fact that while more students than ever are developing some sort of language skills at post-16, fewer students are choosing to specialize in foreign languages; that although foreign languages have recruited strongly at AS level, numbers at A level continue to fall.

It remains to be seen to what extent the revised A/AS level and the reforms at 11–14 and 14–19 prepare students better for foreign language study in HE and what effect they will have. One already discernible impact is the change in academic profile of students choosing foreign languages pre- and post-16 and an attendant striking increase in top grades at A level (see Kelly and Jones 2003: 20). The question to be asked is whether this move towards renewed elitism represents a positive trend. Perceptive readers will not have failed to notice that I have my doubts and that, in my view, there is limited hope for optimism.

Sources of information

Association for Language Learning. Online. Available at: www.all-languages.org.uk (accessed 17 May 2004).

Education Guardian Language Learning. Online. Available at: www.education.guardian. co.uk/languageresources/0,11778,667459,00.html (accessed 17 May 2004).

National Association for Language Advisers. Online. Available at: www.nala.org.uk (accessed 17 May 2004).

Nuffield Languages Archive. Online. Available at: www.nuffieldfoundation.org/languages/ home (accessed 17 May 2004).

CILT, The National Centre for Languages. Online. Available at: www.cilt.org.uk (accessed 17 May 2004).

3

Where do our graduates go? Languages and careers

James A. Coleman

At school careers evenings and university open days, we all face two principal questions on careers:

- What kind of jobs do language graduates get?
- Does a language degree offer good job opportunities?

As a university course becomes less a matter of individual intellectual development and more an investment decision taken by would-be students and their funders, increasing attention is being paid to the employment prospects which attach to a given degree path. Employability is also one of the keystones of the European Union's Bologna Process, to which all EU states are signed up. And in the face of the current recruitment crisis, university Modern Languages have sometimes responded by looking to graduate employability and to an argument – often rather a narrow argument – based on foreign language proficiency qua skill.

A two-pronged recruitment campaign mounted by university language departments since the mid-1990s sought, first, to dispel the myth that a language degree was good only for teaching, translating or interpreting, and, second, to suggest that language graduates' career prospects are better than average. Thanks largely to the efforts of Keith Marshall at Bangor, reliable data have been gathered, disseminated and updated, to be widely used in presentations and press articles across the land. The initiative has been partially effective, not least in countering the narrow and inaccurate views held by some school careers advisers and a fortiori some potential applicants regarding careers followed by language graduates. The exceptional employability of language graduates was even highlighted in the QAA Subject Benchmark Statement. However, as will be seen below, this employability question is less clear-cut.

What careers?

Accurate and up-to-date information is now easily available. CILT, The National Centre for Languages, produces regularly updated information sheets, most recently including one on *Employability of Languages Graduates: Statistical sources* and another on *The Use of and Need for Language Skills in Employment: Statistical sources*. CILT also offers downloadable advice leaflets targeted respectively at school careers advisers, university students, and school students. The Association of Graduate Careers Advisory Services (AGCAS) each year adds informed commentary to first destination statistics gathered by the Higher Education Statistics Agency (HESA), publishing the results on the Prospects website (www.prospects.ac.uk). From the vast amount of data gathered, there is no doubting the importance of language and intercultural skills for UK businesses, or that a language often features in job advertisements. At the same time, proficiency in one or more foreign languages is, in most cases, complementary to the principal characteristics of the job – although frequently carrying a modest salary premium.

Marshall's most recent data showing the domains in which language graduates work (www.lang.ltsn.ac.uk/resources/resourcesitem.aspx?resourceid= 1640) are for 2002.

From Table 3.1, it can be seen that fewer than one graduate in ten follows a stereotypical language career in teaching, translating or interpreting.

The Prospects website for 2002 language graduates (Prospects 2002) shows just 50.3 per cent in UK employment and 10.0 per cent in overseas

Table 3.1 Employment of language graduates

Employment sector	Percentage of language graduates employed
Business services	25.3
Wholesale and retail sales/ maintenance services	11.5
Banking/finance	10.8
Public administration	9.2
Manufacturing	9.0
Education	8.0
Community/social/personal/ services	6.9
Transport/communications	6.9
Health/social work	5.3
Hotels/restaurants	4.4
International organizations	0.2
Other areas	2.4

employment, with 24.5 per cent pursuing further training, 8.1 per cent unavailable for work or training, and 7.1 per cent unemployed. Of those in UK employment, the largest single group (29.8 per cent) is in clerical and secretarial occupations, followed by commercial, industrial and public sector managers (15.9 per cent). AGCAS also reports that the proportion of graduate jobs open to all graduates regardless of subject specialism continues to rise, from around half in the 1990s to 65 per cent of all UK graduate jobs today. In summary, most language graduates go into jobs for which a language is not essential. At the same time, a language degree is a key that opens many different doors.

How employable are language graduates?

Repeated generic studies show that graduate employers value transferable skills most, and subject knowledge least (e.g. Coleman and Parker 1992: 10, Harvey *et al.* 1997). Additionally, there is some evidence that in the past, the skills inculcated by traditional Modern Language degrees were an imperfect match for the skills required in employment (Phillips-Kerr 1991 for 1985 data, Meara 1994 for 1986 data, Coleman 1996: 116–23 for 1994 data). Nonetheless, the latter study confirmed students' awareness of the skills they will need after graduation, and over the past decade personal transferable skills have been systematically integrated into the programme specifications of languages degrees, into learning activities, and into assessment. Chapters 10 and 14 show how today's language graduates, both specialist and non-specialist linguists, can be expected to offer, at a high level:

- communication skills including written and oral presentations, negotiating, receiving feedback;
- interpersonal skills including teamwork and dealing with people;
- 'self' skills including self-awareness, self-motivation, organization and time management;
- intellectual skills including critical reasoning, problem-solving, analysis and synthesis;
- information handling skills including identifying issues and locating, synthesizing and presenting data.

There is abundant anecdotal evidence that employers value the combination of these abilities with foreign language proficiency, which allows language graduates – uniquely – to operate effectively in diverse cultural and linguistic contexts across the world.

However, the national campaign seeking to promote the employability of language graduates rested initially on HESA figures for unemployment six months after graduation. Tables showed French, German and Modern Languages overall second only to notoriously selective professional specialisms such as Medicine, Dentistry, Law and Veterinary Medicine. Marshall usefully brought together the 1996–2002 statistics for the website of the Subject Centre for Languages, Linguistics and Area Studies.

Their value remains nevertheless problematic in many ways.

- These HESA First Destination Statistics do not distinguish between types of jobs, between bankers and bar staff, between temporary and permanent posts, or even between work and postgraduate training.
- Data at six months after graduation are less informative than longer-term trends.
- Graduates, especially in Arts and Languages, tend to be over-educated for the first destination jobs (Connell 2002: 15).
- Tables can look impressive with languages near the top, but distinctions between subjects are unlikely to be statistically significant.
- The charts produced highlighted French, German and All Modern Languages, but omitted Spanish which came much further down the table.
- Individual years produced good-looking tables until 2002 (when the decision was taken to integrate tables for the last seven years) and 2003: current patterns look far less favourable.
- Degree subject is only one of the factors determining graduate employability.
- Data only apply to Single Major Honours, not the majority of language students.

Kingston (2003) first drew attention to the changes in positions brought about when greater discrimination is brought to raw HESA first destination data, and the results were very disappointing for languages. The *Times Higher* league tables, based upon *The Times Good University Guide*, in which graduate employability is one important measure among several others, have, since spring 2003, distinguished between graduate, graduate-track and other jobs, a change that 'excited little criticism and much interest' (ibid.). In the new, more discriminatory rankings for each of the last five years, the bottom ten for graduate employment in graduate/graduate-track jobs include Italian (consistently) and Russian and Iberian Studies (intermittently). The table of ten subjects with an above-average profile in the old methodology and a below-average profile in the new include French and German. It is certainly possible to criticize the taxonomy of jobs used by HESA as being more simplistic than the classification of Elias and Purcell (2003), but we can no longer argue employability on the basis of raw first destination unemployment figures.

In vocational areas, the single most important determinant of graduate employment prospects is subject of study. However, for students of non-vocational subjects such as languages, two other factors may be equally significant: a degree from a 'good' university, and prior educational and socio-biographical background (Brennan *et al.* 2003: 7). Since entrants to degrees in languages in the UK have a lower percentage of 'poor' postcodes, higher representation of independent schools, and higher A level grades than almost any other subject except Medicine, social background may well enhance employability. It is also the case that, with falling numbers of applicants, well-established universities with high research reputations – Oxbridge, the Russell Group institutions, other respected civic universities – are recruiting better than the lower-status new universities. They have also been able to sustain single and combined honours degrees – i.e. those that figure in official statistics – while institutions with modularized degree pathways (once again, the new universities) have dropped them. In other words, 'language graduate' is often shorthand for 'highly intelligent young person from a privileged school and social milieu with a degree from a prestigious university': the oft-repeated argument that language graduates are highly employable may have nothing whatever to do with their choice of degree subject. Put bluntly, if you come from a good family, a good school and a good university, you will get a good job whether or not you choose a language degree.

Conclusion

The inescapable conclusion is that the 'languages = employability' argument was not only relatively ineffectual in recruitment terms, but also based on false premises. However, a review of longer-term surveys of language graduate careers and incomes (Connell 2004) suggests that a languages degree is far better than no degree, and that the prospects are indeed better than in many disciplines. Meanwhile, the data already available, to which will shortly be added the CILT-AGCAS Languages Work project, the Subject Centre's Employability Research Project and other reports, indicate the huge range of careers to which a language degree can open the door. If employability remains, as it surely will, a key argument in student recruitment, it now needs to build on three elements:

- the scope of employment opportunities;
- the solid evidence concerning the employability benefits of residence abroad (see Chapter 15 and Connell 2002: 16);
- the unique combination of practical, intellectual, personal, inter-personal, communication and linguistic skills which language graduates offer to future employers.

Sources of information

CILT, The National Centre for Languages information sheets. Online. Available at: www.cilt.org.uk/infos/cilt_infos.htm (accessed 19 June 2004).

CILT, The National Centre for Languages promotional leaflets. Online. Available at: www.cilt.org.uk/careers/pdf/factsheets/colour_advisers.pdf (accessed 19 June 2004); www.cilt.org.uk/careers/pdf/factsheets/bw_students.pdf (accessed 19 June 2004); www.cilt.org.uk/careers/pdf/factsheets/bw_school.pdf (accessed 19 June 2004).

AGCAS. Online. Available at: www.agcas.org.uk (accessed 19 June 2004).

Languages Work project. Online. Available at: www.agcas.org.uk/partners/docs/cilt_making_languages_work.doc (accessed 19 June 2004).

Prospects. Online. Available at: www.prospects.ac.uk (accessed 19 June 2004).

HESA. Online. Available at: www.hesa.ac.uk (accessed 19 June 2004).

HESA First Destination data. Online. Available at: www.hesa.ac.uk/holisdocs/pubinfo/fds.htm (accessed 19 June 2004).

Keith Marshall's data at the Subject Centre website. Online. Available at: www.lang.ltsn.ac.uk/resources/resourcesitem.aspx?resourceid=1640 (accessed 19 June 2004).

4

Who teaches our students? University teachers and their professional development

John Klapper

Modern Languages is a diverse discipline taught by a correspondingly varied range of staff. This chapter provides a brief sketch of today's modern linguists, examines their training and professional development needs, and surveys the resources that are available to support them.

Staff in Modern Languages

Modern Languages staff include:

- traditional, research-intensive academics, whose main teaching areas are non-language elements of the programme;
- research-active academics, who teach both language and non-language modules;
- teaching-only tutors, fellows or instructors, whose role is to coordinate language teaching;
- foreign language assistants (FLAs), often, but not always, still students themselves (see also Chapter 12);
- postgraduate teaching assistants (PGTAs), usually research students who are employed for a few hours each week.

The extent to which staff are designated 'research active' varies greatly, and, especially in language centres, there are increasing numbers of non-research staff employed on the Other Related (or Academically Related) scales. In all academic categories one finds a substantial number of native speakers of the target language, as well as a number of former secondary and further education (FE) teachers.

As seen in Chapter 1, Modern Languages has been in crisis for a few years now. One of the problems in this shrinking market is the typical academic profile of staff. Recruited on the basis of a recently completed PhD and perhaps a few publications, many languages staff are the product of a postgraduate research world still dominated by literary and cultural topics. With a few exceptions, such a profile is not suited to the changing needs of the discipline, in particular the increasing amount of language service provision for 'integrated' degrees, such as European Studies, and the concomitant reduction in the range and viability of non-language elements.

Besides evincing a genuine interest in language pedagogy (as opposed to seeing it as a necessary evil to be kept to a minimum and fitted in between the 'real' teaching in one's specialist area), today's modern linguist needs to be able to look beyond his or her narrow research field, to seek synergies and common ground with related fields (history, cultural studies, film, politics, gender studies, business) and to be prepared to develop and teach on interdisciplinary courses. The number of departments in which a narrow specialism, especially a literary one, can still thrive is limited; elsewhere university teachers have had to become more flexible and adopt a broader view of their role. The response of some departments over recent years has been to employ experienced, dedicated teaching fellows, instructors or tutors, who coordinate and take the lion's share of the department's language teaching. Often effectively second-class citizens on temporary or part-time contracts, with limited career prospects despite holding professional qualifications, such individuals serve in part to protect non-language aspects of the programme. Where this has not been possible, linguists have had to become 'jacks of all trades', with inevitable implications for their academic self-image, their research profile and often their research output.

Cuts and mergers have also reduced the numbers of FLAs and, where they are still to be found, their role is now very different. Many are no longer just small-group conversation facilitators, teaching 10–12 hours per week, but have become general language teachers, with up to 15 or 16 hours of teaching, are frequently heavily involved in marking of all types, carry out departmental administrative tasks, take partial or full responsibility for language modules and sometimes get involved in teaching aspects of contemporary society. And yet, in spite of all this, they are now often only paid for 9 rather than 12 months of the year.

Finally, in those departments with a postgraduate research culture, it is not unusual for research students to gain some professional experience by giving language classes under the supervision of an academic member of staff.

Professional development needs

Quality assurance-inspired developments in the sector have meant that most universities now require their FLAs and PGTAs to undergo some form of initial training, typically an intensive pre-sessional course with subsequent workshop-style follow-up (see Adam *et al.* 2001, Gray 2001). In stark contrast to this, until the last few years, most academic staff in Modern Languages never received any formal teacher training. For *new* staff, this situation will soon change as all inexperienced lecturers and tutors appointed from 2006 will have to complete a general programme of teacher development, approved and accredited by the new Higher Education Academy. There will be no such requirement for *existing* academic staff, although the Government has stated it expects institutions to ensure all staff are engaged in continuing professional development (CPD) (see HEA 2004).

However, Modern Languages staff are not especially well served by current staff development provision. Training is usually generic, with little or no specific reference to the distinctive activity of language teaching, in effect the core activity of the discipline (Klapper 2001b). Clearly, many academic staff also deliver lectures and conduct seminars on the non-language elements of degrees, and thus shared generic training with other disciplines, on topics such as lecturing, small group teaching and project supervision, can prove economical. Yet junior lecturers are required to spend a lot of their time teaching language classes, and it might be thought unsatisfactory, not to say unprofessional, that they are not being better prepared for what is a complex task. In the absence of dedicated training, most new academics are likely to remain only vaguely aware of the substantial pedagogical research base of their subject, reinforcing perceptions among colleagues in English language teaching and second language acquisition, of a less than serious approach to what we frequently (and rightly) proclaim to be the sine qua non of our discipline, namely effective teaching of the target language.

While language centres are able to draw on a reasonable pool of trained teachers, often with experience in secondary schools and FE, and regularly promote an active culture of CPD in language pedagogy, academic language departments face a tougher task. Postgraduate research into language pedagogy and applied linguistics is still a minority pursuit in Modern Languages. The consequent lack of any culture of language pedagogy in most departments means there are few academics able or willing to organize and deliver training courses on language learning and instructed second language acquisition. Given that very few new appointments are being made to language departments, this has to be a major cause for concern.

▶ Take a few minutes to reflect on any professional training you have had in your career. How relevant was it to your current role?

▶ List three areas of your current teaching practice in which you feel you need support.

What opportunities are there?

The future of professional development in languages must lie in some form of collaborative distance learning, whereby resources and expertise are pooled and small numbers of disparate and far-flung academic staff can access online training. The Languages Subject Centre (Languages Subject Centre 2003a) is the principal focus of professional development in Modern Languages. It organizes a rich programme of activities across its three principal areas of concern, including seminars, workshops and conferences; commissions studies and surveys; and issues a monthly mailing list to the sector. It has also developed a substantial set of language-related web links and a major online collection of over 120 commissioned articles by specialists in the various fields (Languages Subject Centre 2003b). Furthermore, the Subject Centre maintains a varied bank of teaching materials donated by practitioners, which are available to all language teachers free of charge (Languages Subject Centre 2003c).

Other examples of good collaborative practice include the module on 'Supporting Residence Abroad', part of Portsmouth University's MA/ Postgraduate Certificate in Learning and Teaching in Higher Education. This is available as a distance-learning module and is ideal for staff involved in foreign placements of any kind. The University of Hull's distance-learning Postgraduate Certificate in Advising for Language Learning (University of Hull 2003) is also highly recommended for those keen to explore the changing role of the language tutor, in particular e-tutoring and language learning support. The materials produced by the ten language projects that collaborated under the umbrella of the Fund for the Development of Teaching and Learning, the largest ever single investment in Modern Languages (Coleman 2001a), are still available (for an overview, see www.cilt.org.uk/infos/51to75/info51.htm).

HEFCE's National Teaching Fellowship Scheme (NTFS) has produced some valuable resources for the sector. These include 'Communitec' (Byrne 2002), which offers support to tutors using language learning technology and aims to help them upgrade their skills in this area, as well as the PORTAL project (Wyburd 2002), which is looking at the role of the language portfolio as both a learning environment and a mechanism for formative and summative assessment.

A more comprehensive approach has been tried in a third NTFS initiative, the DELPHI project (DELPHI 2002). This is a web-based distance-learning package for teaching languages, available free of charge to all staff in the sector. The programme comprises 14 modules on a wide range of topics relevant to the teaching of foreign languages, both in specialist and less specialist settings, including teaching vocabulary, grammar, translation, the 'four skills', second language acquisition, task-based learning, assessment and language testing. Each module involves 20–25 hours of participant effort and incorporates assessed tasks for those who wish to use the modules to count towards their university's initial training programme (see below). The materials are accessed via a website that includes a large number of electronic links to further sources of training, as well as pedagogical resources, including a review of all the latest books in the field.

Based on principles of constructivist teacher education (Roberts 1998) and reflective practice (Zeichner and Liston 1996), the DELPHI programme builds reflection on participants' own beliefs and practice into the process of learning about different classroom approaches. Through tasks, some reflective and others interactive, participants are encouraged to engage with the material presented and to think about it in the context of their own teaching.

A key feature of the materials is their flexibility, in particular their relevance to both novice university teachers and more established academics seeking to refresh their knowledge of specific aspects of language teaching.

To date, over 200 individuals in 20 countries have registered as DELPHI users and four UK universities have integrated the materials into certificates of teaching and learning. While it is not possible to determine precisely how the materials are being used in each case, it is clear the modules are meeting a demand. The programme is no more than a start but it provides a model of how the sector can collaborate to provide for its own initial and continuing professional development in a rapidly changing environment in which traditional face-to-face training on an institutional, possibly even a regional, basis is no longer viable.

The Higher Education Academy

The Academy is only just being established. It is intended to be the single professional organization for staff teaching in higher education, superseding and incorporating the Institute for Learning and Teaching in Higher Education (ILTHE). It has stated (HEA 2004) that it will recognize all the ILTHE's previously accredited programmes. This means that those who successfully complete a university's ILTHE-accredited certificate or diploma of teaching and learning are automatically eligible for membership of the new Academy. Full-time staff whose role involves comprehensive expertise across a number of areas of professional activity can apply for 'Membership', while part-time and temporary staff, or those with a restricted role, can apply for 'Associateship'.

Alternatively, staff can become Academy members via the Individual Entry Route by submitting evidence directly, to demonstrate they have satisfied the criteria for membership through professional experience. For 'Membership', this involves providing information for *all* of the following six Areas of Professional Activity:

1   Teaching and/or the support of learning in higher education.
2   Contribution to the design and planning of learning activities and/or programmes of study.

3   Assessment and/or giving feedback to learners.
4   Developing effective learning environments and learner support systems.
5   Evaluating practice and personal development.
6   Using research, scholarly activity or relevant professional work to inform and impact on teaching.

The normal expectation is that those applying via this route will have at least *three* years' experience of teaching or learning support in higher education. Applicants for 'Associateship' (e.g. PGTAs and FLAs) must have at least *one* year's experience and need to provide evidence for Area 5 plus two others.

Sources of information

Arthur, L. and Hurd, S. (eds) (2001) *Supporting Lifelong Language Learning: theoretical and practical approaches*, London: CILT/The Open University.

Website of the Higher Education Academy (HEA 2004). Available at: www.heacademy. ac.uk (accessed 5 February 2004).

Generic Subject Centre. Online. Available at: www.ltsn.ac.uk/genericcentre (accessed 5 February 2004).

Website of the Subject Centre for Languages, Linguistics and Area Studies (Languages Subject Centre 2003a). Available at: www.lang.ltsn.ac.uk (accessed 5 February 2004).

The HE Resources Collection at CILT – The National Centre for Languages. Available at: www.lang.ltsn.ac.uk/resources/resourcesitem.aspx?resourceid=601 (accessed 5 February 2004).

Part II

The theory and practice of language teaching

5

Research into language learning

James A. Coleman and John Klapper

For many years there has been a serious discrepancy between second language acquisition (SLA) research findings on the way foreign languages (FLs) are learned and the way many universities have continued to teach them to students. This chapter presents findings from SLA research and seeks to relate them to classroom practice. It looks first at universal aspects of learning an FL, the major concern of SLA research, and then considers the crucial role of individual learner differences and their influence on the acquisition process.

Learner errors and interlanguage

According to behaviourist views (Bloomfield 1933, Skinner 1957), language learning is environmentally determined and is a consistent process of stimulus and response. By contrast, 'mentalist' approaches, prompted by Chomsky's theories of an innate 'language acquisition device' (Chomsky 1957, 1965), have popularized the view that our brains are uniquely well equipped to learn language and that acquisition is 'triggered' by (quite limited) linguistic input.

Research into learner errors has been a key area of exploration for SLA research, as error has come to be seen as a natural, indeed essential, part of the acquisition process. Contrary to early claims of behaviourist-inspired contrastive analysis (Lado 1964), according to which teaching should practise intensively aspects of the FL affected by 'negative transfer' from the mother tongue (L1), empirical studies showed that L1 interference fails to account for a large number of learner errors. 'Error analysis' (Corder 1967), by contrast, sought to explain the origin of errors, especially non-contrastive ones deriving from the FL itself. Given that these often resemble neither FL nor L1 forms, it was hypothesized that they must be part of an internal learner system and must be *developmental*. Thus such variants as 'bringed' or 'goed' represent quite natural transitional stages, which all second language learners pass through on the way to formulating the respective correct form.

Numerous SLA studies have confirmed the regularity and systematicity of learner error. Selinker (1972) gave this system and its transitional stages the name 'interlanguage', by which he meant an autonomous system dependent on its own rules, which changes constantly as learners integrate new hypotheses about the FL into their interim competence. Interlanguage is known to be variable (Tarone 1988) and at any stage of their development learners will sometimes use one form and sometimes another, depending on the language context a structure is used in, on whether language use is formal or informal and on whether it is planned or not (see Ellis 1997: 25–28).

Staged development and teachability

> ► Do you think the order in which students acquire linguistic items reflects the order in which students are taught them, e.g. the order of the textbook or your teaching syllabus?

Early interlanguage research investigated *inter alia* whether FL learners developed in consistent ways, whether there was a *natural* route of development. Studies of the acquisition of English structures showed a clear accuracy order that was independent of formal teaching, of learners' L1 and of age. However, problems were identified with this research, in particular its conception of language acquisition as a linear, once-and-for-all process. Acquisition has been shown to be a lengthy, complicated affair that bears little resemblance to a steady learning curve, is dependent on a number of factors, and is very likely to be characterized by periodic regression.

Building on such insights, research has posited that learners move gradually through transitional constructions, in which an initial attempt to form a past tense such as 'she see' might become 'she saw', then 'she seed' and 'she sawed', before the correct form enters the learner's interlanguage. These sequences of acquisition (Ellis 1997: 23) illustrate the so-called 'U-shaped' behaviour of foreign language learners (Kellerman 1979), in which error frequency is first low, then high, then low again. Such *apparent* regression is the result of learners reorganizing their existing knowledge so they can accommodate new knowledge. Thus, in the example above, the past tense may initially be used correctly but then followed by forms which show learners developing and over-generalizing past tense formation rules ('seed', 'sawed'), until eventually the correct forms are used again as learners move closer to FL norms. This suggests that FL learning is to a considerable extent universal, that there are cognitive processes at work in the learner that are largely independent of both the way in which the language is learned (instructed or naturalistic) and the learner's L1.

For this reason, language teachers need to be aware that what we teach is not always what students learn, that language is not acquired in the order of the grammar syllabus. As suggested by Pienemann's (1984) 'teachability hypothesis', teaching a form or rule will result in correct automatic use only when the learner is developmentally ready to process the particular structure, that is when the learner's interlanguage is close to the developmental stage at which the structure would be acquired in naturalistic acquisition.

Cognitive approaches to SLA

▶ Think of a particular skill you have mastered or at least can perform with a degree of proficiency (e.g. riding a bike, juggling, knitting or playing tennis).
▶ How did you learn the skill? What were the learning steps involved?
▶ Do you still think about those individual steps now when performing the skill? If not, why not?

Researchers working in the cognitive tradition consider language acquisition to be broadly comparable to all the other kinds of information the human mind processes. Language learning is seen as a complex skill, in which a range of sub-skills must be practised in 'controlled' processing until they can be integrated into 'automatic' or fluent performance. According to Anderson's Adaptive Control Theory (Anderson 1983), learning involves transforming 'declarative knowledge', i.e. explicit knowledge of facts and memorized rules, or knowledge *about* something (e.g. the correct way to grip and swing a tennis racquet), into 'procedural knowledge', which denotes knowledge of *how to do* something (e.g. play a back-hand return over the net at speed).

For McLaughlin (1987) language learning is a move from controlled processing, in which considerable attention is paid to the different elements of the action, to automatic processing via repeated practice, in which automatized sequences are made available very quickly with limited attention on the part of the learner. Repeated practice leads to fine-tuning of the particular skill, allowing discrete units to be combined into steadily larger stretches of language, thereby reducing the burden on memory.

In many ways the cognitive approach corresponds to most learners' experience of learning and using mechanical rules (Johnson 1996). In apparent contradiction of Krashen (see below), elements learnt consciously *can* gradually become part of subconscious application of language: there comes a stage at which learners produce utterances on the basis of what they feel to be right even though they may not be able immediately to recall or formulate the relevant rule.

Universal Grammar

Proponents of Universal Grammar (UG) have sought to build on Chomsky's theoretical construct of an innate Language Acquisition Device to address the question: if L1 acquisition results from a unique language faculty, is FL learning a manifestation of the same phenomenon, or is it governed by general cognitive processes involved in the learning of any skills? The UG view is that young children have *open parameters* (parameters denote the key differences between languages, such as standard English subject–verb–object word order versus Japanese subject–object–verb). Parameters become fixed as soon as young children receive evidence from L1, and these pre-set parameters make FL learning a very different experience: learners automatically seek to apply L1 parameter settings to the FL and, where they conflict with what they discover about the FL, they need to reset them; or, when in the FL they discover an active parameter not activated in their L1, they need to fix the setting for the first time – as learners have to do with all the active parameters in L1 (see Towell and Hawkins 1994: 74–109).

Most language teachers will be disappointed by the UG approach. It is primarily a theory of *language*, not of SLA, concentrating on competence rather than performance, and on syntax rather than psychological and social aspects of language learning.

Input and output

Acquisition clearly depends on learners being exposed to FL *input*, i.e. spoken or written language in either natural settings or in formal instruction. SLA theories differ, however, on the function of this input.

The most (in)famous theory is Krashen's (1985) 'input hypothesis' which presumes a theoretical contrast between 'acquisition' (FL proficiency through naturalistic, non-classroom exposure) and 'learning' (conscious study of the FL, usually classroom-based). The crucial factor here is 'meaningful input': for language to be successfully acquired, as opposed to unsuccessfully learnt, the target-language input must be novel, it must be relevant to learners' interests, it must contain structures that are a little beyond their current level of competence, and it must be understood by them. At all times learners should concentrate on or 'go for' meaning, rather than form. Rules that are formally taught and learnt merely serve to 'monitor' the acquired FL system.

An important contribution to SLA has been made by interaction studies (for an overview see Mitchell and Myles 1998: 121–43). According to these, input is only part of the story: learning a language is the result of learners' internal processing mechanisms interacting with linguistic input, which is frequently modified in some way. Thus, many native speakers engage in 'foreigner talk', simplifying the input they provide to language learners. Alternatively, there may be 'negotiation of meaning', whereby one speaker fails to understand and the other rephrases the particular utterance. Or else 'negative evidence' is supplied as interlocutors correct each other's language in some way.

It is generally recognized that input is a necessary but not sufficient condition for the acquisition of a second language: what is also needed is *output*, as this leads to interaction with speakers of the target-language, and subsequently to further input. As Swain (1995: 247–49) argues, sustained speaking (and writing) 'pushes' learners to produce 'comprehensible output', giving them the chance to test hypotheses about language and to notice gaps in their competence, while forcing them to practise more varied and complex language and to process syntax rather than just the semantics involved in trying to understand input. Contrary to Krashen, this confirms the fundamental belief of most language teachers that, ultimately, languages are learnt by using them.

Communicative language teaching

What use has language teaching made of these various insights from SLA? Although the communicative approach has few clear links to SLA research, it has been much influenced by acquisition order studies and input theories, and its 'strong' version (Howatt 1984) sees communication as both the aim and means of learning: language is learnt through meaningful language use in the classroom.

In the 'weak' version of communicative language teaching (CLT), the version one tends to find in most UK university foreign language classrooms, the aim is the same, but the means used to achieve it are different. Classroom activities are more structured to enable learners to practise communicative functions in a controlled way and gradually to build up to freer, less directed meaningful FL exchanges.

Methodology here frequently centres on the classic lesson structure of Presentation–Practice–Production, or 'PPP', in which presentation of a specific form or structure by the teacher is followed initially by controlled then by freer practice, before learners engage in open language use in which the focus is on meaning. PPP has, however, been questioned in recent times (e.g. Willis and Willis 1996) on the grounds that SLA has shown language cannot be ordered into a syllabus of graded difficulty and linguistic items cannot be learnt and subsequently employed in spontaneous, unmonitored language use within the space of a single lesson or unit.

More generally, CLT has been criticized for promoting communication as a largely formulaic, threshold ability, with emphasis on transactional language within a narrow functional range, for unduly emphasizing meaning over form and thereby failing to provide learners with a generalizable language framework that can facilitate the creation of new or even unique utterances.

Form-focused instruction

Increasing concern with CLT's failure to promote formal accuracy has prompted interest in form-focused instruction (FFI) (Spada 1997, Doughty and Williams 1998), which denotes any approach that draws learners' attention to form, either explicitly or implicitly, including formal teaching of rules and feedback on errors.

Long (1991) has distinguished 'focus on formS' from 'focus on form'. The first involves taking individual linguistic items out of context and isolating them for separate study as part of an a priori synthetic syllabus, while in the latter a primary communicative need, identified as part of meaning-based interaction, draws the learner's attention to a formal aspect of the language and induces 'noticing' (see Chapter 8). The aim is thus to make linguistic forms salient so that learners can 'notice the gap' which results from the mismatch between input (the target-language ideal) and their own output (their current inter-language). The key difference from a focus-on-formS approach is that this noticing of formal linguistic features occurs incidentally, rather than being the principal concern of classroom activity.

Task-based language instruction

An approach that marries thinking on CLT and FFI and seeks to address the shortcomings of PPP is task-based instruction (TBI) (Ellis 2003, Skehan 1996, J. Willis 1996). This is based on the assumption that the communicative inter-action characteristic of task-based work provides sufficient comprehensible input to 'trigger' acquisitional processes. It can thus be seen as an offshoot from or a development of CLT, especially the 'strong' form of the latter, asserting that language learning depends on learners being involved in real communica-tion in which they use language in a meaningful way. However, unlike the strong version of CLT, it crucially insists that acquisition needs to be supported by instruction which ensures a certain attention to linguistic form; that initial fluency work should lead gradually to accuracy-focused activities.

Typically (see J. Willis 1996), TBI adopts a three-stage methodology, involving:

a   a pre-task phase, in which the topic and task are introduced;
b   a task cycle, in which the task is performed and learners plan and deliver a report on the performance of the task;

c   a language focus phase, in which formal aspects that arose in the course
of the task are analysed and subsequently practised.

(For a sample task-based lesson see Larsen-Freeman 2000: 146–50.)

The idea of starting with a task is to create an actual need for language to
be used (an 'information gap' requiring communication among participants is
a standard element of CLT activities) and for learners to identify what language
they need in order to perform the task. There is then a gradual move to a
greater focus on form with supported consciousness-raising (see Chapter 8)
and analysis. In this sense, the overall cycle is a bit like PPP in reverse order.

There have been criticisms of TBI (for a review see Klapper 2003c). These
have focused on uneven oral development, the problem of grading tasks, the
difficulty of ensuring rigorous assessment using tasks, problems designing a
task-based syllabus acceptable to a mass education system and, above all, TBI's
failure to account for language learning as a process of skill development.

Individual differences

While research on universal factors in SLA has radically changed our conception of the language learning process, teachers are well aware that every learner
is an individual. The humanistic tradition of language teaching and learning
has sought to counter the early behaviourist emphasis on how teachers influence learners, and to recognize that students, singly and jointly, bring to the
classroom not just minds, but also bodies and emotions. Research into individual learner differences (Skehan 1989) has done much to shape current
thinking, especially within learner-centred communicative and autonomy-
based approaches, where self-awareness and self-reliance have an important
role. Some of the multiple and interacting factors that influence success in
language learning can be categorized as biographical, cognitive and affective.

Biographical factors

Age, through successive stages of cognitive development, determines many
aspects of *first* language acquisition, and the Critical Period Hypothesis
(Lenneberg 1967) suggests that unless *foreign* language learning begins before
puberty, ultimate attainment levels will be jeopardized. Research clearly shows
that for language learning, the earlier the start the better, yet while later starters
may find it harder to achieve native-like proficiency, especially as regards
accent, adult beginners can out-perform children, at least initially, in naturalistic contexts. Little comparative research has been conducted with adults,
but increased maturity added to self-selection and motivation means that by
graduation those who started to learn a new language at university have often

overtaken those who started the language at school. Previous language learning and residence abroad will have influenced not only target language (TL) competence, but also motivation, attitudes and learner beliefs.

Cognitive factors

Language aptitude

Language aptitude is an innate ability to learn and use both native and foreign languages, related to but distinguishable from general verbal intelligence. According to early studies based on the Modern Language Aptitude Test or MLAT (Carroll 1979), language aptitude consisted of four factors: phonemic coding ability (identifying distinct sounds and associating them with particular symbols), grammatical sensitivity (recognition of structures and their function), inductive language learning ability (inferring relationships between form and meaning from experience of the language) and rote learning. More recent work (Skehan 1998) uses the terms auditory ability for the first factor, linguistic ability for the second and third, and memory, differentiated into initial coding, storage and retrieval. Teachers cannot influence language aptitude: they can only measure it (see Chapter 11) when selecting for specialist training, as at the Foreign and Commonwealth Office (Davies 2003: 45–46), and take it into account when constituting groups. A further limitation is that aptitude tests predict only cognitive achievement, and not the other factors that contribute to language learning.

Learning styles

Despite recent discussion in the academic press about whether learning styles actually exist, there is substantial evidence to show that individuals perceive, analyse, organize and recall information in ways that are both stable and widely different. However, the many conflicting theoretical frameworks and classifications make practical application of the findings difficult. Beyond widespread recognition of the related continua which oppose holistic/global and serialist/analytical, rule-formers and data-gatherers, two popular traditions group learners either according to their ways of thinking (Kolb 1976) or according to which senses are most active in stimulating memory. In the first system, individuals are situated on each of two dimensions: abstract conceptualization–concrete experience and active experimentation–reflective observation. In the latter, learners are classified as visual, auditory, tactile or kinaesthetic (Reid 1997). Through reflective or language awareness activities, learners can be helped towards greater autonomy and effectiveness through identifying and/or extending their learning styles, although styles appear stable and resistant to pedagogical intervention. There is more scope for accommodating learning styles in self-access centres and materials than in the classroom – and indeed most learning styles research tends to ignore the social and interactive side of learning.

Learner strategies

Learner strategies research developed out of an earlier focus on 'the good language learner' (Naiman *et al.* 1975, Rubin 1975). It emerged that while certain characteristics of good language learners might be innate (in particular verbal intelligence and aptitude) and others were related to personality (including the affective qualities motivation, attitude and anxiety – see below and Arnold 1999), much depended not on who learners were, but on what they did. Various taxonomies have been developed to account for all the possible techniques and strategies employed with regard to the four language skills and to vocabulary and morpho-syntax, among which Oxford (1990) has been most influential. But boundaries between cognitive, metacognitive, affective and social strategies can be fuzzy, as is the border between learning strategies and communicative strategies. More recently, research has focused on whether and how learner strategies can be taught as skills (Cohen 1998; see also Chapter 16).

Extroversion/introversion

While introverts generally perform better academically, an extrovert appears more likely to take advantage of social opportunities for foreign language input and use: which is more advantageous for language learning depends on the circumstances and activities involved.

Affective factors

Learners' emotional states have a powerful influence on their behaviour in the classroom and other learning situations, and an impact on their success. Anxiety or negative attitudes can impair performance, while positive motivation, empathy or self-esteem can enhance it.

Anxiety

Probably the most influential factor in language learning, anxiety can reduce both learning capacity and performance by requisitioning cognitive processing resources and preventing memory from operating properly. Like motivation, language anxiety may be a quasi-permanent trait or a state brought about by the situation, e.g. speaking in the classroom, sitting a high-stakes test, or addressing native speakers. Anxiety is more evident in communicative classrooms than in traditional grammar-translation contexts because of the reliance on speaking, which obliges vulnerable learners to rely on an inadequate vehicle in front of their peers, and on meaningful communication which involves greater personal investment. Standard instruments exist for measuring anxiety (Horwitz *et al.* 1986), which reduces with age and after residence abroad.

Although like adrenaline in sport a degree of anxiety can be facilitative, successful learning depends generally on lowering anxiety, and without necessarily adopting the soft chairs and baroque music that characterize suggestopedia, most teachers will want to create a supportive and collaborative classroom atmosphere (Oxford 1999). Working in pairs and small groups is less face-threatening than talking in front of the whole class, as well as more efficient. Error correction needs to be sensitive to minimize damage to fragile self-esteem and self-confidence. In post-pubertal learners, perceived threats to the ego will induce behavioural inhibitions. The language learning situation is, by definition, one in which uncertainty pertains, and tolerance of ambiguity is needed if the learner is not to experience increased anxiety. To progress, language learners also need to take moderate risks, such as guessing the meaning of a noun or speaking despite the likelihood of making mistakes: anxious learners deprive themselves of practice.

Motivation

Motivation research was for a long time dominated by a social-psychological approach, led by Gardner and his team at OISE in Toronto (Gardner and Lambert 1972, Gardner 1985, Gardner and MacIntyre 1993). Analysing the factors underlying measures of attitude, they identified two contrasting orientations: an *integrative* orientation (a sincere, positive interest in a people and culture that use a different language) and an *instrumental* orientation (a recognition of the practical benefits of learning a new language). The two represent opposite ends of a continuum, and studies have confirmed the importance of both for successful language learning, with integrative orientation more significant in most learning contexts.

The motivation research agenda was broadened in the early 1990s (Crookes and Schmidt 1991, Oxford and Shearin 1994) to incorporate insights drawn from individual, educational and even industrial psychology. The picture we now have is complex and dynamic, embracing semi-permanent traits of character, shorter-term states, and situation-specific factors. The most widely accepted model of motivation is that of Dörnyei and Ottó (1998). This builds on Crookes and Schmidt's levels of motivation (micro, classroom, syllabus and extracurricular), and, in a masterly synthesis, incorporates ideas on feedback and reward, goal orientation, self-efficacy and self-determination, group dynamic, intrinsic/extrinsic motivation and the development of motivated behaviour over time. Dörnyei's explication of the model (Dörnyei 2001:

85–100) is linked to a recognition that teachers must contribute actively to generating and maintaining positive student motivation by multiple techniques, including enhancing learners' language-related values and attitudes, making the curriculum relevant to them, creating realistic learner beliefs, and using ice-breakers and warmers to recreate a supportive group dynamic (Dörnyei 2001: 116–40). The 'Ten commandments for motivating language learners' (Dörnyei and Czisér 1998: 215) are deceptively self-evident and simple, but based on extensive research:

- set a personal example with your own behaviour;
- create a pleasant, relaxed atmosphere in the classroom;
- present the tasks properly;
- develop a good relationship with the learners;
- increase the learner's linguistic self-confidence;
- make the language classes interesting;
- promote learner autonomy;
- personalize the learning process;
- increase the learners' goal-orientedness;
- familiarize learners with the target-language culture.

Attitudes to the learning situation, the teacher, the materials and activities, and especially the target-language community are key factors in learner motivation: 'positive attitudes towards the L2, its speakers, and its culture can be expected to enhance learning and negative attitudes to impede learning' (Ellis 1994: 200).

Willingness to communicate

Willingness to communicate (WTC) is 'the probability of initiating communication, specifically talking, when the opportunity arises' (MacIntyre et al. 2003: 590). It represents an attempt to integrate linguistic, psychological and communicative approaches (MacIntyre et al. 1998), and is both a learning outcome (particularly of residence abroad) and a powerful influence on success in language learning. It embraces stable personality traits such as extroversion, evolving factors, notably communication anxiety and perceived communication competence, and situation-specific elements such as formality, number of people present, and topic of conversation.

▶ List ten things you do in your own classroom practice to increase motivation and to reduce anxiety.
▶ How do these compare with the recommendations of researchers?

Social interaction

The learner is also a social being, learning through interaction with others. Sociocultural theories of learning, according to which all learning is first social and then individual, are thus especially relevant to us. Although Lev Vygotsky died in 1934, it is only in the last two decades that his work on child development has been widely applied to language learning. The knowledge possessed by children and unskilled learners is advanced by interaction with others (parents or teachers), whose guidance through successive steps of a problem is known as scaffolding. The ZPD or Zone of Proximal Development is defined as 'the distance between the actual developmental level as determined by independent problem solving, and the level of potential development as determined by problem solving under adult guidance or in collaboration with more capable peers' (Vygotsky 1978: 86). Even among adults, the role of interaction remains crucial: new language knowledge is not transmitted, but rather co-constructed and then internalized as learners collaborate in authentic problem-solving. In this constructivist context, the task-based interactions considered above from a cognitive perspective represent, whether tutor-led or peer-led, collaborative learning through social interaction. Research informed by Vygotskyan theory concerns both classroom and online learning (e.g. Hampel and Hauck 2004).

Conclusion

The principal goal of research into language learning is not necessarily to provide practical guidance for language teachers, although research insights can help us to understand why one approach might work better than another in particular circumstances. Awareness of some of the findings briefly outlined in this chapter, and of the factors that promote success in FL learning, can help conscientious teachers to understand the learning process, and perhaps even to enhance their own practice.

Sources of information

For accessible introductions to several of the areas covered in this chapter, see the DELPHI distance-learning programme:

> Module 2: E. Broady, *Understanding Second Language Acquisition*;
> Module 4: C. Edwards, *Task-based Language Learning*;
> Module 12: J. Littlemore, *Learner Autonomy, Language Learning Strategies and Learning Styles*.
> Online. Available at: www.delphi.bham.ac.uk (accessed 11 June 2004).

An important database of current UK research into language learning also includes surveys/ guides and bibliographies. Online. Available at: www.languagesresearch.ac.uk (accessed 4 July 2004).

The Association for French Language Studies has published *A Brief Guide to Research in French Language and Linguistics*. Online. Available at: www.north.londonmet.ac.uk/afls/ resguide.html (accessed 4 July 2004).

Byram, M. (ed.) (2000) *The Routledge Encyclopedia of Language Teaching and Learning*, London: Routledge.

6

Curriculum design

James A. Coleman and Elizabeth Hauge

Introduction

The present chapter focuses on the *language* curriculum, since Chapters 22 to 26 deal specifically with the 'content' in terms of cultural, literary, linguistic, business and area studies. It also addresses broad issues, since subsequent chapters deal at a more detailed level with the concerns and activities appropriate to different strands of the curriculum – the four skills of speaking, listening, reading and writing (Chapter 7), grammar (Chapter 8), vocabulary (Chapter 9), assessment (Chapters 10 and 11), using the foreign language assistant (Chapter 12), and translation and interpreting (Chapter 13).

Curriculum design for Modern Language courses is often broadly similar across languages at specific levels in terms of wide goals or aims, narrower learning outcomes or objectives and, at times, forms of assessment (see Chapter 10). However, it can vary considerably in the detail of materials, methodology and delivery at different levels – and, of course, in terms of any single actual syllabus.

It is conventional to distinguish between curriculum and syllabus. The curriculum contains a broad description of general goals and embodies a theoretical orientation, while the syllabus is a more detailed and operational statement translating the theoretical principles into a series of planned steps (course content) leading to defined objectives (Dubin and Olshtain 1986: 34–35). Syllabuses may be built around grammatical structures, around the functions that language performs, or around the situations in which the language will be used, such as tourism or university study.

> ▶ Think about the syllabuses that you followed as a student, or which you are now teaching.
> ▶ Are they functional, grammatical, situational or a mixture of these?

In reality, curriculum designers rarely start with a clean slate – indeed, there are advantages in seeing what was done before and what is done in similar circumstances elsewhere – but we prefer to set out all the considerations to be taken into account. Initial questions that must be addressed include:

- What student *levels* are expected?
- Are these *specialist* or non-specialist learners?
- What are the long-term *goals* that the courses hope to achieve?
- What *materials* will be used?
- What methodological *approach* will be used?
- Will *delivery* of the courses be face-to-face, online or blended, i.e. a mixture of these?
- Is the language course *integrated* with one or more content courses?
- What kind of *assessments* will be used?

Levels are important since language students range from complete beginners to virtual native speakers. In order to demonstrate progress between the objectives for each semester in a degree programme, it may be necessary to make provision for courses at six or seven different levels.

The level of the students also influences the answers to most of the other questions. Longer-term goals will clearly differ according to level, while materials at the lower levels will not only be less complex, but also probably more tightly structured than at higher levels where students will be given greater freedom to express themselves. As for choice of materials, many tutors at lower levels opt to use course books, while at higher levels there is usually a greater preponderance of authentic materials from a variety of sources to provide comprehensible input (Krashen 1981, 1982) and help students to become familiar with the discourse features of different text types.

The approach may also vary, with the materials chosen, from a more traditional focus upon grammar and translation to a more modern focus on communicative language teaching (Brumfit 1984, Johnson 1982, Littlewood 1984, Savignon 1991), often using a topic-focused, task-based approach (Ellis 2003, Nunan 1989, Skehan 1996, J. Willis 1996). Again, although much of the delivery of Modern Language teaching is done face-to-face in seminar groups, tutors today are being encouraged to supplement this with independent learning (see Chapter 16) and online support, using a platform such as Blackboard or WebCT (see Sources of information for an example). Students can access such Virtual Learning Environments (VLEs) on site or from home to check course information, retrieve documents, do practice exercises, submit work or communicate with their tutor and/or fellow students. Computer-Assisted Language Learning (CALL) and Computer-Mediated Communication (CMC) are covered in Chapters 18 and 19. The balance between whole-class, small-group, one-to-one and independent work is a crucial decision, subject as much to resource as to pedagogical concerns.

A principal constraint on mainstream foreign language syllabuses is what is happening in the rest of the course. Although integration of language and content is less prevalent than in the past (see Chapter 1), the language syllabus often has to accommodate other parts of the curriculum such as study skills, CV writing or residence abroad preparation.

Finally, while students may be assessed according to common criteria across the levels, specific forms of assessment at individual levels will obviously differ too, according to what students are able to do with the target language (TL) at any given point in their language-learning (see Chapter 11).

Other constraints on curriculum and syllabus design include staffing, access to resources such as language labs, computer labs or video equipment, and scheduling – an alternation of classes with independent study or homework is more flexible than a whole afternoon in class once a week. Traditionally, resources allowed for one piece of work to be handed in, corrected and returned each week, but some departments have to manage with a student dossier or portfolio on which less frequent formative feedback is provided.

Quality Assurance processes mean that, unlike their predecessors and their contemporary peers in some other countries, UK academics need to familiarize themselves with the Quality Assurance Agency for Higher Education (www.qaa.ac.uk) and its policy on programme specifications. This is the framework in which curriculum design takes place. It embraces the specification of learning outcomes in terms of knowledge and understanding, cognitive skills, key skills and practical/professional skills as well as programme structures, and will from the start require close liaison with other parts of the institution. The processes involved are too complex to cover in the present volume (but see Chapter 10 on learning outcomes and assessment). Familiarity with the benchmark statement for languages and related studies (QAA 2002) is also essential.

> ▶ Obtain course documentation (programme specifications) for several courses in different languages in your own institution – and if possible from others – to help inform your own choices. What are the common features? What are the key terms that are repeatedly used?

The remainder of this chapter provides a snapshot of seven possible levels and lists some common activities and tasks.

Levels

Level 1

Most Modern Language (ML) departments have courses for Beginners (aka *ab initio* learners), who comprise three groups:

- non-specialists (see Chapter 14) who wish to add a foreign language to their main focus on, say, Engineering or Economics;
- specialists who are fast-tracking to catch up with post-A level entrants within one or two years;
- Modern Languages students who are continuing their study of one or two (usually European) languages at degree level, but who wish to add another language (such as Chinese, Japanese or Arabic) to their repertoire while at university.

Typically, the non-specialists have 2–3 hours of study a week, the fast-trackers up to 6, compared to around 3–4 for conventional entrants.

At Beginner level, the overall goals are to give students an understanding of – and the opportunity to practise – the basics of the language, and a course book is generally used since this gives students an overview of the structure of the course and enables them both to review work done and to prepare work in advance. Tutors will also ensure that there is cyclical reinforcement of structures and vocabulary throughout the course, and they may supplement the course book with additional materials. Initially, some tutors may prefer to teach through the medium of English, gradually introducing TL instruction as the course progresses. Delivery at Level 1 will probably be face-to-face, but online resources may be available for practice tasks outside classes. Variety in activities is essential at all levels, but especially so for Beginners.

Assessments (see Chapter 11) will take the form of short tasks done in-class or for homework with an oral and a written exam at the end of the year or each semester. The ultimate aim might be for students to reach GCSE level, which would be equivalent to the Common European Framework (CEF) level A2, by the end of the academic year.

Level 2

Tutors will again typically use a course book, building in cyclical reinforcement of structures and vocabulary throughout the course. Face-to-face classes (with online practice materials) will be in the TL, and reinforced by dedicated oral classes with the foreign language assistant (see Chapter 12).

Assessments will comprise in-class and homework tasks with an oral and a written exam. By the end of Level 2, students will be expected to have reached the equivalent of a good AS Level or a grade below C at A Level, the equivalent of CEF B1.

Level 3

This is the lowest level of entry for ML students who have studied the language prior to starting their degree. Language teaching from this level up is normally conducted entirely face-to-face through the medium of the TL (with the exception of some translation classes). Course books are often replaced with a dossier of authentic materials from the broadcast and print media of the TL country. It may include background reading texts; comprehension questions for written or video texts; grammar and/or vocabulary work; lists of further useful material in print/video form or available on the internet. The advantages of producing a dossier are similar to those of using a course book, but tutors have more control over what is included and they can tailor the materials more precisely to the needs of particular cohorts of students.

Many tutors adopt a communicative approach, but a great deal of traditional teaching, involving close study of texts, grammar (see Chapter 8) and translation (see Chapter 13) still takes place. By the end of Level 3, students should be reasonably competent users of the language who have reached 'A' or 'B' standard at A Level or CEF B2.

Level 4

Post-A level ML students start here, and by the end of the academic year should be able to comprehend and produce a reasonably wide range of TL structures and vocabulary with a good standard of accuracy in a variety of situations: CEF B2/C1.

Level 5

Students will become familiar with spoken and written discourse on issues of contemporary importance and will be able to present, verbally and in writing, accounts of complex topics, their opinions on these and the justification for their views. In addition to these advanced communication skills, they will also be highly competent, independent language learners with well-developed research and organizational skills.

Activities at this stage are more likely to be of the integrated- rather than the discrete-skill variety (see Chapter 7), and assessment may include project-based research tasks. Target level upon completion: CEF C1.

Level 6

Level 6 students should be extremely competent users of the TL who are ready to explore TL varieties in greater depth and become truly creative in their use of the TL. By the end of this year's study, they should be able to understand quite easily most authentic written and spoken texts in many registers and genres in the TL. They should also be able to produce the TL as required in analytical, specific and informative situations. At the same time, their pronunciation should be approaching native speaker standard. Target level: CEF C1/C2.

Level 7

Students at this level are near-native speakers of the TL, understanding virtually everything they hear, including nuance, and managing linguistically complex interactions fluently and accurately. They should be able to translate between their native language and the TL accurately, maintaining style and idiom as well as content. In class, they should be able to cope with any linguistic challenge in their studies, and therefore more complex literary, political, cultural and technical written and spoken texts can be used. Target level: C2.

Readers should note that level descriptors will vary across institutions and types of courses, and should be set realistically, bearing in mind the proficiency level of entrants.

A note on Languages for Specific Purposes

Whatever the commissioning department may intuitively believe, LSP (Languages for Specific Purposes) is rarely appropriate in courses for non-specialists. A course in law with French may legitimately stress legal French, but mechanical engineers, even those preparing for a placement abroad, will not normally require mechanical engineering French. They can usually cope with the technical interactions, but need generic French for more important social interactions: talking over meals or going out in the evenings.

Principles

Several principles should be borne in mind when designing the curriculum.

1   Language *learning* at all levels is more effective when students:
    ● find themselves in a TL-rich environment where they are motivated to use the TL in different contexts;
    ● feel confident enough to take risks, to make errors and experiment with the TL;
    ● are made aware of appropriate language-learning strategies and are encouraged to put them into practice both in and out of class;
    ● have opportunities to use the TL out of class.

2   Language *teaching* at all levels is more effective when tutors:
    ● provide materials that students perceive to be interesting and relevant;
    ● organize in each class a variety of ways to work (individually, in pairs, in small groups, as a whole class);
    ● incorporate task-based activities and some problem-solving contexts in which students can activate – and build on – their existing general knowledge;
    ● provide formative feedback on all assessed coursework.

At lower levels it is also particularly important for tutors to encourage the development of a positive self-image by providing success-oriented tasks and positive feedback.

Activities and tasks

At all of the levels discussed above there should be a certain amount of experiential learning balanced by analytical work (Stern 1990); a topic-focused, task-based approach with specified learning outcomes is often most motivating, whether based on a course book or tutor-selected materials. When topics are carefully chosen (for example, if they are linked to the cultural, political or social situation in the TL country), it is usually possible to build before and during the course a bank of materials at an appropriate level for use either in class or for support outside class. Activities based on these will be set for pedagogic reasons to help students to acquire and practise the TL.

Some examples of activities and tasks that might be used at the different levels – with increasing degrees of difficulty as the levels progress – are as follows:

Pedagogic tasks to exploit written, aural or visual texts include:
- gap-filling;
- labelling;
- multiple choice;
- completion;
- matching;
- true/false/not given.

Although mainly used in class at lower levels, such tasks also appear in online practice materials at higher levels.

Speaking tasks can include:
- asking and answering questions in various situations (including quizzes);
- peer correction;
- peer teaching;
- information-gap tasks;
- simulation or role play tasks in various 'real world' contexts;
- informal discussions;
- conducting a survey and presenting the results;
- giving formal individual/group presentations on researched topics or projects;
- organizing and taking part in formal debates.*

Writing tasks can take the form of:
- writing sentences, paragraphs, notes, instructions, descriptions, guidelines, etc.;
- writing letters of different kinds, summaries, reviews, etc.;
- researching a topic and writing reports, articles or various kinds of essay;
- drafting speeches for debates.*

(* These are generally more successful from Level 5 on.)

In conclusion, as we have seen, curriculum design for university ML courses involves consideration of level, learner profile, goals, learning outcomes, materials, methodology, delivery, course integration and assessment. There are differences between the levels, but there are similarities across languages at each level in terms of goals, learning outcomes and, in many cases, forms of assessment.

Staff new to curriculum design would be well advised to consult existing course descriptions, look at other institutions' programmes, build on the experience of others, and implement change gradually. They should be keen to accept external examinerships: the best form of professional development available in this domain.

Sources of information

The Subject Centre offers a range of information on curriculum and syllabus design. Online. Available at: www.lang.ltsn.ac.uk (accessed 19 June 2004).

Example of learning management using Blackboard, with differentiated information for staff and students. Online. Available at: www.iss.soton.ac.uk/landt/elearn (accessed 19 June 2004).

Example of level descriptors. Online. Available at: www.lang.soton.ac.uk/cls/stages.html (accessed 19 June 2004).

7

The four language skills or 'juggling simultaneous constraints'

Elspeth Broady

The caricature of the French professor who could dissert on the French imperfect subjunctive, but who could not order a meal in Paris has long been used to champion a more 'practical' or 'communicative' approach to language teaching. However, language teachers in these post-communicative days also evoke the problem of the over-confident communicator who engages fluently in colloquial routines, but who is restricted by over-simplified grammar and cannot produce accurate written text. Put simplistically, the problem in both cases has to do with the integration of knowledge and skill: the learned professor possessed knowledge but limited skills while the superficially fluent student possesses some skills but little knowledge.

Effective language skill requires the integration of knowledge (grammar and vocabulary) in the performance of a task, e.g. asking for directions, answering a comprehension test or contributing to an oral discussion. The task imposes constraints – processing constraints we shall call them – on how quickly and effectively we can access our language knowledge: language knowledge that might be easily available for use in some tasks may not be so easily available for others. Processing constraints are about the limits on how many things the human brain can do at once. For example, if I engage in conversation while trying to use the new photocopier, I usually end up with enlarged copies when I want them reduced. I 'know' which keys to press, but conversation competes for my attention and I may press the wrong key or forget to set a particular option. It will, of course, come as no surprise that the repeated practice of a task generally makes the knowledge required for it easier to access: for example, I can use the old photocopier successfully even while engaged in animated discussion with several colleagues! This process of making access to knowledge more efficient through repetition of a task is known as automatization. However, in the process of automatizing, we tend to lose awareness of what we know, such that it can then be difficult to update and modify. For example, I can't tell anybody my old photocopier code: I just type it in automatically without thinking. If someone told me to 'change the third number in your code to a six', I would not be able to do it without thinking very hard and performing the task slowly. Using language can be similar: it takes time and mental effort to develop knowledge of the target language (TL) grammar and vocabulary, it takes time and mental effort to automatize use of that knowledge in performance, and language knowledge is a lot more complex than knowledge of a photocopier! Trying to develop accurate and more complex language knowledge and its use in performance is about 'juggling simultaneous constraints' (Flower and Hayes 1980: 31), to use an expression originally coined for the process of writing.

> ▶ Skehan (1998) captures this same idea when he says that language teaching needs to focus on developing learners' accuracy, fluency and complexity, but that these three areas may not always be developed simultaneously. What do you think he means?

As with all complex skills, the problem we face in trying to develop communicative ability in a second language is that there are trade-offs between different aspects of the skill. For example, if, as an intermediate level learner of a second language, you wish to give a really fluent oral performance in that language, you may have to sacrifice some level of grammatical accuracy and conceptual complexity, i.e. the ideas you can express and the range of vocabulary in which you can express them will need to be more limited. Conversely, if you have to perform an unfamiliar task requiring highly complex knowledge, then you may not initially be able to perform that task very fluently. One of the ways in which we 'juggle constraints' is by developing strategies for coping with the demands of different tasks.

Language task difficulty and the four skills

> ▶ Is holding a conversation in a foreign language easier than making a formal presentation on a complex topic, e.g. explaining a social phenomenon, such as racial discrimination? Why? Why not? Jot down the factors which, in your opinion, determine the difficulty of a language task.

A number of authors (Brown *et al.* 1984, Skehan 1998) have attempted to identify what makes a language task difficult. The following seem to be the key factors:

- the complexity of the language involved;
- the complexity of the knowledge being expressed;
- the degree of predictability of the content and the structure of the task;
- the degree of familiarity with the task itself, and the topic of the task;
- the speed of delivery required and time pressure;
- the opportunities to control the task.

Language tasks may not be difficult just because of the inherent complexity of the language involved. Learners may, for example, be able to understand more complex language if they are familiar with the topic being expressed. Similarly, if they are familiar with a particular type of task, such as making a presentation, then they may find that presenting an unknown topic with new vocabulary is not so daunting. And, of course, the difficulty of processing any language will also be determined by which of 'the four skills' – speaking, listening, reading and writing – are involved.

> ▶ Thinking generally, which skill would you say is easiest in a foreign language? Why? What are the differences between the four skills?
> ▶ Which skills do you think your students find easiest?

The differences between the four skills are typically determined by speed of delivery and time pressure. Speech sounds are transient and thus have to be processed sequentially in real time. Individual sounds and words cannot be given too much attention; instead, the listener and speaker need to focus on ensuring that the main message is communicated. For this reason, informal spoken language is frequently repetitive and redundant as the speaker revises, reorganizes and reiterates for the benefit of the listener. Speakers and listeners change roles frequently. If we have to speak for a longer turn without interaction, most of us have to bring to mind a predictable organizational framework – a plan – to allow us to structure our thoughts and maintain fluency. Such predictable formats help listeners too: we expect a lecture to begin with an introduction outlining the key questions and to end with a conclusion where these questions are revisited. Whatever the type of interaction, then, speakers and listeners have to base comprehension at least partially on guesswork strategies because they simply do not have enough time to process each word individually.

Written language, on the other hand, can in principle be processed at greater leisure. A reader can go back over a text to check understanding. A writer can spend time selecting the exact word and revising an earlier portion of text in the light of a later portion. These processing conditions mean that written text is typically more dense than spoken text, more grammatically and lexically complex. However, it would be wrong to imagine that there are no time pressures involved in processing written language. If a reader spends too much time decoding individual letters and words, then insufficient attention will be available to make sense of the sentences and paragraphs of a text, i.e. to access its real meaning. Similarly, if a writer gets bogged down in 'polishing' a sentence, it is then easy to forget how that sentence fits in with the overall plan of the text. So, written text also has predictable features so as to ease the processing burden on both readers and writers. A further challenge is that written forms typically carry more explicit grammatical information than spoken forms. For example, a regular French verb such as 'chanter' may have around 12 inflectional endings distinguished in speech, depending on pronunciation, but over 25 distinguished in writing. As many language learners will attest, putting pen to paper in a foreign language is like stepping into a minefield where 'mistakes' – and the depressing red-pen marks they trigger – loom at every step.

As well as distinguishing spoken from written language modes, we need to distinguish productive and receptive language skills. Speaking and writing involve producing language, i.e. retrieving language knowledge from memory and activating the relevant motor skills programmes to produce sounds, or letters on paper or a computer screen. Listening and reading involve processing sounds or letters and matching that information with language knowledge stored in memory. If we take it as a general principle that recognition of knowledge is easier than recall, then it is obvious that receptive skills should be experienced as less demanding than productive skills. But reading and listening should not be seen as 'passive'. Effective comprehension requires active involvement in interpretation. In what follows, we review some of the tasks and strategies that are relevant to each of the four skills.

Speaking

▶ In what circumstances do you talk most fluently? In what circumstances do you find yourself 'drying up', even in your first language? How do you keep communication going if you can't find the word you are looking for?

Speaking is usually considered the core skill in language learning; it is what learners generally want to be able to do. But as we have seen, speaking is demanding in that it requires production of language knowledge under severe time pressures. It therefore requires a lot of practice. The challenge for teachers then becomes providing extensive practice without losing learners' motivation through the boredom of repetition. At the very early levels of language development, learners may be aiming to produce typical phrases and structures that can be used in short exchanges. These can be modelled first in an audio or video dialogue and then isolated for repetition. Repetition drills are the 'scales' of language learning: not very exciting, but important opportunities for learners to build up control over the complex sequencing of movements required to produce a phrase. Small variations can be introduced into drilling to keep learners focused and involved: for example, orchestrate repetition from different groups in a class (pairs, groups of four, half the class); get learners to repeat loudly or softly or simply get them to practise saying key phrases in pairs. Repetition is also something that is well supported by computer-based independent learning materials: replaying phrases is easy to control and some computer-based materials have the possibility for students to record themselves and check their pronunciation.

Once learners have some knowledge of the language to draw on, the information gap principle (McDonough and Shaw 1993: 164–66) is a useful one in providing varied speaking practice. What motivates people to initiate talk? Usually, it is to share information that is not already known. Of course, there are all kinds of other language functions, but this principle of information exchange seems fundamental. Thus, one way to stimulate language use is to set up an information gap which learners have to fill, using the TL. For example, if your learners are practising asking personal information questions, an information-gap activity might involve giving each student a card with such instructions as 'Find someone whose birthday is in January' or 'Find someone who likes cats', or even 'Find someone who shares your views on education funding'! You can vary the seriousness or the levity of the topic depending on your learners' interests and language needs. Other information-gap activities might involve:

- getting students to describe a picture to their partners so that the partners can identify the picture from a set;
- checking partial information with a partner who also has partial (but different) information in order to complete a booking form;
- asking for directions to a particular location from a partner who has a map.

One of the most difficult spoken tasks to orchestrate effectively in the classroom is what is usually termed 'discussion'. You can invite students to 'discuss' a text or a video recording in class; what often ensues is an embarrassing period of limited communication. The failure of discussion may be because the task of expressing opinions is too demanding to start with: as we mentioned earlier, trying to express complex ideas is likely to reduce fluency of communication. In everyday conversation, we tend to start exchanges with very down-to-earth topics: narratives about activities, judgements about simple issues such as preferring red to white wine, enquiries about feelings. Only gradually do we build up to more complex topics. So if you want to engage your students in discussion, you might try starting with some very simple questions such as 'If you could live anywhere you wanted, would it be in a town or the country? Why?' This could serve as a prelude to a deeper discussion, e.g. on the depopulation of rural France! Furthermore, if you want your students to express more complex ideas, then explore giving them clear guidelines for organizing their thoughts. For example, if you are asking them to discuss an article, then you might suggest they select the three most important sentences in the passage and explain why they have chosen them. You might ask them simply to identify the problem and the solution raised in a particular article, or to summarize a narrative. In general, the more concrete the task, the more likely it will generate spoken communication.

As native speakers, we command a variety of devices to help us manage the complex task of speaking. We hesitate, using 'um' or 'er'; we fill the pauses with 'filler phrases' such as 'y'know', 'sort of thing' and 'kind of like'. These expressions give us time to think and yet maintain contact with the person we are talking to. You could make your students aware of these devices in recordings of authentic TL speech and encourage them to use them to support their own fluency. There are also strategies for coping with vocabulary gaps: as native speakers, we effortlessly navigate our way around temporarily forgotten words by paraphrase, often using general words such as 'thing' or 'wotsit'. This ability, which is part of what Canale and Swain (1980) term 'strategic competence', is a fundamental component of communicative skill. A useful way to get students to practise this could be by means of a drawing information-gap task: one learner has to describe a drawing to another so that they can reproduce the drawing. You may need to introduce a time limit in order to focus learners on communication and you'll need to be prepared to debrief such creative expressions as 'un chat tabé' (a tabby cat) or 'Spendengeld' (spending money)! While it might be claimed that encouraging learners to solve problems in this way could lead to fossilization, i.e. students never learning more accurate expressions, there is no doubting the importance of such strategies in maintaining fluency.

One way of overcoming the risk of communicative fossilization is to get learners to practise oral tasks several times over. Bygate (2001) researched the impact of task repetition and found that on second performance, learners improved on measures not just of fluency but also of complexity of language used. We may be concerned that repeating exactly the same task again will be boring for learners, but if we can introduce some new element into the repetition, then we can offset that concern. You could, for example, do a short debriefing of key vocabulary items between task performances; learners might then move round to a new partner to practise again, this time with the challenge of integrating the new vocabulary.

A simple oral fluency task that lends itself well to repetition is the 'speaking challenge': invite your students in pairs or individually to try speaking fluently on a given topic for a very limited period of time, i.e. 30 seconds or one minute, depending on level. It is best *not* to allow much preparation (e.g. between 10 and 20 seconds) in the first instance in order to emphasize the task as a light-hearted challenge. For lower-level students, you could set challenges such as: 'tell me five things about yourself in German, starting now' or 'speak for 15 seconds about your town'. If the speaking task is clearly time-limited, learners tend to stop worrying about the content or accuracy of what they say and concentrate on achieving fluency. As is the case for all challenges, succeeding in such tasks can be highly motivating. This motivation can then sustain a repeat of the task where learners can improve on their performance.

▶ Why do you think second language learners may be reluctant to participate in class oral activities? Note down all the reasons you can think of, and consider how they might be addressed in your teaching.

In planning speaking activities, there is always a need to consider the social-affective setting of the classroom. We all feel embarrassed when our ability to communicate effectively breaks down or we say things that we believe reflect badly on ourselves. Second language learners are particularly sensitive to this because they may feel they are unable to communicate their thoughts and ideas fully, and that what they can communicate may appear trivial or ridiculous. One way of addressing this, as indicated above, is to use brief oral tasks, presented as games or challenges, and to keep the classroom atmosphere light and friendly. Small group work, e.g. in pairs, multiplies opportunities for practice and allows learners to gain confidence before speaking out in front of a larger group. In managing discussion and oral question-and-answer, you could explore using what Thornberry (1996) calls 'wait time', that is simply extending the pause you allow when addressing an oral question to a student. It seems that teachers typically only pause for around one to two seconds after asking a question before expecting a student to reply or moving on. Thornberry found that if teachers systematically paused for longer (around four seconds), then learners responded for longer and initiated more questions.

Reading and listening

▶ How would you define 'understanding'? If we assume that 'understanding' a text means knowing the meaning of the words used in it, why is it that we sometimes experience 'not understanding' a text in our first language? What is it that causes that 'not understanding'?

Reading and listening involve the matching of linguistic knowledge and knowledge of the world. As Bartlett (1932) established, comprehension takes place when we match the input we hear or read with our existing frameworks of understanding. These frameworks, stored in long-term memory, are termed 'schemas'. If we cannot link incoming information to an existing schema, or if we select the wrong schema, comprehension can be severely hindered. For example, you will probably find making sense of the following passage difficult: but why?

> An approach based on sampling abilities . . . will probably regard processing and contexts as things to be handled by extension once the underlying pattern of abilities has been measured. In contrast, a processing approach will regard the capacity to handle real language use as the dominant factor, with abilities playing a subservient, servicing role.
>
> (Skehan 1998: 155)

Even though you probably understood each word in isolation, you may have had difficulty making sense of the text as a whole. This is arguably because you have no schema for making sense of it. The vocabulary used is abstract, and if you cannot access a schema for this passage, it is impossible to know what these terms refer to. While you can try to understand the message by interpreting each individual word – what is called bottom-up processing – you really need to have some idea of what the text is about *before* you do this. That would allow you to process top-down, that is, predict what the author is trying to say and check those predictions against what you understand from the text.

To demonstrate how schemas influence interpretation, take a look at the passage below. Read through the text and then note down synonyms for the words in italics.

The Creature

Jim ran on and on. He hardly dared turn around. He felt the *grofulous* animal gaining ground, coming up behind him faster and faster. As he ran along the *cramp* edge, he heard the *sprangian* sea *ranking* against the rocks. Terror gripped him and he felt *holf* . . .

Now, in principle, you should not have been able to understand this text because it contains five randomly invented words. But you probably *did*. The schema for this text – 'hero pursued by threatening creature' – is relatively straightforward: generations of my students have come up with it just from looking at the title. Having brought to mind a schema, you can quite easily fill in the gaps. You probably gave synonyms such as 'grotesque', 'huge' or 'terrifying' for 'grofulous' but definitely not 'happy', 'comforting' or 'peaceful'! Those adjectives do not fit in with the scary story schema. Similarly, you may have thought of 'crashing' or 'beating' for 'ranking', but not 'lapping' or 'playing'. In this way, our schemas help us to interpret text quickly. Bottom-up processing and top-down processing interact all the time in our comprehension. Your ability to come up with a schema for the above text would obviously have been reduced if there had been a much greater proportion of unknown words, but conversely, we saw with the earlier extract how 'knowing the words' does not guarantee understanding.

Tasks practising listening and reading need to encourage learners to engage in both bottom-up and top-down processing. To do this, it is useful to plan listening and reading comprehension work as a cycle of activities (see Broady 2002). It makes sense to start with activities favouring top-down processing since learners need to access a schema for a written text or a recording as quickly as they can in order to have a framework for more detailed listening/reading. Such activities might involve predicting the content of the text from just a headline or from a global view of the text, or 'skim-listening' to a news bulletin to identify two or three key points. If a text or a recording contains challenging key vocabulary, this key vocabulary can be clarified first and students then asked to predict the content of the text. The same thing can be done with key phrases. Students' predictions can then be used to guide a first reading or listening, providing a kind of information gap. Activities favouring bottom-up processing focus attention on linguistic information more intensively. This might mean:

- listening for specific words;
- finding synonyms and translations;
- identifying who said what;
- correcting an erroneous summary of the text;
- filling in blanks in a transcription.

At lower levels of language proficiency, over-reliance on bottom-up processing seems to hinder task performance, while at higher levels it may be the reverse (O'Malley *et al.* 1989, Long 1990). As learners gain basic fluency in processing spoken or written language, so they may be tempted to gloss over details, particularly where these conflict with a straightforward schema. Integrating bottom-up and top-down processing is essential for effective skill development (Broady 2002). For more listening activities see White (1998).

> ▶ Have you ever watched a TV news bulletin in a language you do not 'understand'? How much of the news bulletin were you able to interpret? How did you do this? What information sources were you drawing on? What information do you think you were missing?

Video recordings can be particularly useful for encouraging top-down guess-work strategies. Through the visual channel, video provides rich and accessible contextual information for the interpretation of language. We can often guess the gist of a conversation just by looking at where the interaction takes place, the clothing and manner of speakers involved and the whole range of paralinguistic cues, in particular gestures and facial expressions. The visual and the sound channels can thus be usefully separated. Students could be asked to watch a conversational exchange between two characters. From the visual channel, they can predict the nature of the dialogue, either giving the gist of what is being said or actually predicting the phrases used. In this way, learners' own productions serve as an advance organizer to focus their attention on the language channel during a subsequent viewing. Conversely, another group of students could focus first on the language channel without vision and from what they hear, predict the age of the speakers, their relationship and the exact context of the exchange. The two groups then swap predictions and view the full recording to check their understanding. In extracts from news bulletins, the visual channel can be particularly helpful in getting learners to establish the likely gist of the item before they are exposed to highly dense language, delivered at speed. It is important to remember that the dominance of the visual information may sometimes cut across detailed bottom-up processing. Getting students to focus, with no other support, on the detail of the language used in a video recording may not prove to be very effective in the classroom, but then, if you base video activities on detailed printed worksheets, students' attention is in any case likely to be divided between the worksheet and the screen. Significantly, a number of researchers (Vanderplank 1988, Garza 1991, Danan 1992, Borrás and Lafayette 1994) have claimed the value of video input with TL subtitles, particularly for vocabulary retention. For examples of sequences of video activities, see Loftus and Loftus (1992), Broady and Meinhof (1995) and Broady and Shade (1996).

Of course, video is now a digital medium. As such, it can be easily delivered on a computer screen along with any other digital resource. Video can be linked to on-screen text comprising activities and exercises with little danger of attention being divided: transcriptions and subtitles can be called up, on-line dictionaries can be consulted at the same time as viewing. Small sections of the video can be replayed easily and endlessly. In this way, the advent of digital video has enabled much more detailed use of video material in language learning. You will find more ideas on exploiting audio and video activities in Broady (2002) and Coleman (2000).

> ▶ What would you prefer to read on a train journey? An encyclopedia, a book of poetry, a holiday brochure or a novel? Why?
> ▶ Would you say you listen 'differently' to (a) a weather forecast, (b) an interview with a famous actor, and (c) a friend telling you about a bad day at work? If so, in what ways?

Different types of comprehension task lend themselves to different kinds of comprehension strategy. Very few of us read encyclopedias from beginning to end in the same way we would a novel: we listen to weather forecasts differently from interviews. Nuttall (1996) distinguishes usefully between 'skimming' and 'scanning', primarily in relation to reading comprehension, but the terms are equally useful for listening practice. In scanning, the reader rapidly runs over a text to identify a specific piece of information required. This is the strategy we might use for checking in a holiday brochure whether a flat has central heating or not, or in listening in a weather forecast for the details for our area. Skimming has a broader focus, involving running through a text to get the general gist, and can be easily applied to listening comprehension. As suggested above, this strategy is particularly important for language students since it can allow them to set up a schema for further detailed reading. Training learners to skim a text at speed or just to listen for gist can help to restore confidence for students daunted by 'all those words I don't understand'. But it is a skill that needs repeated practice.

As with all skills, listening and reading benefit from extensive practice, so it is useful to encourage learners to incorporate listening and reading for meaning in the TL into their everyday lives. This could be listening to the radio in the TL, regularly watching TL television and reading novels and newspapers in the TL. Encourage your learners to read and listen for pleasure: if you feel you need to motivate this by providing a focus for the activity, invite learners to write brief reviews of TL novels and films for other students and to post them on your institution's website. Depending on the level of your students, reviews could be written in English or the TL. Other students could then add their opinions. To encourage regular viewing and listening of TL broadcasting, you might start every class by inviting learners to report back on, for example, the week's most interesting news story. In this way, regular target-language reading and listening are integrated into some kind of task which potentially involves other target-language skills such as speaking and writing.

Writing

As well as being a skill in its own right, writing is a significant support for learning. In other words, it supports the retention and organization of target-language knowledge. As we mentioned above, writing involves making very explicit the grammatical role of words. In this way, it requires more intensive bottom-up processing than, say, listening comprehension. A number of authors (e.g. Nunan 1999: 181–82, Wajnryb 1990) have proposed exploiting this in dictation-type activities such as 'dictogloss'. In dictogloss, students listen to a text read out twice and note down as many words and phrases as possible. They then try to reconstruct as much of the text as possible through pooling notes in small groups. There are then subsequent readings for groups to check their texts. This type of activity can work very well as practice for bottom-up processing, but also for the kind of detailed checking of written forms that is central to effective writing.

But writing is not just about checking grammar and spelling. It is about expression of ideas in a coherent form. Having to maintain a coherent plan of the intended text, find appropriate words to express the component points and endlessly check grammar and spelling can make writing a very demanding task in a second language unless students have strategies for breaking it down. The so-called 'process' approach to writing practice proposes just this. In the same way that we have stressed above that reading and listening comprehension tasks are best planned as a cycle of activities, so White and Arndt (1991) have argued that writing tasks should be planned as a cycle of activities involving generating ideas, planning, drafting, structuring and reviewing. Students, for example, might start out brainstorming in groups the points for a particular piece of writing. They then consider how these points might be organized most effectively, possibly reviewing models of similar texts. Gradually, individual students or groups put pen to paper, but that is not the end of the process. Drafts are then circulated among the group for various levels of revision until a final draft is produced for evaluation. Even proficient writers rarely produce effective text without going through multiple stages of drafting, and White and Arndt (1991) argue that second language writers need familiarization with writing as an iterative process, rather than a one-off production. For more writing activities, see Hedge (1988).

Increasingly, writing takes place via a computer keyboard rather than paper and pen. The computer environment, which facilitates drafting and redrafting as well as dissemination of text to multiple reviewers, is increasingly being advocated for second language writing practice (Broady 2000). For example, many institutions provide electronic learning environments where learners can post texts for each other to read and comment on, or where they can engage in written exchanges. Students can also write for websites and for bulletin boards. Such electronic environments can be powerfully motivating as learners realize they have an audience for their writing. They also provide extensive opportunities for collaborative writing where groups develop a text, adding different sections and reviewing/proof-reading those already written.

General guidelines for skills work

1 *Be aware of overload*. When designing skills-based activities, beware of overloading your learners. Provide support for the task they are to engage in. Determine the support based on the language level and confidence of the learners. Where learners need to comprehend a complex text, for example, try to keep the production task simple. You might allow answers in English

or set several sequences of questions. Where the production task is complex, allow planning time. In planning speaking activities, start with simple triggers to communication.

2 *Use frameworks and schemas.* Setting clear and simple frameworks for the organization of content in speaking and writing tasks helps learners 'know where they are going'. For instance, a 'problem–solution' framework can help students plan out an essay or present a report: they can organize their ideas under the headings 'Situation' (a background context is described), 'Problem' (a particular issue is raised), 'Solution' (possible ways of addressing the issue are reviewed) and 'Evaluation' (the most effective solution is identified). Similarly, helping learners access their existing 'schemas' should facilitate comprehension skills, so before listening/viewing, use questions to get learners thinking about the topic of the passage they are about to hear/view. Get them to predict its contents from their general knowledge (existing 'schemas') and then listen/view to check predictions.

3 *Stimulate engagement through information gap.* We mentioned the information-gap principle in relation to speaking tasks, but it applies equally well to comprehension tasks and writing. The kinds of prediction activities suggested above in relation to reading and listening create an information gap: students' guess-work functions as the gap which they can fill by listening or reading again. Texts can also be divided up into sections with the different sections distributed among a group of learners. The group then has to assemble the information from the various individual members in order to complete some kind of task, e.g. answer a set of questions.

4 *Use time limits.* Faced with the demands of a complex task in a language that is not automatized, learners will instinctively focus on bottom-up processing, i.e. concentrate on individual words. In speaking tasks, they might try to write out every word they wish to say, even in response to a simple question. In listening and reading, they might try to decode every word of a text. In writing, they might spend too long checking and rechecking for word-level errors, and possibly trying to translate word for word from their first language. To encourage learners to practise language under more 'realistic' processing conditions, set time-limited tasks, such as skim-reading or one-minute oral presentations with minimal preparation. Get them to 'write down five sentences about . . . in five minutes'. Then use these products as the focus for a further cycle of work – checking understanding, clarifying expressions, etc. Surprisingly, time limits seem to force many learners to panic less about the detail of their language as they have to redirect their attention to performing the task efficiently.

5 *Plan work in 'process' cycles.* When practising skills, design cycles of activity that allow for 'rehearsals', 'repetition', 'drafts' and different levels of compre-

hension. In other words, do not expect learners to produce an error-free written text, a coherent contribution to a discussion, a detailed comprehension of a television news bulletin first time off. Build in cycles of feedback and reflection and 'trying again', based on the learning from the previous cycle. And, most importantly, encourage learner involvement in tasks through guesswork and strategy use.

6 *Integrate skills.* Link work on different skills together in a task or cycle of tasks. For example, work on written texts and listening passages may lead to an oral presentation or discussion, which in turn could be the basis for a written report. In planning skills work, particularly at more advanced levels, it pays to link tasks so that students practise communicating similar ideas but through different skills. In this way, vocabulary knowledge can be reinforced and the cognitive load of expressing new ideas can be relieved to promote more confident performance. Furthermore, such integrated tasks are usually experienced by learners as 'real' uses of language in a way that gap-fill exercises and comprehension questions are not. In this, they are motivating, but they also support learners in developing 'transferable' language skills, in other words, skills that can immediately be used in the 'real world' and, in particular, in professional contexts (see also Chapters 10 and 14).

7 *Always plan an outcome to promote progress.* Plan language classwork so that it leads to some kind of outcome, such as a short oral activity, a written text, even a summary in English of a TL written text or a video extract, where learners can demonstrate their achievement. Language is a tool for doing things: to sustain motivation, students need to know what they can do, and how well.

By regularly practising skill-based tasks of the kinds discussed above, students should be better able to gauge their own progress in their second language. But they also need to have realistic expectations: fluent language skills do not develop immediately in the context of the once-a-week language class. Further, fluency is not the only consideration in effective language performance, as we mentioned at the start of this chapter. Regular practice is essential, but so is the ability to review one's performance and improve it. Students need to be willing to accept the limitations of novice performance while continuing to aim at more expert performance. And of course, supporting all these different aspects of second language skill development as a teacher is, itself, a complex skill – or, rather, a stimulating challenge!

Sources of information

For ideas on information-gap activities, see: Klippel 1985, Pattison 1987, Neu and Reeser 1997, Ur and Wright (1992).

For classroom discussions, see Ur (1981).

For examples of brief oral discussions as pre-viewing exercises, see Broady and Meinhof (1995) and Broady and Shade (1996).

For ideas on developing communication skills, see Nolasco and Arthur (1987) and Klippel (1985).

8

Teaching grammar

John Klapper

The place of grammar in foreign language (FL) teaching has always been the subject of much debate. Moves in the second half of the twentieth century from the structural syllabuses of grammar–translation and audiolingualism towards more meaning-based approaches to language teaching, principally in the shape of a 'strong' version of communicative language teaching or CLT (see Chapter 5), went hand in hand with a rejection of the primacy of grammar. This found its most extreme expression in so-called 'natural' approaches that rejected any direct link between the teaching of grammar and the acquisition of grammatical forms (Krashen and Terrell 1983). Even in the less controversial 'weak' version of CLT championed by many mainstream FL textbooks, grammar has tended to be seen as a subsidiary or non-core element of language learning. In recent years, as dissatisfaction with excessively meaning-based approaches has spread, especially with learners' apparent inability to generate accurate language independently of formulaic expressions, the methodological pendulum has swung back towards a (modified) emphasis on grammar and structure (e.g. Engel and Myles 1996, Doughty and Williams 1998, Hinkel and Fotos 2002).

This chapter first defines what we mean by 'grammar' and provides a justification for teaching grammar. It then considers what grammar we should be teaching and, finally, discusses how tutors can best approach the task.

What is grammar?

A key distinction is made in applied linguistics between *implicit* and *explicit* knowledge of grammar. Implicit knowledge is knowledge *of* grammar that is intuitive and allows correct grammatical forms to be deployed automatically, without the user being aware of why a particular form is correct – e.g. a native

French speaker's awareness of *je le lui ai donné* or a native German's awareness of *ich habe es ihm gegeben* as correct formulations based on implicit knowledge of the relevant word order rules. Work in second language acquisition (see Ellis 1990) shows that it is not possible for language teaching to influence the development of implicit knowledge in any direct or immediate way.

Explicit knowledge, on the other hand, is knowledge *about* grammar, i.e. the conscious knowledge we use in checking the accuracy of our language production or in employing rules to formulate (usually written) utterances. Explicit knowledge is not immediately available in unmonitored language use but is called upon slowly and deliberately, either by an FL learner or by a native speaker when employing a 'careful style' in such tasks as essay or report writing.

Ellis (2002b) has argued that explicit knowledge can assist the processes involved in using and acquiring implicit knowledge, in particular by drawing FL learners' attention to specific forms and structures, encouraging them to monitor their language production and thus to notice the 'gap' between language input and their own output. For this reason, grammar teaching should be aimed at the development of learners' explicit knowledge.

Grammar and second language acquisition (SLA)

SLA research has been much concerned with the development of learners' grammatical knowledge and how this relates to the growth of overall language competence. Views on the precise detail of the process vary but can be summarized in the following simplified model:

Input ⇨ Noticing ⇨ Intake ⇨

Structuring and restructuring ⇨ Proceduralization

For language to be acquired, spoken and written input – spoken and written samples of the target language – needs to become intake. A key role here is played by 'consciousness-raising', or getting learners to 'notice' features of input in some way (Rutherford 1987, Schmidt 1990). This can be achieved either by direct grammar teaching about structures or by enhancing the input during meaning-focused work, e.g. by making the grammar we want students to focus on stand out in some way, either aurally or visually.

On a cognitive view of language learning (see Chapter 5) repeated noticing is claimed to promote 'structuring' and 'restructuring' (McLaughlin 1990) of the learner's implicit system of linguistic knowledge. Here, learners gradually start to work out how form and meaning map on to each other, first sorting the new information about a particular structure, then comparing it with, and unconsciously accommodating it to, their existing system of language knowledge, and formulating new hypotheses to account for the differences, or 'gap', between the two. The unconscious process continues as learners test their new hypotheses by attending further to linguistic input and receiving feedback on their use of the new form.

Through repeated use in meaningful communicative interaction, grammatical knowledge becomes internalized, i.e. it becomes organized in such a way that the learner is able to draw on it readily and quickly, allowing production to become increasingly automatic; this is known as 'proceduralization' (Johnson 1996, and see Chapter 5). It is believed that, in this way, consciousness-raising and noticing play a major part in allowing explicit knowledge of grammar to develop gradually into implicit knowledge.

However, language learning is rarely as predictable or uniform as the above suggests. In particular, we should remember (see also Chapter 5):

- Noticing and reasoning place a heavy cognitive burden on learners who may require a considerable period of assimilation before they can actually produce the particular form themselves.
- Restructuring of learners' existing 'interlanguage' system, to accommodate information about new grammatical items, can lead to a temporary drop in grammatical performance in other areas – a source of much frustration to tutors who may have thought the particular areas had been 'mastered'.
- Research shows that grammatical structures are acquired in a particular order but that each form develops very gradually and passes through transitional interlanguage phases in which non-target language forms are prominent and alternate with correct forms (Ellis 1997).
- Consequently, the attempt to teach a particular grammatical form or rule will not automatically result in correct usage if the learner is not developmentally ready to process the structure. Automatization is *not* an inevitable consequence of practice: it can only occur when a student's language system has matured to the developmental stage at which the structure that is being taught would be acquired in naturalistic language acquisition.

Grammar and the language curriculum

The notion of an innate learner syllabus impervious to grammar instruction, including the order in which structures are taught, raises serious questions about contemporary FL textbooks and grammar practice manuals based on a supposed order of grammatical difficulty. Many such volumes appear to assume that acquisition is a function of clear contextualization and abundant practice

– usually first in controlled or restricted exercises, and then in freer communicative activities, following the well-established sequence of Presentation–Practice–Production (PPP) (see Chapter 5). Unfortunately, it is not possible to circumnavigate or transform fundamental natural acquisition processes in this way.

Nor can language syllabuses be based on the natural acquisition order (even assuming it were possible to determine this with any accuracy). Developing a group of students' grammatical competence is not like constructing a series of walls where one brick can follow another in the same fixed sequence on each wall. Rather, it is a much more organic affair in which each *individual* learner evinces considerable variety in his or her ability to use new grammar accurately, first progressing, then apparently inexplicably regressing, before slowly moving forward again.

So how can we know what specific items of grammar to include in the curriculum? The obvious starting point is those areas in which FL learners are known to experience difficulties. For example, with near-beginner English learners of German as an FL, this would include:

- present tense conjugation (*du/Sie* versus *ich* forms);
- accusative case;
- article declension;
- variable prepositions (*in den* versus *im*);
- past participle formation;
- auxiliary *haben* versus *sein*;
- strong verb forms.

Added to these would be general developmental errors that apply to all learners of German, of which the most intensively researched is word order (Clahsen *et al.* 1983, Ellis 1989).

► Make a list of the five areas of grammar in your FL that cause greatest problems for:

a near beginners;

b post-A level students.

However, 'difficulty' is not a straightforward concept. Some aspects of grammar that are easy to convey as explicit knowledge may be deeply problematic from the point of view of implicit knowledge. An example of this is use of the German accusative case to denote the direct object, which is a simple rule to teach, but getting students to use it accurately in fluent and unmonitored production (i.e. as implicit knowledge) is far from easy.

In the light of this, Ellis (2002a) suggests some general criteria for judging language complexity. Table 8.1 adapts this for German as a foreign language:

> ▶ Complete the categories in Table 8.1 with reference to *your* FL. Try to include at least two grammatical items for each of the six categories. In which order would you present these items in a structural syllabus?

Table 8.1 Criteria for judging language complexity

Criterion	Definition	Example
1 Formal complexity	The extent to which the structure involves just a single or many elements	Accusative *den* is formally simple; perfect tense *er ist ausgegangen* involves several elements
2 Functional complexity	The extent to which the meanings realized by a structure are transparent or opaque	Subjunctive I forms *sie sei* and *sie gehe*, and masculine accusative *den* are transparent; subjunctive II *machte* and accusative feminine *die* are opaque
3 Reliability	The extent to which the rule has exceptions	Weak verb conjugation is very reliable, strong verb forms are much less reliable
4 Scope	The extent to which the rule has broad or narrow coverage	Weak/*der* declension and mixed/*ein* declension of adjectives have broad scope; zero declension has narrow scope
5 Metalanguage	The extent to which the rule can be provided simply, with minimum metalanguage	Comparison of adjectives is simple; word order generally is more difficult; relative clauses still more so
6 Mother tongue/ FL contrast	An FL feature that corresponds to a mother tongue feature is easier than a feature that does not	For English learners of German, word order is difficult, but the position of adjectives is not; for Spanish learners of English, however, the latter is a problem

Source: Adapted from Ellis (2002a: 28)

Approaches to teaching grammar

Traditional approaches to language teaching adopted an overt approach to explaining grammar, usually involving extensive language description, meta-language and intensive practice. Such explicit – and often ineffective – teaching is based on erroneous assumptions about how language is acquired. (See, in particular, Alderson *et al.* (1997) on the lack of any strong relationship between language competence and knowledge of grammatical terminology, and D. Willis (1996) for a short critique of the limitations of the PPP approach.) Although there are occasions where explicit teaching may be desirable as a way to focus attention on a specific structure and to prompt subsequent noticing of the feature in input, it has clear limitations and its use should not become too protracted.

Much contemporary language teaching assumes less explicit approaches to grammar, with a considerably reduced role for formal language description and an enhanced role for contextualized, meaningful use of target structures. Among the wide range of possible approaches involving more meaningful, contextualized use of grammatical structures, some of the most common include:

- pictures or drawings to illustrate specific grammar points (e.g. street maps or building layouts for prepositional use);
- dialogues (e.g. friends discussing what to give a third person for his or her birthday as a way of introducing indirect objects);
- visual organizers (e.g. a person's appointment book or diary to introduce the 'passé composé' or perfect tense);
- texts: short parallel texts might be used to compare and contrast key structures (e.g. one featuring imperatives, the other with the same ideas expressed less forcefully via modal expressions).

The approach to grammar that most closely accords with what we know about language acquisition is *discovery learning*. This is a much less direct and less directed technique, which engages students' critical powers and problem-solving capacity by encouraging the scanning and analysis of language data, the noticing of key forms, the formation of hypotheses concerning the relevant grammatical rule and the testing of this rule in further analysis of data. Examples of activities here include:

- identifying grammar items in a short passage, categorizing them in some way (e.g. in French, putting all the verbs under '-er', '-re', '-ir' headings; in German, allocating verbs to separable and inseparable columns), and articulating rules of use;
- comparing formulations: students are given a text full of, say, French passive constructions and then receive key sentences from the text rewritten

so as to avoid the passive; they have to compare how the ideas have been expressed and formulate rules for the construction and use of the passive;

- identifying what is wrong in a set of incorrect sentences (perhaps a composite of the group's own recent written work) and explaining structural norms and rules;
- examining concordances of grammar items taken from a language corpus (see Chapter 21) and formulating rules; at advanced levels, students might also compare the rules for use offered by standard prescriptive grammars with the evidence provided by corpus data.

Grammar practice

> ▶ Do you think grammar practice activities are important?
> ▶ Would you say most of the activities you employ are of the 'controlled' or 'free' variety?
> ▶ Do you believe free practice should always follow on from controlled practice?

Controlled practice of grammatical structures is of value because:

- it means students provide additional input for each other;
- the frequent re-occurrence of structures ensures plentiful opportunities for noticing key linguistic features;
- in written practice, in particular, students can monitor their output more consciously and carefully;
- it increases explicit knowledge about grammar and this is an important step on the way to accurate and automatic use of a rule.

Most tutors will be familiar with the options for practising grammar, including such techniques as oral and written drills, gap filling, substitution, re-ordering, sentence reconstruction, etc. These are all covered at length in any good practical grammar manual and tutors are likely to have experience of them from their own FL learning. There are also numerous suggestions to be found in EFL manuals, such as Rinvolucri (1984) and Ur (1998) which are both excellent sources of ideas for practising grammatical structures within a communicative framework.

However, drilling and practice should not dominate. Controlled practice can facilitate the proceduralization of language knowledge, but it must be linked to meaning-based and natural language use in which the student is forced to move beyond knowledge of a small segment of language and to employ a wider range of skills, including the ability to improvise. Tasks such as information-gap activities, situations, role play, discussions and free writing, in which the focus of students' attention is not exclusively accurate structural knowledge but rather conveying a message, are especially important in this regard.

When employing practice activities, it should be remembered that the development of structural accuracy in fluent, unmonitored communication, the process of proceduralization, is a gradual and complex process. However, by employing a mixture of varied and appropriately pitched practice activities and tasks, both controlled and free, the tutor can ensure that all learners are sensitized to key grammatical features, that all learning styles are appropriately engaged and thus that all interlanguage systems are provided with the optimum conditions for development.

Conclusion

There are good reasons for teaching grammar. However, insights from language acquisition research do not support an exclusively structural syllabus that assumes learners acquire implicit knowledge through intensive practice of carefully graded structures. The building of grammatical competence is, rather, a developmental process, which teaching can only indirectly influence.

After years of conflicting methodologies and competing philosophies, it seems sensible to state that there is no single 'best approach' to grammar teaching. Grammar instruction is a means to enhance and refine input by inducing noticing and consciousness-raising and, thus, to help language become intake in readiness for eventual acquisition. Provided we keep this in mind, we are justified in adopting a varied and eclectic approach to grammar teaching, with the exact mix of activities depending on the nature of the module, the students and their particular learning needs and individual learning styles. Ultimately, these are things only the individual tutor can judge.

Sources of information

Module 3 in the DELPHI distance learning programme is devoted to the topic of grammar (access via www.delphi.bham.ac.uk/modules.htm – password required).

Shortall, T. (2003) *Grammar Rules: teaching grammar in the foreign language classroom*. Online. Available at: www.bham.ac.uk/delphi/private/Module%203/index3.htm (accessed 5 February 2004).

9

Teaching and learning vocabulary

Paul Meara

It has become something of a cliché in Applied Linguistics to describe vocabulary as one of the neglected aspects of language teaching. Recent years have seen a considerable growth in research on vocabulary acquisition – though rather less on vocabulary teaching – but there are few signs that this research is having much impact on the way people who teach languages actually think about how they should teach vocabulary.

Part of the problem is that people have only vague ideas about what sorts of vocabulary targets are useful for language learners, and even professional language teachers are often uncertain of the basic parameters.

▶ Ask yourself the following questions before you go on:

- How many words do you know in English?
- How many words do think a first-year undergraduate knows?
- How many different words do you use in a day?
- How many words do you know in your best foreign language?
- How many different words did Shakespeare use?

If you put questions like this to typical groups of language teachers, you get a huge range of replies (see Zechmeister *et al.* 1993). Ask a group of language teachers how many words they think they know in their mother tongue, for example, and you will get answers ranging from a few thousand to a few million. These huge disparities have practical implications, of course. If you think that your own vocabulary is around 5,000 words, and you teach your students 2,500 words then you will believe that your students know about half as many words as you do, a pretty satisfactory outcome for most teachers.

Recent research in English suggests that as a broad generalization native speakers will acquire about 1,000 words a year up until the age of 25 (Diack 1975, Nagy and Anderson 1984, d'Anna *et al.* 1991, Nation 2001). This vocabulary is made up of a hard core of words that almost all speakers know, and a looser peripheral vocabulary made up of specialist vocabulary in fields that are relevant to the individual. There is no real agreement about the size of the core vocabulary, but 5,000 words is probably a safe lower limit (Goethals 1992).

Foreign language students entering higher education (HE) language courses in the UK have target language vocabularies that are very much smaller than these figures for native speakers. One of the reasons for this is that extensive reading is the main route by which people enlarge their vocabularies (Nagy *et al.* 1989, Krashen 1989), but the shift away from literature in language teaching at secondary level means that students have often not been challenged in this way, and their vocabularies are relatively small as a result. Another contributory factor is the current methodological emphasis on 'communicative' language teaching (Brumfit and Johnson 1979). Communicative approaches tend to emphasize oral skills, but spoken language is lexically less rich than written language, so students are probably exposed to a narrower range of lexical input when they learn a language in this way. Furthermore, whereas English language teaching is informed by a long tradition of vocabulary studies and several corpus-based frequency counts, the same cannot be said of foreign language teaching (in the UK at least). The sole exception is French where a substantial body of research is available to inform the selection of vocabulary for textbooks (Gougenheim *et al.* 1964), but is not routinely known or used.

It is difficult to avoid the conclusion that current practice in the UK regarding vocabulary teaching is based on the assumption that students will somehow just pick up the vocabulary that they need. In practice, a lot of the necessary vocabulary expansion occurs during the year abroad, and there is some evidence that most students expand and deepen their vocabularies massively at this time (Milton and Meara 1995). However, students themselves often complain that they quickly lose these gains once they return, and again there is some evidence to show that these perceptions are correct. What seems to happen is that vocabularies rapidly undergo attrition if they are not used, and most language departments do not provide an environment that is rich enough to prevent this attrition from setting in. There is surely something odd about a course that leaves students less competent at the end of their fourth year of study than they were at the end of their third year. This strongly suggests that good practice ought to include a final-year environment that is rich enough at least to delay vocabulary attrition, one that, for example, involves extended projects requiring extensive use of authentic texts on different topics.

Techniques for teaching vocabulary vary enormously, and require different levels of autonomy on the part of learners. A useful collection of techniques designed for teaching vocabulary in class is Nation (1994), which includes an extensive range of teacher-driven activities, as well as suggestions for peer-teaching. Some people argue that the effectiveness of these techniques varies with individual learning styles (see Chapter 5), but there is little hard evidence that individual learning style is a serious factor in vocabulary. Most people agree, however, that it is not possible to teach in class all the words that students need because the number of words required is simply too great, particularly where advanced learners are concerned. This implies that learners should take responsibility for their own vocabulary learning. There are a number of ways in which they can do this. Traditional list learning is surprisingly effective – though it seems to work best when the words to be learned are semantically unrelated, rather than when they are made of words from a single semantic domain. Vocabulary notebooks are also an effective approach.

Computers have an important role to play in teaching vocabulary. Computerized databases (see Chapter 21) look like being a particularly important learning tool. Computer programs can present new words in both oral and written form, and in a variety of contexts; they can also implement sophisticated rehearsal schedules, which significantly reduce the chances of new words being forgotten. For very advanced learners, computer programs like Wordsmith Tools (Scott 1996) provide access to detailed information about the way words in a corpus behave. Programs of this sort can be used to generate concordances for target words, and this reveals what other words collocate with the target words, and what syntactic patterns the target words occur in. They also allow students to compare the contexts that differentiate synonyms. Using a concordancer is a particularly effective way of working with authentic texts from a single specialized genre.

In general, however, the best way to acquire a large vocabulary is for students to engage in extensive reading – and this is perhaps the single most compelling argument for preserving a hefty literature component in HE language courses. A productive approach at this level is for students to learn texts off by heart – a technique that was widely practised in the early part of the twentieth century, but is only rarely used today. This technique works particularly well when the text to be learned is a translation of a text you already know well in your L1 (see Chapter 13). Even when literature is not a major part of the programme, students can be encouraged to read widely – for leisure as well as for their studies – and should be advised to take an *active* approach to vocabulary learning.

One approach to vocabulary learning that works especially for learners with a visual learning style is the 'keyword method' (Pressley *et al.* 1980). This mnemonic approach to vocabulary acquisition is based on the idea that there are two sides to learning a word: one is learning the meaning of the word, while the other is concerned with learning the physical attributes of the word, its spelling, its pronunciation, and so on. Proponents of the keyword method argue that learning the meanings is actually not so difficult, since we mostly know the concepts anyway. What *is* difficult is learning new labels for these familiar concepts, and this implies that vocabulary teaching should really be focusing on helping learners acquire the new word *forms*. The keyword method addresses this issue by using images.

Imagine that you want to learn the Spanish word for 'banana': *plátano*. The first step in learning this word is to find a familiar English word that looks a bit like *plátano*. 'Plate' looks like the first syllable, so let's work with that. This is the keyword for *plátano*. We next make a strong visual image that involves both a plate and a banana. A simple image of a banana on a plate would do, but images that are funny, or otherwise striking, work much better, so let's imagine a cartoon banana spinning a plate on a stick like a circus performer. We now have a complex link that connects 'banana' to *plátano*.

At first sight, this method seems to involve a lot more work than traditional ways of learning words. However, the visual image acts as a sort of temporary cement; it fixes the physical form of the word, makes it more resistant to forgetting, and provides a way of recalling the word via the image when you need it. In time, as the association between 'banana' and *plátano* becomes stronger, the image becomes superfluous, and it just fades away.

▶ Try to invent keyword images for the following Croatian words:

brzo – quickly	dobro – good	mleko – milk
brod – ship	ulica – street	kasno – late
verovatno – probably	hleb – bread	novac – money

You may find that it is easier to develop images for concrete nouns than for the other words. Good examples of the keyword method can be found in the Linkword books – e.g. Gruneberg (1993).

Large-scale, systematic research on the keyword method – mostly published in the 1980s (for a summary see Rodríguez and Sadoski 2000) – shows that learning words in this way can be the most effective of all. The keyword method allows students to learn very large numbers of words in a short space of time – as many as 200 words in a single day (Atkinson and Raugh 1975). This suggests that learning a very large vocabulary is not as difficult as we think it is, and the implication is that good practice should involve all students being taught how to use this type of mnemonic approach as a matter of course. This, in turn, would enable us to raise significantly the vocabulary targets that we expect students to reach, particularly in the early stages of their leaning.

▶ Now try to recall the meaning of these Croatian words:

mleko	dobro	kasno
brzo	novac	brod
ulica	verovatno	hleb

You should find that you remembered almost all of the words, even though you were not necessarily trying to learn them as you read the chapter. There is some research (Beaton *et al.* 1995) to show that words learned by the keyword method are extraordinarily resistant to attrition, and can easily be reactivated years after they were originally learned.

Sources of information

For further information about vocabulary teaching, search the Vocabulary Research Group Archive. Online. Available at: www.swan.ac.uk/cals/calsres/varga (accessed 21 April 2004).

10

Assessment in Modern Languages

John Klapper

Introduction

Assessment is arguably the single most important element in language teaching in higher education (HE) and it is certainly one that causes much anxiety for staff new to the profession. This chapter first considers the important link between learning outcomes and assessment and looks at the key features of effective assessment. It then discusses the use of essays, presentations and projects, and finally explores the role of peer assessment and the assessment of transferable skills.

Learning outcomes and assessment

Academic Review, as promoted by the Quality Assurance Agency, empha-sizes the notion of 'alignment'. This refers to the process of bringing into line and linking to each other intended learning outcomes (sometimes called 'objectives'), methods of learning and teaching, assessment tasks, criteria, marking and feedback (Brown 2001: 4–6). All parts of the process should serve to support appropriate learning. It is particularly important that manageable learning outcomes are linked to appropriate methods of assessment, so that our students, colleagues and quality monitors can be clear about, and have confidence in, the standard and coherence of modules.

When writing learning outcomes it is a good idea to think in terms of what we hope students will be able to do once they have completed the course. The learning outcomes should serve as an outline for assessment, and if we find it difficult to know how to assess something, this may well mean we need to rethink the outcome and link it to specific, measurable evidence of competence. It is also important that all outcomes that are included should be assessed in some way; they need not necessarily all be measured to the same degree, but if it is a significant element of the module, it deserves to be assessed.

▶ Consider the following outcomes for a fictional Level 2 German literature module. What is wrong with them?

By the end of this module, students will:

- be familiar with post-war German social, political and economic history;
- understand the development of literature in the post-war period;
- know about the role of the Gruppe 47;
- understand the continuing influence of the Nazi past and the war in post-war writing;
- have read a selection of representative texts from the period;
- have in-depth knowledge of one set text;
- be able to appreciate textual nuances.

The module is assessed by one essay and one individual seminar presentation. There will also be one non-assessed group seminar presentation.

There are two major problems with this scheme. First, most of the outcomes are too general and are inappropriately expressed, failing to tell us what students *will be able to do* upon completion of the module: words and phrases such as 'understand' and 'be familiar with' are too vague to be of much use. Second, and more importantly, it makes no attempt to link the outcomes to assessment procedures: we need to be told how precisely each outcome will be assessed. For example, some of these outcomes might more helpfully be presented as follows:

Table 10.1 Sample module description

Outcome	Assessed by
1 Demonstrate knowledge of specific aspects of post-war German social, political and economic history	Essay
2 Identify and explain key issues in the development of literature in the period 1945–1949	Group presentation
3 Show in-depth knowledge of one of the set texts	Individual presentation and essay

Key features of assessment

▶ Have you ever set an assessment which:

- failed to assess what you had intended?
- proved too easy or too hard?
- turned out to have an inappropriate mark scheme?
- showed students were not clear about what they were being assessed on?
- proved unduly cumbersome or time-consuming?

▶ Or have you ever taught on a module in which the type of test or exam you set has affected the way students learned or the way you taught?

These effects are common in varying degrees to all attempts to assess students and they can be summarized under the following headings.

Validity

This includes:

- face validity: does the test *look* as if it measures what it is meant to?
- content validity: does it contain a representative sample of the skills and knowledge it is meant to be assessing?
- construct validity: can it be shown that the test measures the ability it is supposed to measure?
- criterion-related validity: to what extent do test results agree with those derived from an independent and dependable measure of a student's ability?

The latter two aspects are research procedures, which are most relevant to the production of mass standardized tests. For Modern Language degree purposes, the first two are more important.

Face validity is important because tests that do not appear to have anything to do with the supposed purpose of assessment may not be accepted by students and this may reflect how they perform on them. For example, a speaking assessment may not be thought relevant to a reading knowledge course, or a factual multiple-choice test may not be considered appropriate to a course on the history of ideas.

Content validity is even more crucial: if assessment ignores whole areas of a syllabus, this will have a negative effect on learning (e.g. only assessing one or two specific periods in a module on nineteenth- and twentieth-century history). The key is to start with the learning outcomes (knowledge or skills) we want to assess, and then to decide how we are going to test them. By doing this, we are more likely to measure effectively what it is we aim to assess, that is to make our assessment *valid*.

Reliability

Assessment also needs to test students in a consistent way. A student should get the same mark regardless of when he or she sits a test and regardless of who is marking the work. Similarly, when we are marking 60 essays (or conducting 60 oral exams), the first student to be assessed should be treated in the same way as the last. And if more than one marker is involved, all must apply the same criteria and standards. This is what is meant by assessment being *reliable*. See Knight (2001) and Hughes (2003) for a range of practical techniques to increase reliability.

Transparency

Clearly, in any assessment task it is crucial that students know what they have to do, but it is just as important that they know what the marker is looking for. They also need to know by which standards their work will be assessed, i.e. they need to see and understand the marking criteria. Thus, for an essay, they should know which categories we are assessing, for example:

- acquisition of knowledge;
- interpretation and analysis;
- construction of argument;
- relevance of material;
- documentation and presentation.

Ideally these should appear in a grid with grade descriptions for each category.

Besides making the process transparent to students, this approach is central to demonstrating to external reviewers the coherence and quality of assessment procedures.

Practicality

Assessment in HE is usually subject to certain practical constraints. For example, we rarely have time to trial our tests and exams before letting students loose on them. Similarly, timetable and resource constraints may well mean it is not possible for all students on a module to be assessed via individual seminar presentations twice a year, and group assessments may have to be used instead. In other words, whatever assessment instrument we use also has to be *practical*.

Washback on teaching

Finally, we must ensure that what we test is not only relevant to what we have taught and what students have learnt, but also that the assessment process serves to promote that learning. When assessment has beneficial effects on teaching and learning, it is common to talk about 'positive washback', whereas if assessment fails to further the learning outcomes, one would see this as 'negative washback' (Alderson and Wall 1993). Positive washback can be achieved by:

- testing the learning outcomes directly: if we teach students to write summaries, analyse films or review books, then they must be tested on those skills;
- ensuring students know what is expected of them in the exam or test;
- testing a representative sample of the syllabus by choosing items from a wide range of topics, rather than just one narrow area.

It is rarely possible to satisfy all the above demands simultaneously. For example, a multiple-choice test to assess 100 students' performance on a cultural theory module may be reliable, practical and have a degree of content validity, but its face and construct validity would be very doubtful. Similarly, a single essay task to assess students' understanding of detailed phonetic and phonological issues on a linguistics module might be acceptable in terms of face validity but its content validity (narrow sampling) and possibly its transparency (difficulty of formulating appropriate criteria) could be questionable. In practice, we are likely to have to compromise in reconciling the five key features of assessment, but we should nevertheless always remain aware of them in devising tests and exams.

Essays

Essays are still the dominant form of assessment on non-language modules. Provided they are supported by clear and precise criteria that increase consistency and limit the element of subjective judgement that is inevitably involved, they can discriminate effectively between students and allow the most able to demonstrate their knowledge and understanding.

However, we should not forget that some students have never been taught essay-writing skills and find it difficult to structure their responses and even to lend expression to their knowledge. While all universities offer students some form of study skills support, including essay writing, the most an individual module tutor can do is to vary the mode of assessment, so that essays are not the sole instrument and those who are good at essays are not repeatedly at an advantage; for example, by assessing seminar presentations and re-worked seminar papers (informed by tutor feedback) or setting a formative essay plan task prior to an assessed essay.

It is especially important with essays to allow students an insight into how their work will be marked. Providing students with clear criteria in advance of the task and discussing what these mean (e.g. typical words such as 'coherent' or 'cogent' may not mean a lot to some students) is just one part of it. It is also a good idea to show students anonymous samples of good and poor essays from previous iterations of the module, so they can see more clearly what is required. After obliterating marks on the scripts, the tutor could ask students to work in groups and apply the marking criteria to a couple of essays. This might be linked to peer assessment of each others' practice essays (see below).

Other ways to improve the effectiveness of assessment via essays is to offer a strictly limited number of titles. It may seem fairer to offer a wide choice, but in fact this reduces severely the reliability of essays as a testing technique. For the same reason, Race (2001a: 58) suggests breaking up the title into sub-questions and indicating the marks available for each part. This shows students what is required by what are often abstract and open-ended essay titles, and it stops them drifting off the point and including irrelevant material – one of the most common weaknesses with undergraduate essays.

Some consider essay an inauthentic form of writing (since, unlike other genres, it is uncertain who the reader is supposed to be) with no existence outside academic contexts. You might therefore consider other options too. Reports, summaries or briefings, for example, have greater real-life validity and can be equally demanding, particularly where both language and content are to be assessed.

Presentations

Assessed oral presentations can supplement more traditional written assessment tasks and are perceived by many staff and students to be more relevant to the real-world skills required by employers (see 'Transferable skills' below).

As with other forms of assessment, it is important that students understand the criteria by which their presentation is to be assessed, including what marks are to be allocated to:

- content: evidence of research, relevance of material, coherence of arguments, exemplification and illustration, response to subsequent questions;
- effectiveness of presentation: voice projection, eye contact, use of notes, use of visual aids, quality of handout;
- target-language use: accuracy, fluency, etc. (see Chapter 11).

Since many students are likely to find an assessed oral presentation a demanding experience, it is sensible to allow a 'dry run' in advance of the assessment to provide formative feedback and build confidence.

Race (2001a: 71) points out a number of practical difficulties with presentations, which represent distinct disadvantages:

- With a large group, individual 20-minute presentations for all can prove time-consuming; this might mean using group presentations instead, with the problem of allocating marks fairly between participants.
- Evidence is transient, making second marking and quality assurance difficult; this really means presentations need to be video-recorded, adding to the organizational burden of the tutor.
- Presentations obviously cannot be anonymous, making it more likely that subjective elements will enter the assessment process.

In spite of this, oral presentations are worth serious consideration, since:

- they vary the mode of assessment and thus prevent certain students being unduly advantaged by a particular assessment instrument;
- experience suggests the exposure that comes with public presentation tends to focus students' minds on detailed preparation;
- presentations encourage the development of vocationally relevant skills.

Projects

Most degrees in Modern Languages feature elements of projects or dissertations, especially in the final year. At level 3, such tasks are an important method of fostering research skills, while at any point in a degree they serve to enhance autonomous learning. Projects are an excellent method of developing deep learning, encouraging students to engage more thoroughly with the subject matter for its own sake, rather than merely to jump through a particular assessment hoop. They are also likely to help the student develop information retrieval skills more effectively than other tasks and to access diverse media (books, journals, reviews, film and other visual material).

However, for it to be effective as both a learning and assessment instrument, a project requires considerable support:

- Deep, as opposed to mere surface learning, a sense of real commitment to the project, will be greatly enhanced if students have a relatively free hand in choosing their own topic. This does, however, place extra demands on tutors in terms of their knowledge and expertise, the provision of material and/or advice on accessing appropriate sources.
- While many of the expected learning outcomes for a project will be shared across all students' work (e.g. demonstrate knowledge of a specialist area, evaluate a range of different sources), each individual project will need

distinct outcomes appropriate to the topic. For example, in a project on language variation in Switzerland: identify the official languages and their geographical distribution, demonstrate recent trends in language use at state level, explain the historical relationship between Swiss German and High German, present a case study of language use in one German-speaking canton, etc. These individual outcomes require considerable initial tutor input.

- Projects need structuring: few students at undergraduate level are able to cope with a completely open-ended task. Projects should therefore be broken down into phases with intermediate deadlines (e.g. initial plan, revised plan, first draft, second draft), ideally with tutor consultation and feedback at each stage.
- Projects should not simply replicate other course assessment methods. There is a danger that assessment may focus too much on the ability of students to write up their findings – essentially the skills assessed in essays or other written tasks. Criteria should, rather, reflect the project as a whole and the process the student has gone through, e.g. information gathering, analysis of sources, presentation of data or illustrative material, overall coherence and the relationship of the parts to the whole.
- Marking is time-consuming, and reliable assessment requires double-marking.

Project work is thus a valuable element of undergraduate learning and assessment, but it is not to be seen as a sort of short-cut or labour-saving device.

Peer assessment

Many in HE are sceptical about the benefits of peer assessment. However, encouraging students to engage with marking criteria and to apply them to mark others' work does help them understand more clearly what we expect of them. Moreover, students can learn a lot from looking closely at work that is better than their own and thinking about why it is superior.

Possibly the strongest reason for using peer assessment is that it promotes deeper learning than traditional tutor assessment, which all too often encourages students to 'learn to the test' and thus remain surface or tactical learners. Exercising judgement and applying criteria forces students to engage more closely with the subject matter (Race 2001a: 94–100; 2001b).

Even if we feel uneasy about allowing peer assessment to count towards course marks, it can be a rewarding experience for students to be involved in evaluating each others' (non-assessed) essay plans prior to writing the assessed essay to which the plan relates, or in making judgements about each others' seminar presentations. Apart from learning from superior work to their own, this type of task allows students to see others' weaknesses or errors and to become aware of potential pitfalls that they need to steer clear of in future.

A further, pragmatic reason for including elements of peer assessment in our work is that with larger classes and a generally heavier teaching and administrative load, we cannot devote as much time to assessment and feedback as we would like, or perhaps once did. Feedback from peers can supplement the written comments and oral feedback we provide students on their assignments.

Peer assessment requires the investment of considerable time and effort and it is very unlikely to save tutors any time. Nevertheless, it does have clear benefits in terms of student engagement with, and improved understanding of, the assessment process. So, if only occasionally, it is probably worth including in our teaching.

Transferable skills

All degree courses are nowadays expected to indicate which transferable or graduate skills they promote. Being based on communication, Modern Languages has always been especially strong in developing these key skills, although it is probably fair to say they have not always figured prominently or explicitly in assessment procedures. (For transferable skills in institution-wide languages programmes, see Chapter 14.)

Transferable skills can be usefully summarized under the following headings (King and Honeybone 2000: 18–20):

- communication (e.g. speaking, presenting, receiving feedback);
- interpersonal (e.g. teamwork, negotiating, managing people);
- self-management (e.g. self-reflection, time management, organizing);
- intellectual (e.g. critical reasoning, synthesizing, problem-solving);
- practical/applied (e.g. formulating hypotheses/arguments, reporting findings, referencing).

When designing a module and its assessment scheme, it is important not just to align outcomes with assessment tasks but also to ensure that the chosen assessment instruments measure those transferable skills developed during the module. Often this will be a strong argument in favour of a *diverse* assessment strategy, since a single method, such as an essay, is likely to sample a narrow range of transferable skills.

Two effective tasks for assessing transferable skills are projects and portfolios. In projects, skills that students are likely to draw on, and to be assessed on, include:

Communication:	reading, writing, foreign language skills
Self-management:	time management, self-reflection and self-discipline
Intellectual:	reasoning, analysing, synthesizing, evaluating, summarizing
Practical:	formulating problems/arguments, information gathering and handling, interpreting and evaluating information, reporting and referencing, and C & IT skills.

If the project entails group work, then, in addition, teamwork, leadership and negotiation skills may be required, while vivas linked to the project will involve oral presentation and use of graphics.

In portfolio work (see also Chapter 11), reflection on learning is a central formative feature of the assessment task, and the inclusion of a wide range of transferable skills in the assessment criteria will encourage students to reflect on the role these skills have played in their work on the module as a whole.

Since students are more likely to attend to transferable skills when they are assessed explicitly, there are grounds for separating out their assessment from other criteria. To avoid an excessive marking burden, however, it is sensible to adopt a simple pass/fail/good judgement on individual key skills (James 2000). Inevitably, the assessment of transferable skills always involves a degree of compromise.

Sources of information

Modules 13 and 14 in the DELPHI distance learning programme are devoted to some of the issues covered in this chapter (Klapper 2003a, 2003b).

LTSN Generic Centre (2001) *Assessment Series*, LTSN, York. This set of four guides and eight briefings is aimed at HE staff and provides succinct, readable overviews of important generic issues and practices in the field of assessment. The *Guide for Lecturers* and the briefings on *Key Concepts, Formative and Summative Assessment, Criterion- and Norm-referenced Assessment* and *Self-, Peer- and Group-Assessment* are especially recommended. Online. Available at: www. ltsn.ac.uk/genericcentre (accessed 20 June 2004).

11

Assessing language skills

John Klapper

Following discussion of the various purposes of language testing and different test types, this chapter considers the use of oral assessment procedures, language essays and translation. It looks at how the results of assessment can be benchmarked against European-wide standards of language proficiency and considers the role of language portfolios. The chapter complements and develops some of the more general assessment issues raised in Chapter 10 and should be read in conjunction with the latter.

Purposes of language testing

Which of the statements in the box below apply to your department?

In my department, testing is used . . .	Yes	No	Not sure
1 as a selection process			
2 to help students learn material more effectively			
3 to increase motivation			
4 to help the tutor discover what the students do not know or cannot do			
5 to show students what they can do			
6 to provide evidence of whether students have progressed			

It is impossible to be prescriptive about assessment methods. Each situation is different and requires a different approach, depending on the learning outcomes, the purpose, status and importance of testing, and on the time and resources (physical and human) that are available.

We can distinguish six main language test types:

1 *Aptitude*. These tests assess a student's capacity for learning *any* language. Language aptitude is a complex (and controversial) topic. Elements of aptitude testing are found in 11+ and some intelligence tests. There are commercially produced tests available and a good discussion of issues relating to aptitude can be found in Skehan (1998).

2 *Placement*. These are sometimes confused with diagnostic tests and indeed they often serve both purposes. Strictly speaking, however, a placement test is designed to identify which level in a multi-level programme a student should be allocated to. Normally one would expect the test material to be related to the curriculum or syllabus of the various levels. For example, the University of Birmingham's Centre for Modern Languages has a web-based multiple-choice placement test in five languages for its Open Access programme (CML 2003) which enables students to find which of eight possible levels they should enrol on.

3 *Diagnostic*. These tests identify strengths and, in particular, weaknesses in the FL, so that tutors can devise appropriate programmes of work and students can take remedial action. Diagnostic testing can be helpful in assessing entrants to a degree course or IWLP where doubts exist about levels of competence. Computer-based testing can be useful here, saving time and being more manageable during the busy start-of-year period. The DIALANG suite of tests (DIALANG 2002) is especially to be commended. This is a substantial EU-funded project that aims to diagnose language competence in 14 languages. It offers assessment in listening, reading, writing, structures and vocabulary, and makes extensive use of self-assessment and feedback. Once they have familiarized themselves with the tests, university language departments could easily use DIALANG as a placement test for their courses.

4 *Progress*. As a course develops, a tutor needs to have information on how students are coping and developing linguistically. Coursework on most modules will include some such check on progress, possibly in the form of informal recap exercises or quizzes, possibly in the shape of more formal class tests at the end of each unit of work. Both will be closely linked to the teaching content.

5 *Achievement*. These are the most common tests found in university language programmes. They usually occur at the end of a module or year of study and

aim to assess how well students have assimilated course material and whether they have achieved the learning outcomes of the course. In the later stages of a degree programme, as students' linguistic proficiency becomes more varied and advanced, such achievement tests can take on the appearance of proficiency tests (see below) which, strictly speaking, are inappropriate for anything other than a summative final-year exam intended to attest to a student's overall linguistic proficiency. In other circumstances it makes little educational sense to test students on substantial amounts of material that have not been covered in the course syllabus.

6 *Proficiency*. Unlike a test of achievement on a particular course, a proficiency test aims to assess all-round ability in a language in varied contexts, independently of the setting (naturalistic or classroom-based) in which the language was acquired. Examples in the UK are the Institute of Linguists' exams or the Diplomatic Service Language Allowance exams, which accredit language skills at a number of levels of proficiency. Such tests are notoriously difficult to set. A finals exam is probably the closest university language programmes get to such professional tests, but there is still a clear difference between the two, given the bias towards translation and 'academic' writing tasks in the final year of many language degree courses.

Test types

An important distinction in language testing is made between 'direct' and 'indirect' tests, that is between those that involve learners in actually performing the skill that is being assessed (e.g. an oral as a direct test of speaking) and those that assess the language elements that are thought to support or underpin the four main language skills (e.g. a multiple-choice test of discrete grammatical items as an indirect test of FL writing).

The advantage of indirect tests is that they are thought to be a more precise and objective method of assessment, allowing linguistic features to be tested separately and ensuring assessment is transparent and highly reliable (see Chapter 10 for these terms). Moreover, such tests are simple to administer and are thus very practical.

However, producing effective indirect tests can prove challenging (see Bailey 1998). With multiple-choice items, it is not easy to provide credible distractor answers and it can be difficult sometimes to isolate just one element of language. Another problem is that no one really knows if indirect tests are valid tests of the skills they claim to measure: is someone with a good knowledge of FL vocabulary necessarily a good FL reader? Furthermore, indirect tests can lead to negative washback (see Chapter 10) since, in preparing for an indirect test of writing, students are likely to spend time studying decontextualized grammar rather than actually doing any FL writing.

Growing recognition of the fact that language performance involves the integration of these discrete aspects of linguistic knowledge led to the development of direct skills testing, i.e. separate tests of actual speaking, writing, listening and reading activities. This was given impetus by the spread of communicative language teaching and the need for tests that could assess the ability to apply knowledge of the linguistic system in the achievement of communicative goals. (For detailed discussion of approaches to skills-based testing, see Hughes 2003, and Klapper 2003b: 14.2–14.4.)

A strict separation of skills is, however, unnatural and rather than assessing each of the four skills in turn, many language modules in HE nowadays feature *integrative* tests that assess students' ability to use a combination of skills. An example of integrative testing would be a task requiring students to listen to a simple telephone message and to draft a memo in reply. This involves the linguistic elements of phonology, grammar, vocabulary and discourse, as well as the skills of listening and writing.

▶ For each of the four skills of listening, speaking, reading and writing, think about how you would assess students' ability through one direct and one indirect test.

▶ Consider also which criteria would feature in the marking scheme for each of the resulting tests.

The indirect/discrete-point versus direct/integrative contrast can usefully be seen as a continuum, with the choice of test type ultimately a pedagogical one. In addition to the pedagogical reasons for choosing a particular test type, however, tutors need to consider the value of employing a *variety* of testing techniques with any one group of students. There are good reasons for doing this:

- No single test can be absolutely reliable; therefore the more varieties of testing that are employed, the less likelihood there is of bias or distortion.
- Students are known to have different learning styles and to respond differently to styles of teaching and techniques of testing; only through variety can we make allowance for this.
- Different students excel in different areas of language. So the wider the range of areas covered by our testing, the fairer this is to all.

Language essays

Free writing in the FL reveals very clearly students' underlying weaknesses in the language, ones which, in spoken communication, might be labelled 'performance error' or put down to 'communicative pressure'. Moreover, essays or summary writing are an especially effective vehicle for assessing higher-level language skills, or cognitive academic language proficiency (Cummins 1980), since they allow students space for distinctive treatment of a complex topic and give them scope to show what they can do linguistically, i.e. to employ varied structures, a wide range of vocabulary and idiom.

In spite of these positive features, there are grounds for questioning the status of the academic essay in FL teaching. With over half our linguists now non-specialists (see Chapter 14), we ought to take greater note of the argument that, as a form of assessment, the FL essay unduly favours those who have mastered the art of essay writing in L1 and know how to structure an academic essay. At the very least, non-specialists are likely to need support with this task. Forms of support include:

- practice in writing short essay plans, introductions or conclusions in the FL, including both pro–contra and linear essay structures, with appropriate feedback;
- occasional use of other writing tasks, such as providing counter-arguments to a paragraph of FL text promoting a particular issue, or developing an argument begun by a short FL text.

Apart from this, many of the recommendations relating to essay writing in non-language elements of Modern Language degrees (see Chapter 10) apply equally to language essays, including sharing precise criteria with students, limiting the range of titles offered and breaking titles down into sub-sections.

The assessment of essays should ideally involve a combination of analytic and objective marking schemes (for a fuller discussion, see Klapper 2003b). The former involves criteria for each of the sub-components of writing (e.g. content, structure, accuracy and range of language), weighted equally or differentially. Objective marking can take various forms but essentially involves some form of error quotient to assess accuracy and command of language; for example, divide either the total number of words used or a standard minimum by the number of errors made, possibly penalizing certain errors more than others, and deducting a set percentage of the marks available for under-length essays.

Assessing speaking skills

Oral exams

▶ Take a moment to think about your questioning technique in oral exams:
- Do you prepare your questions in advance?
- Do you consciously vary the *type* of question you ask?
- How can we ensure reliability in oral exams (see Chapter 10)?

The purpose of an oral exam is to allow students to demonstrate what they are capable of. Questions should therefore be open rather than closed. To guarantee fairness, each student is entitled to expect questions that are similar in number, range and difficulty. However, assessors will quickly gain an idea of each student's level, and can, when appropriate, introduce more challenging topics to evaluate the best performers' ability to cope linguistically with intellectually demanding content.

It is surprisingly difficult to focus on accurate assessment, while also keeping track of the conversation and checking all the relevant areas of a topic have been covered. It is therefore a good idea to prepare a list of sample questions in advance, or at least a checklist to ensure you cover key uses of language that are to be assessed, and prompt each student to produce the same sort of language. Such an approach serves to increase the reliability of marking. For example, at low to intermediate levels:

- can narrate a sequence of daily events;
- can narrate an event in the past;
- can talk about future plans, etc.

Ideally, two examiners should be involved in oral examining to increase reliability but, if this is not possible, performances should be video- or audio-recorded. The latter provides tangible evidence to support decisions (e.g. in case a mark is queried) as well as evidence for external examiners.

Group orals

A useful variation on the traditional oral exam is a discussion between students in which the examiner is not involved. This is a good all-round assessment of the ability to communicate in a foreign language in a realistic setting. It is the responsibility of the students themselves to develop the discussion and to reach agreement on some outcome. Ideally, the task will have no single 'right' answer and the topic will involve various possibilities. To avoid the situation where students have to depend on general knowledge or their own inventiveness, they might be asked in advance to look through relevant source material to help inform the discussion.

Tasks might include:

- choosing a holiday for a particular person from a range of brochure options;
- choosing the best candidate for a position in a company;
- discussing a proposal for using a derelict public building from a range of developers' bids.

To avoid the danger of students not contributing enough to the discussion, a structured approach might be adopted, as for example in The Open

University's speaking test, where each member of a group of four has to make a brief initial 'pitch', in which he or she outlines a view or position on the topic, prior to a general discussion to which all group members are expected to contribute.

Role play

The usual approach to role play is to give students just before the test a set of instructions explaining what they have to do. For example:

> You are on a visit to St Petersburg. You want to visit Petrodvorets and so you go to a tourist information centre. Ask how to get there, find out the cost of travel and of entry to the Palace. Ask how long it will take to get there and see if the person serving you has any advice on when you should go. Describe what you are going to do and make the necessary booking.

Providing such instructions in L1 will avoid any ambiguity about what is required and, with near beginners, this approach may be the only practical one. Otherwise, it is probably more common for instructions to be given in the target language. However, it should be noted that this can often provide linguistic support (e.g. in the above scenario, 'Palace', 'costs', 'advice'): with weaker students this might be desirable, while in other circumstances it could make the task too easy. One way round this is to phrase the instructions in more general terms:

> You are on a visit to St Petersburg and want to go to Petrodvorets. Find out from the person at the tourist information centre details of travel, cost and availability, and make the necessary booking.

Role plays are an effective means of involving students in particular types of language use, ranging from basic social situations to complex negotiating ones, such as convincing a company representative in an interview that you are the right person for the job. They are also the best way to test students' ability to ask questions, to use certain social address formulae, to vary linguistic register and to employ functions such as persuading, objecting, explaining, etc.

Apart from the type of low-level situation above, role play can be made more complex by including unexpected elements or 'twists'. Here the examiner throws in something the candidates are not expecting, to see how they cope linguistically when they are forced to 'think on their feet'.

Criteria for role plays are difficult to write; sometimes they may need to include slight variations to recognize the demands of different situations. They have to take account of how well the task has been performed, the relevance of the information provided and/or given, the appropriateness to the situation of the language used (lexis and register), as well as the usual criteria for oral assessment, such as accuracy of language and the quality of pronunciation and intonation.

Besides these three common tasks, there are numerous other possible approaches to oral assessment, including individual and group presentations, integrated skill tests, picture stimuli, information-gap activities, explaining/providing instructions, and reading texts out loud (for a comprehensive discussion, see Underhill 1987: 44–87; for a more succinct overview, see Klapper 2003b; see Chapter 10 on presentations).

Translation

> ▶ What do you see as the principal function of translation in language teaching?
> ▶ When used in assessment, is translation mainly a test of linguistic accuracy?

Although translation is relatively easy to prepare and *seems* to most of those who use it to be a suitable test (i.e. has face validity), there is little research to suggest it correlates with other measures such as speaking, reading or writing (Newson 1998). Many consequently believe that translation should serve primarily to train translators, rather than function as a vague means of language acquisition support (see Chapter 13). Such an approach emphasizes the communicative role of translation, its function as cultural mediation, and assumes that developing translators can learn much from real-world translation activity. This also implies that students should only translate into their L1.

With regard to assessment of translation as a communicative vehicle, marking needs to be concerned with the extent to which the target text:

● conveys the function of the source text;
● reflects the form or text type of the source text;
● observes appropriate linguistic conventions;
● observes culture-specific conventions;
● is coherent;
● observes the rules of the language system.

In practice, most language degree programmes, at least in the final year, still feature translation as a test of language proficiency and tutors therefore need to ensure the task is made as valid and reliable (see Chapter 10) as possible.

Content validity can be achieved in part through the following:

- translation texts should be on topics covered in the module;
- they should provide a clear context (i.e. students should be told the source of the text);
- there should be a clear purpose (i.e. students should know why the text was written and for whom);
- texts should cover a range of registers and styles to reflect the materials encountered on the course.

Reliability can be best achieved through the use of clear criteria. One way to structure these is to consider, first, how well the student has *understood* the source text, and second, how well he/she has rendered it in the other language. Yet, since holistic assessment of translation is very difficult to implement fairly, marking also probably ought to feature some more analytic or mechanical system for counting (and possibly weighting) different types of error.

Achievement and the Common European Framework

In the European Language Portfolio, described below, proficiency is intended to be recorded in terms of the Common European Framework for Languages (CEF) assessment scale (Council of Europe 2001). This records language competence on a six-point scale. The scale is increasingly being used by textbook publishers across Europe to describe the target levels of their products.

The CEF can also be used to compare the levels of UK public exams with the accredited national tests of other countries, which are slowly gaining in popularity. For example:

- In France, the internationally recognized Test de connaissance du français offered by the Centre international d'études pédagogiques, and its two diplomas for foreigners in French as a foreign language, DELF/DALF.
- In Germany, the four qualifications offered by the Goethe-Institut: Zertifikat Deutsch, Zentrale Mittelstufenprüfung, Zentrale Oberstufenprüfung and the Kleines Deutsches Sprachdiplom.
- In Spain, the three diplomas offered by the Instituto Cervantes and the Universidad de Salamanca: the Diploma de Español (Nivel Inicial), Diploma de Español (Nivel Intermedio), Diploma de Español (Nivel Superior).

Information on these and all the other European countries that produce examinations and certification for language learners can be found via the website of the Association of Language Testers in Europe (ALTE 2004).

Similarly, many university language centres and language departments are now pegging their courses to the CEF levels. See the following case study:

University of Southampton Language Stages

Find your language level: the seven language stages
Language degree options are offered at seven levels or stages of proficiency. Entry levels are stages 1 to 4. You would normally expect to progress at the rate of one stage each year, but the scheme is flexible enough to permit you to jump a stage if you make exceptional progress at some point.

Stage	Starting point	CEF upon completion
1	complete beginner	A2
2	post-GCSE	B1
3	post-AS/A level	B2
4	good A level standard	B2/C1
5	A level + one year of study	C1
6	A level + two years of study	C1/C2
7	virtually native speaker	C2

Detailed descriptors exist for each language stage, describing learning outcomes under the headings 'Listening, Reading, Speaking, Writing, Other Skills'. (Compiled from information available at: www.soton.ac.uk/cls/stages.html.)

(See also Chapter 6 and Chapter 14.)

Language portfolios

One of the more significant developments in assessment in recent years has been the introduction of learner portfolios (Baume 2001, CIEL Language Support Network 2000, Wyburd 2002). A portfolio is a collection of work produced by a student that demonstrates achievement, progress made, as well as effort invested in the task. The student usually decides what is to be included as evidence and provides an accompanying self-reflective piece of writing. Students may sometimes also be involved in helping to formulate the criteria for assessing the portfolio.

From the student's point of view, the variability of what one might consider acceptable output is probably the greatest strength of the portfolio. Depending on the topic and level, it might include:

- marked work, both spoken and written;
- a list of learning materials used;
- learner diaries;
- correspondence;
- reports on activities, surveys or investigations undertaken in the target country (maybe during residence abroad);
- reflection on issues, etc.;
- the results of internet searches.

With lower-level language tasks, one might include with the completed tasks reflection on perceived weaknesses and an indication of remedial action taken.

The advantages of portfolios for tutors are that they reveal how a student has developed linguistically and they are thus more informative than one-off, 'snapshot' language assessments. They also show if and how students have responded positively to feedback.

On the other hand, a major problem is that one can never be sure that all the work is the student's own. To address this concern, it may be necessary to conduct a viva in the FL linked to the portfolio. Furthermore, the individualized and therefore extremely diverse nature of portfolios can make it difficult to formulate reliable marking criteria. While they can have huge motivational benefits and provide positive washback on classroom learning, portfolios are thus probably not ideal as the *exclusive* instruments of summative assessment. However, they clearly have a role to play in formative assessment and they also have considerable potential for helping in the assessment of residence abroad. For ideas on designing portfolios, and issues to consider when marking them, see Baume (2001) and Race (2001a: 68–70).

A significant recent development in the use of portfolios is the appearance of the Council of Europe's European Language Portfolio (ELP) – see Little and Perclová (2001), Gauthier (2002). This provides a lifelong record of the learner's developing language skills, designed to be shown to prospective employers and to act as a stimulus for learners to reflect on their FL competence and identify future needs. The ELP consists of three parts:

- a small-format 'Language Passport' containing details of qualifications gained in various FLs;
- a larger, A4-format 'Language Biography' for recording both formal and informal language learning experiences (i.e. educational as well as travel-, placement-, and work-related), and current language learning;
- a 'Dossier of Evidence' in which learners file proof of FL competence, such as recordings or documents they can understand or have themselves produced.

Sources of information

Clapham, C. (2002) 'Principles of assessment', article in the Subject Centre for Languages, Linguistics and Area Studies *Good Practice Guide*. Online. Available at: www.lang.ltsn.ac. uk/resources/goodpractice.aspx?resourceid=1398 (accessed 6 February 2004). Contains several useful links and references, and provides a full glossary of assessment-related terms.

DIALANG (2002) Diagnostic tests. Online. Available at: www.dialang.org (accessed 6 April 2004). A set of computer-based diagnostic tests available over the internet, with immediate feedback on test scores, as well as advice on how learners can improve their proficiency to the next level of the CEF.

Hughes, A. (2003) *Testing for Language Teachers*, Cambridge: Cambridge University Press. The most accessible volume on the subject.

Module 14 in the DELPHI distance learning programme covers in greater depth the issues raised in this chapter (Klapper 2003b).

The Cambridge University Press series on assessment in languages represents the most up-to-date and authoritative statement on the subject (see Alderson 2000, Buck 2001, Douglas 2001, Luoma 2004, Purpura 2004, Read 2000, Weigle 2002).

12

Using the foreign language assistant

Agnès Gower

At a time when more and more institutions are reducing or axing their foreign language assistant (FLA) posts due to falling student recruitment, it is important to point out the value to language departments of their FLAs. As they are usually students themselves – except in German departments where they may be trained teachers (Adam *et al.* 2001: 77) – and are also native speakers of the language, they are more likely to be able to relate to students and to engage with them in conversation on current aspects of the target country's culture than some of their more senior academic colleagues. They will thus be better equipped to prepare second-year students for residence abroad. They may also bring new teaching ideas to a department through what they have experienced in their own country. Some may even, in the course of their studies, have taken a module in teaching their own language as a foreign language and may be keen to put their learning into practice.

Their principal function is to provide intensive small-group oral practice. Increasingly, the once traditional semi-detached 'conversation class' on a random topical theme has been replaced by thematically integrated work involving structured discussion and/or individual and team presentations, as well as programmed reinforcement of language topics. However, practice varies widely across the sector and will depend on the skills and experience of the individual FLA.

To be able to make good use of the valuable resource that FLAs represent, a number of issues need to be addressed.

Recruiting FLAs

There are several ways to recruit FLAs. Some institutions have reciprocal agreements with partner language departments in the target country, often alongside SOCRATES-ERASMUS links. Such arrangements are beneficial, since each institution selects its own candidates, usually from students in their fourth year at university, and then submits the names to the partner institution. Interviewing costs are thus minimized and home graduates are helped towards an academic or teaching career.

Some posts are sponsored directly by governments, especially in languages such as Portuguese, Italian and Catalan, which are not commonly studied in schools around the world and for which a university, unsure of the potential recruitment, may be reluctant to bear the cost of a post. For instance, through the Ramon Llull Institute, the Catalan government with support from the Spanish Foreign Affairs Ministry pays the salary of the Catalan assistants in posts in universities around the world. There are currently 18 spread around Great Britain (see www.llull.com/llull/estatic/eng/quisom/lectorats-dades.shtm). For German assistants, the DAAD, the German Academic Exchange Service, plays a prominent role by awarding scholarships to students wishing to gain teaching experience abroad (Lektorships) while raising awareness of German language and culture.

Finally, language departments may receive spontaneous applications from foreign students wishing to have a part-time job to fund themselves through a British PhD, to get a taste of the British education system before embarking on a Postgraduate Certificate in Education or simply to stay in England for a couple of years to improve their English before returning to their own country to teach English.

Briefing FLAs before they come to the UK

First of all, since FLAs come from education systems that are significantly different from the one in which they will have to operate, they require some insight into the ways of the British system. For instance, the personal tutoring system will be totally alien to them; they may be surprised by the relatively informal student–tutor relationship that prevails in the UK; they will also be unfamiliar with terms such as Single Honours, Joint Honours, institution–wide language programmes (see Chapter 14), electives and the whole degree classification system. This briefing should be undertaken before they come, in the form of a letter and a supporting documentation pack, and reinforced through an induction course once they are in the UK (see below).

Briefing FLAs is key to ensuring that they feel valued by their host department. Before they take up their post, they need to know:

- when they should arrive;
- where they are expected to report to;
- who the Head of Department is;
- who they can contact in case of difficulties.

Furthermore, FLAs will appreciate being told what precisely their duties will entail; for example:

- how many hours of work per week;
- how many weeks per year;
- what type of students they will teach;
- what kind of classes they will be expected to take (oral classes, area studies, aural or language laboratory classes);
- whether they will be on their own with students or will work together with a member of staff;
- whether they will have to prepare their own material or teach a pre-established programme.

They also need to be aware of the resources that will be at their disposal: whether they will have access to audiovisual equipment and information technology; what newspapers or magazines their host department subscribes to; what videos, books and reference material will be available on-site so that they can best select what to bring with them (remember: they usually fly to the UK so they are limited in what they can bring with them). Similarly, the department could tell them what types of material would help them most in their teaching, as it is very difficult for someone with little or no experience of teaching to anticipate what might be useful in class.

Finally, before they arrive, future FLAs should be given information about accommodation, pay and taxation, banking, health and other practical arrangements such as car parking and insurance. One point that is often overlooked is supplying the name and contact details of the previous post-holder (assistantships are usually one-year contracts) so that they can ask questions they would not dare ask a future and more senior colleague. It can be both useful and reassuring if the person who writes to the future FLAs provides his or her email address, as email is a far less intimidating medium than the phone or a formal letter, especially for a foreigner.

All this practical information is paramount in enabling FLAs to settle quickly in their new country. Needless to say, it is in the department's own interest to help FLAs find their feet quickly, since a settled assistant who feels welcomed and valued will be far more productive.

The importance of mentoring and induction

All departments should provide FLAs with a mentor, who may or may not be their line manager (the latter is far preferable). The mentor will be there to support the newcomers, to help them settle in, but also to guide them in their teaching choices, especially in the first few weeks. The mentor should be approachable, could be the same for all FLAs (if a department has several) or a different one for each. The mentor needs to be experienced in teaching, but someone very senior could be too intimidating and might have forgotten what it is like to start teaching in a foreign country. In addition, ethnicity and gender are possible factors influencing the choice of a mentor (Partington 1998: 31–32).

The mentor must not, however, be a substitute for a more formal induction programme. This may be offered across language departments and, ideally, should take place shortly before the start of term, with some reflective sessions following the FLAs' first few weeks of teaching. The DOPLA course (see Gravestock *et al.* 2000), a form of which now operates in over 30 higher education institutions across England and Wales (Adam *et al.* 2001, Gray 2001), is a good example of such a programme. It is a far more efficient way of making an assistant productive within a short space of time than the traditional 'throw them in at the deep end' approach (Partington 1998: 43). Inviting FLAs to follow an induction programme gives them – especially those with no experience of teaching or teacher training – ideas on methodology (making a lesson plan, using text, audio and video stimuli) and a forum for reflection and discussion on class (especially small-group) dynamics, both of which will enhance their confidence and make them less apprehensive about facing the students for the first time. Increased confidence leads to a more relaxed class atmosphere and makes it more likely that FLAs will start off on the right foot with students.

Organizing training sessions for FLAs also indicates to them that their work is taken seriously and that their classes are an integral and valued part of the students' learning experience, not some questionable 'added extra'. Moreover, if the induction is run across language departments, it enables FLAs to meet other assistants, with whom they can discuss common problems and exchange possible solutions.

Once the induction is over, the mentor and the tutors in charge of the modules that FLAs are teaching on must remain available, should the assistants need advice. FLAs should be made to feel sufficiently at ease to ask at any time for help or clarification.

Equally, mentors and convenors should see it as part of their job to offer guidance, especially where marking may be involved. If marking is required of FLAs, they must be provided with adequate marking criteria and the department must ensure their marks are monitored by a senior member of staff (either their mentor or the convenor for the module concerned).

Finally, it is essential to institute regular meetings with FLAs, whether formal or more relaxed occasions. Having lunch with the assistants can be one of the most effective and efficient ways to field questions and deal with problems as and when they arise.

Monitoring the work of FLAs

The department must monitor the effectiveness of the assistant as a teacher, at the very least through class-observation and student questionnaires, both of which should feature during the first term or semester (rather than the second, as is often the case for more senior colleagues on year-long modules) in order to give sufficient time for areas of concern to be addressed. Observations could most usefully be carried out by the mentor, with whom a certain level of confidence is more likely to have been reached. Similarly, it is probably best if the mentor (after consultation with module convenors, where necessary) discusses with each assistant the results of student questionnaires. Feedback should be constructive, drawing attention to positive features, as well as making suggestions for improvement.

Building for the future

It is a good idea to ask FLAs to keep a record throughout the year of what they have used with their students (including lesson plans, materials and comments on what worked and what did not) and to file these. This means that, when future assistants arrive, they find in their offices a ready-made bank of materials and ideas, as well as a record of, for instance, what current second-year students did in Year 1, which is invaluable in avoiding duplication and ensuring continuity.

During the examination period, and following a full briefing, FLAs can usefully contribute to the oral and aural examinations at Levels 1 and 2, and can undertake invigilation duties. Besides this, assuming they are not more heavily involved in the examination process, they could be asked by language module convenors to prepare new material (aural, oral or written exercises).

It might also be worth considering a final general meeting with the FLAs before they return home to solicit feedback on the course and the year as a whole. This could be done as part of the normal end-of-year module review process.

Sources of information

Gravestock *et al.* (2000). Copies of this comprehensive training pack are available free of charge from the University of Birmingham's Centre for Modern Languages.

DOPLA, website of the DOPLA project. Online. Available at: www.bham.ac.uk/dopla (accessed 17 April 2004).

DAAD, website of the German Academic Exchange Service (Deutscher Akademischer Austausch Dienst). Online. Available at: www.daad.de (accessed 17 April 2004).

Ramon Llull Institute, website of the Catalan consortium in charge of the external promotion of Catalan language and culture. Online. Available at: www.llull.com/llull/estatic/eng/quisom/lectorats.shtm (accessed 17 April 2004).

13

Translating and interpreting

James A. Coleman and Isabelle Perez

Although the general public may be unaware of the differences, translation and interpreting are often contrasted by professional practitioners as distinct activities requiring different skills. The former usually involves written target texts which can always be revised, whereas the latter deals with fleeting messages, conveyed orally by the interpreter under time constraints, and therefore with little room for error repair or stylistic improvement. Both activities take place within a social context (Hatim and Mason 1990), and represent an act of communication which attempts to relay across cultural and linguistic boundaries another act of communication (Hatim and Mason 1997). Both involve careful analysis and understanding of meaning in context as well as attention to extra-linguistic aspects of communication. In what follows, we distinguish vocational training from the use of translation (and more rarely interpreting) as a technique for language learning and transferable skills acquisition.

Vocational training

Globalization has increased the demand for communication professionals in all domains, and triggered an expansion of vocational training programmes and postgraduate courses in translation and/or interpreting. Full-time employees of national or international organizations (such as the United Nations or European Union institutions) tend to be specialists in either translating or interpreting. The latter domain divides into *conference interpreting* (simultaneous or consecutive) and *liaison interpreting* between interlocutors with no shared lingua franca. But new tasks demand integrated skills: bilingual précis-writing for the UN, for example, involves gist translation on the basis of audio-recordings of meetings.

Computers, long essential for word processing, desktop publishing and glossary databases, now also offer Computer Aided Translation (CAT) and Machine Translation (MT). MT systems, including TRADOS, DéjàVu and SDLX, memorize segments of text that have already been translated and subsequently propose them to the translator. MT is cost-effective for specific types of texts comprising set structures and limited lexis (manuals, software specifications and commercial websites) or regularly updated content such as quarterly reports or contracts. But most translation tasks require a human to edit the computer's efforts and resolve any remaining ambiguities.

Vocational courses cover both the practical aspects of the translation/ interpreting process and the underlying theoretical issues. Practical modules increasingly include training in 'translation technologies': machine translation, translation memory, terminology management, software and world wide web localization. Editing and publishing skills feature prominently, in particular pre- and post-editing required by translation programs. Theoretical modules might dwell on the face-to-face setting of liaison interpreting and its implications for the interpreter's role and visibility, and on the ethical obligations of the public service interpreter.

Translation and interpreting as learning activities

> ▶ Think back to your own foreign language learning. What role did translation play in this? How was it handled in class? What was expected of you in written translations?

The translation tradition

As a teaching exercise, translation goes back at least to the Renaissance. Close study and stylistic imitation of the Greek and Latin writers of Antiquity was to bring to European vernaculars the precision, qualities and status of classical languages. The scholars who effected translations from and into the classical tongues slowly gained mastery of the structures, vocabulary, registers and prosody of Greek and Latin.

Over four centuries, prose largely supplanted poetry. But the fundamental approach to teaching modern and classical languages, retrospectively labelled 'grammar-translation', remained the same: the target language was acquired through explicit learning of grammatical rules and exceptions, reinforced by repetitive and decontextualized drills, and supplemented by translations of short extracts from great writers. The venerable exercise relied on other elements in the teaching context:

- prior mastery of virtually all the morpho-syntactic features of the target language, so that the focus was not on basic accuracy but on style and nuance of meaning;
- near-exclusive focus on a single mode and register, high-status writing of publishable quality, which even in the native language demanded the leisurely attention to detail of a wordsmith;
- the parallel reading by the student of vast quantities of literary and critical target-language texts from all periods, and an unspoken assumption that the students would already have familiarity with the literary canon of their native tongue;
- reliance on students working intelligently and independently with a battery of reference works.

Why translation?

> ► List what you feel are the advantages and disadvantages of transla-
> tion as a language teaching exercise.

In today's very different context, what is the role of translation? Since the emergence of Applied Linguistics as a scientific discipline about 40 years ago, much criticism has been heaped on the grammar-translation approach (for its history and characteristics, see Stern 1983: 453–56):

- the inevitable link with students' mother tongue can intensify problems of interference – anglicisms which writing directly in the target language would not have triggered;
- the emphasis on knowledge about the language rather than practical ability to use it;
- the concentration on a particular written register that graduates rarely, if ever, need;
- the debatable link between translation and actual language skills.

Actual practice has sometimes tended to encourage word-for-word translation rather than emphasizing cultural equivalence and appropriacy. And teachers have too often used isolated, decontextualized sentences or fragments, so that translation takes place in a vacuum: a fundamental principle of translation studies is the role of contextualization (written by whom, when, as part of what longer document?) and purpose (target text to be published where, for what sort of readership?).

Even among those who teach through translation, voices have been raised against its over-use, and in particular its inefficiency in helping students acquire morpho-syntactic fundamentals (see Chapter 8 on grammar). It is, rather, once these have been internalized that translation can stretch students' proficiency. Recurrent errors are better remedied by other means, and translation as a linguistic exercise is arguably most useful with advanced learners after their year abroad has provided enhanced morpho-syntactic, sociolinguistic and socio-cultural insights.

Nonetheless, old habits die hard, and translation is still widely used, especially at more advanced levels. And in many ways, translation does meet the requirements of contemporary second language acquisition (SLA) theory. The constraints of the source text oblige learners to produce target-language output containing particular lexis or structures, in a particular register. Exploration of synonyms and near-synonyms enhances their lexical range. Monitoring of TL production becomes instinctive and automatized.

In fact, a rationale for the use of translation across general-purpose language courses in today's communicative and task-orientated classrooms rests on two learning objectives – intercultural communication and linguistic proficiency.

Many now argue that the real role that a language learner will play is not that of a pseudo-native speaker, adopting all the linguistic and cultural behaviours of the target-language community. Rather, in a globalizing world, linguists are intermediaries, facilitating communication between individuals and groups from differing linguistic and cultural backgrounds. The essential purpose of translation is to communicate, to convey a message across linguistic and cultural barriers. Successful translation and interpreting therefore depend on – and their practice develops – mastery of both the source and the target language and culture in all their diversity.

SLA research has shown a universal tendency for an individual's foreign language proficiency to reach a plateau once they feel that their communicative needs are being met. This is very evident among some migrant communities, but has also been evidenced among final-year students after a period of residence abroad. If students are to continue to expand their active range of structures and lexis, they need to be pushed to explore and use all the complexities of the target language: judicious selection of translation passages can oblige students to draw on sophisticated resources when they might be tempted in spontaneous use to rely on an adequate but incomplete spread of expressions which they have already acquired and automatized.

Translation *from* the target language presents students with models of target-language use, develops an awareness of how skilled users fine-tune their meaning, and enhances students' written skills in English.

Interpreting can foster multiple language and transferable skills (see Chapters 10 and 15) including personal development and self-management (e.g. multi-tasking, reflective/critical thought, development of self-confidence), analytical skills (e.g. understanding and analysing, perceiving structures, problem solving, extracting key information), and oral communication skills (e.g. public speaking fostered through the development of short-term memory skills, the technique of note-taking, and the ability to produce coherent speech using the appropriate register).

How translation?

Traditionally, a passage for translation has been set in week 1, submitted for marking in week 2, and returned in week 3. The student works with dictionaries and grammar books, and perhaps other reference books, to produce a draft which renders the source text as faithfully as possible. In correcting the students' work, the tutor will consider all the alternative ways of expressing the original author's intention, balancing accurate rendering with cultural and stylistic appropriacy and sensitivity to native-speaker usage. Feedback on the page and especially during the hand-back class will cover the potential variants and the reasons for preferring a particular version, which may even be handed out as a 'fair copy'. But such an approach, however systematic and intellectually satisfying, may not yield the best results.

You could try asking students to provide a commentary or discussion of the tricky points, and why they opted for one solution rather than another – this is a standard exercise with more advanced and professional training. As with other learning activities, group work can provide opportunities for productive discussion and reflection: arguing one's case deepens the learning and accelerates the internalization of the point under discussion. The group work can take place in small groups in class, with one group using the OHP or electronic whiteboard and leading the summary discussion. Alternatively, work on the first and successive collaborative drafts can take place between classes, with paper and pencils, or using the many online tools available in Virtual Learning Environments such as Blackboard or WebCT, or through e-mails and attached Word files with proposed changes tracked and comments added.

Word processing also facilitates a third technique: rather than correcting every error a student makes, the tutor initially only indicates *where* an error is located, or perhaps the type of error (vocabulary, verb tense, adjective agreement, etc.). The student then has to submit a revised version: intervening work with reference books will have automatically focused on areas of weakness.

The wide range of different approaches, based on the identification of a variety of transferable skills and knowledge developed through translation classes, embraces use of parallel texts, summary translation, focus on difficulties specific to individual language combinations and much more. The Subject Centre's *Good Practice Guide* contains lots of other good ideas: see the articles by Nott (2002), Perez (2002) and Sewell (2002). Issues of principle and practice are addressed in Sewell and Higgins (1996), in Malmkjaer (1998), in encyclopedia articles by Rogers (translation) and Bassnett (translation theory) in Byram (2000), and more polemically in Phipps and Gonzalez (2004: 149–65). Module 11 in the DELPHI distance learning programme (Millan 2002) is devoted to the topic of translation.

Translation for testing?

Translation still forms part of assessment in many universities: even ten years ago it was still by far the favourite form of final language examination. But as an assessment exercise, it is problematical. In formative assessment – which is effectively one function of the weekly 'prose' – the repeated focus on short-comings (especially if the tutor still clings to red ink, undifferentiated squiggles and marginal 'Oh!!!'s) can be very demotivating. Marking schemes are conventionally negative – minus 2 for grammar, minus 1 for agreement, minus ½ for spelling – and positive rewards for 'good' translations difficult to systematize. It is pedagogically preferable to provide detailed and supportive feedback without a mark. Experienced teachers also know from interminable arguments over stylistic minutiae that translation is also a highly subjective topic! Criteria must be transparent and known to students, and must focus more on effective communication, fluency, register and style than merely on accuracy of morphology and syntax (see Chapter 11). However, if appropriately used, translation can be an effective assessment tool (Buck 1992), and both translation and interpreting tasks can complement other examinations.

Sources of information

Subject Centre for Languages, Linguistics and Area Studies. Online. Available at: www.lang.ltsn.ac.uk/index.aspx (accessed 19 June 2004).

National Centre for Languages. Online. Available at: www.cilt.org.uk (accessed 19 June 2004).

Institute of Linguists. Online. Available at: www.iol.org.uk (accessed 19 June 2004).

Institute of Translators and Interpreters. Online. Available at: www.iti.org.uk/indexMain.html (accessed 19 June 2004).

CIUTI (International Permanent Conference of University Institutes of Translators and Interpreters). Online. Available at: www.ciuti.org (accessed 19 June 2004).

AIIC (International Association of Conference Interpreters). Online. Available at: www.aiic.net (accessed 19 June 2004).

Part III

Modes and contexts of university language learning

14

Institution-wide languages programmes and non-specialist learners

Derrik Ferney

Introduction

Institution-wide languages programmes (IWLPs) are organizational structures that aim to maximize opportunities for language learning within institutions by providing a comprehensive and viable language programme that can take into account the needs of a wide spectrum of non-specialist language learners. They may be located in language departments, language centres or other central units with responsibility for general education, 'broadening' and electives programmes.

Nomenclature

IWLPs and the learners they serve are known by different names according to institutional preference. At the level of the programmes themselves the most widely used term remains 'IWLP', though a commonly used alternative is 'Languages for All'. There are similar issues of nomenclature at the level of the learner. It is generally agreed that the term 'non-specialist' is not ideal insofar as it is both faintly pejorative and potentially misleading. Other terms have been tried. Hartley (1992) suggested 'non-mainstream linguists' and more recently the terms 'students of other disciplines', 'specialists in other disciplines' and 'less specialist language learners' have been used, but none seems to have achieved the currency of 'non-specialist', which has been further legitimized by its use in the 1997–2001 TransLang[1] (Transferable Skills Development for

Non-Specialist Language Learning) survey and in the Quality Assurance Agency (QAA) Subject Benchmark Statement for Languages and Related Studies (QAA 2002). For these reasons the term 'non-specialist' is used in the remainder of this chapter. Having said this, we should bear in mind that IWLPs are a sub-set of non-specialist provision, and not vice versa. This is reflected in TransLang's findings that in 1996–97 the majority of non-specialist students were *not* enrolled on IWLPs (Pilkington 1997: 19–44) but instead were 'minoring' in the language, studying it as part of specifically international degree programmes in areas such as Engineering, Law, Tourism or Business, or simply studying it on an entirely voluntary basis with no institutional accreditation.

Student profile

IWLPs work by aggregating or consolidating disparate demand into unitary provision. Some deal with in excess of 2,000 students, which requires a management structure that is both robust and simple. They may offer up to 15 languages to students from several faculties (possibly in different locations), and the majority of the provision is likely to be sub-A level.[2]

IWLPs achieve this by teaching students from different disciplines together and, ideally, using the resulting economies of scale to increase the range of languages and levels available. O'Leary sums this up neatly when describing the establishing of an IWLP in 1990:

> In order to ensure viable groups in a range of languages and offer different levels of study within these languages, students are taught in groups homogeneous in terms of prior achievement in the target language and heterogeneous in terms of subject specialism.
>
> (O'Leary 1998: 117)

This is not quite the full story, since the need to achieve economies of scale can result in students from different years as well as different disciplines being placed in the same language module.

Curriculum design

Because their student clientele is so diverse, IWLPs have tended to opt for relatively general purpose (GP) curricula that are likely to be relevant to the needs of most students. While some IWLPs do have privileged links with specific faculties which provide enough students for a languages for specific purposes (LSP) orientation to be used with closed groups at all levels, the general picture is of languages for general professional purposes at the lower levels, with opportunities for the introduction of LSP, possibly in the form of 'add-ons', at the higher levels. There is evidence that this is what students want, and the IWLP community has given considerable thought to *when* and *how* LSP can be introduced into their otherwise generic curricula.[3] O'Leary and Drew (1995) and O'Leary (1998, 2000) provide interesting accounts of how specialist lexis and register can be developed in the higher stages of an IWLP, while Hartley (1994), Ife and Peña-Calvo (2000), and Lewis *et al.* (2000) describe ways in which IWLPs can be enhanced to prepare students for periods of residence abroad.

Accreditation within modular schemes

Language learning on IWLPs may be accredited internally within modular programmes (i.e. the learning counts for academic credit and can contribute towards degree classification) or it may be taken as an 'optional extra' (i.e. it does not count for academic credit, and may or may not be geared to the examinations of an external awarding body). This seems to be a question of institutional preference. While there can be drawbacks in terms of motivation and retention with the 'optional extra' approach, it does appear to be popular with significant numbers of students.[4] Little and Ushioda (1998: 27–30) provide a helpful account of the arguments for and against accreditation (which they refer to as 'integration'). As part of its general policy initiatives regarding the teaching of languages within the European Union, the Committee of Ministers specifically identifies higher education (HE) as having a key role in promoting multilingualism, urging member states to encourage 'teaching programmes at all levels that use a flexible approach – *including modular courses* and those that aim to develop partial competences – and *giving them appropriate recognition in national qualification systems*' (Council of Europe Committee of Ministers 1998; my italics).

▶ Your proposal to establish an IWLP has been broadly accepted by your institution, but concerns have been raised by the Business School and the School of Applied Sciences that the discipline-based needs of their students may be lost in what seems to them to be a general purpose programme.

How would you address this concern? Considerations might include an analysis of student needs (is a period of residence abroad required or optional?) and a review of First Destination surveys to inform the precise relationship between GP and LSP elements at various stages of the provision and to identify ways of customizing provision – either through class contact or additional LSP material for work outside the classroom.

In-service training and team building[5]

In the case of a very large IWLP, the logistics of offering 15 or so languages at different levels by means of 100 classes per week, taught by 30 staff, many of them part-time, require a high level of common understanding among the teaching force and highly efficient, centralized management and administration. (Stewart 1995 provides a witty and informative account of the latter.)

In-service training by means of workshops and away-days has much to recommend it, but it can be difficult to organize on a regular enough basis where staffing is casualized. As a result, most practitioners build and maintain the IWLP team by a combination of written briefing materials issued to staff on commencement of contract, regular team meetings and updates via intranet postings or written memoranda. At the very least, IWLP staff will need a handbook containing information about the staff associated with the programme, key contact numbers (who to contact in case of illness, for example, so that cover can be arranged), language learning facilities and resources including reprographics, the languages and levels available for study, classroom management issues and methods of assessment. Some of the key ingredients in building and maintaining a team of tutors capable of delivering an IWLP to common standards are a shared understanding of:

- The programme as a whole, so that tutors can answer general questions about it or refer students to someone who can.
- The aims and objectives of the programme, its curriculum and target levels of achievement.
- The type of learners taking the programme. For the majority of IWLP students, language learning will be optional (whether it counts for credit or not), and if it is not pleasurable, relevant and productive they may simply withdraw from the programme. Several factors appear to influence success, including varied student expectations about language learning based on previous experience, pressure of work in their main discipline, and different learning styles within mixed groups. The problem of attrition is therefore a very real one, and its scale can be gauged from research by Reimann (2001), among others. Tutors have to be alert to these problems if they are to maintain student interest and commitment and thereby maximize retention.
- The varied and interactive approaches to teaching likely to interest students from a range of backgrounds.
- Assessment instruments and marking standards. Because of the large teaching teams covering several languages and levels in IWLPs, it is extremely important to define precisely the repertoire of assessment instruments so that consistency can be achieved. Students need to know the basis on which they will be assessed – this is the role of *assessment criteria* which should be published in programme literature, and tutors need to

know how the assessment criteria will be applied to specific assessment tasks by means of *marking schemes*.[6]

- The need for continuing evaluation and review using standard HE quality processes.

► Your IWLP is delivered by permanent staff (20 per cent of the delivery) and 23 hourly-paid staff (80 per cent of the delivery). It is managed by a full-time IWLP co-ordinator and has an external assessor for the major languages only. Hourly-paid staff will attend staff development sessions only if they are paid to do so (at half the teaching rate). What are the major staff development issues to be addressed in order to achieve consistent, high-quality teaching and learning? How would you convey them to hourly-paid staff?

Greater student autonomy in learning and assessment

As a result of the downward pressure on class contact hours (two to three per week now seem to be the norm) much energy and inventiveness have been devoted to devising methods of continuing student learning outside the classroom (see, for example, Allen and Graham 1995, Roberts and Shaw 1998, Lewis *et al.* 2000, Morley and Truscott 2001, Walker 2001).

Two such methods are tandem-learning partnerships, where students learning each other's mother tongue team up to investigate topics agreed with and monitored by a tutor (see Chapter 20) and portfolios, where students compile evidence of their language-learning activity over time (Fay 2003). These methods enable students to customize language learning and assessment towards their own needs, such as residence abroad, the language of their specialist discipline or grammar revision. They also lend themselves to continuous and project-based assessment which can promote learning outside the classroom.

There is no single model of IWLP assessment, nor a single set of assessment instruments, but few use examinations alone. Equally, few use entirely open assessment because of the dangers of poor academic practice and plagiarism. Most use a combination of open and closed task-based assessments, with the latter taking the form of invigilated in-class tests or examinations, as appropriate.

The development of metacognitive skills by students – learning how to learn

The heterogeneity of the clientele of IWLPs and reductions in class contact hours have led to the need to encourage learning outside the classroom;

simultaneously, they have led to a greater awareness of the importance of how learners see themselves and how they organize their learning so as to maximize language gain (see Chapter 16). Hurd (2000) describes research into distance learners' perception of their efficiency as language learners. Walker (2001) describes the use of learner diaries in tandem-learning partnerships, where they are used by students to set goals, plan ahead and introspect about their learning. And in the extensive first chapter of their book on institution-wide languages programmes, Little and Ushioda argue that a successful second language pedagogy for IWLPs must develop learner autonomy in two dimensions:

> On the one hand, it must focus on learning how to learn, so that learners develop the means to manage their own learning . . . . On the other hand, our pedagogy must seek to develop learners' capacity for independent language use, for only if they have such a capacity can they carry their target language knowledge and skills beyond the confines of the classroom or the self-access centre.
>
> (Little and Ushioda 1998: 21)

The teaching of grammar

IWLPs tend to use a communicative approach and segment their teaching materials according to topics or functions. This approach poses known problems with regard to the coverage and sequencing of target-language grammar (see Chapter 8). If there is a general trend it is, predictably, towards the downplaying of grammar at *ab initio* and lower intermediate levels, and progressive explication at higher levels. However, Carty and O'Connell (1998) add a further twist to the grammar debate by contrasting the generally weak grammatical knowledge of (GCSE-generation) UK students with the far better developed grammatical awareness of the international students who are now so numerous on IWLPs. They point to the 'complicating effect' this has in the classroom, and conclude: 'These differing characteristics of international and UK students mean that there are effectively two audiences in the classroom when teachers are dealing with grammar' (Carty and O'Connell 1998: 49).

The use of new technologies in IWLPs

It is not clear that the use of Information and Communication Technologies (ICT) with non-specialist students is fundamentally different from their use with specialist students (see Chapters 18 and 19). While most practitioners would agree that the use of ICT has become an important part of the landscape for the latter, there are only occasional references in the literature to the use of ICT in an IWLP context (see, for example, Gilligan 1998, Beavan 2000, Little 2001; see also Sources of information below).

Mapping IWLPs onto language learning frameworks

While there is a good deal of diversity among IWLPs in respect of contact hours, curricula and levels of progression, there is a general feeling that the transparency and 'portability' of qualifications can only be enhanced if they map onto a national or international framework. Historically, the problem for IWLPs has been which framework to map onto.[7] More recently, the 2002 QAA Benchmark Statement (QAA 2002) has provided useful pointers to the Council of Europe's Common European Framework of Reference for Languages: learning, teaching, assessment (CEF) and the European Language Portfolio (ELP). The CEF (Council of Europe 2001) seeks to promote language learning by providing a transparent framework that can be used by educational providers as a European 'yardstick' for their study programmes (see also Chapter 11). It also makes a distinction between multilingualism and plurilingualism which is of importance to IWLPs. By adopting the plurilingual approach:

> the aim of language education is profoundly modified. It is no longer seen as simply to achieve 'mastery' of one or two, or even three languages, each taken in isolation, with the 'ideal native speaker' as the ultimate model. Instead, the aim is to deliver a linguistic repertory, in which all linguistic abilities have a place. This implies, of course, that *the languages offered in educational institutions should be diversified and students given the opportunity to develop a plurilingual competence.*
>
> (Council of Europe 2001: 5, my italics)

The (relative) down-playing of the 'ideal native speaker' model is crucial, as is the CEF's acknowledgement of the value of what it terms 'partial competences', where it is appropriate for sub-sets of language skills to be developed (a reading knowledge of German for engineers or scientists, for example). In brief, it would seem that the CEF potentially has a great deal to offer IWLPs, particularly if students can also be offered the ELP (see Chapter 11). The Department for Education and Skills (DfES) is currently trialling a voluntary recognition scheme called the 'Languages Ladder' which maps UK national qualification frameworks against the CEF with a view to forming a ladder of recognition from beginner level to a standard that sits alongside GCSE, A Level and National Vocational Qualifications. IWLPs may be able to capitalize on these developments by referencing themselves against the CEF/Language Learning Ladder via the QAA's Benchmark Statement and by providing students with the opportunity to document competences using the ELP (see, for example, Davies and Jones 2001).

Mapping IWLPs onto transferable skills frameworks

The work of the TransLang project (Fay 2003) represents the most extensive empirical investigation undertaken so far into non-specialist language learning in general, and IWLPs in particular. In essence the project aimed to show two things: that learners acquire knowledge and not 'just' skills when they learn foreign languages, and that the skills they do actually employ and learn include a wide range of non-linguistic skills that can usefully be transferred to other learning and professional activity. A central hypothesis was that these transferable skills go unrecognized by students, teachers and lecturers alike. In the first phase of the project, the transferable skills identified were self-management skills, communicative and interpersonal skills, cognitive (information processing) and research skills, task-enhancing skills and transferring skills. In its second phase, the project addressed the task of designing models of learning and teaching capable of incorporating these newly identified skills into language learning much more visibly than had previously been the case. The results were collated into the Guide for Practitioners (Pilkington 2000), which contains numerous case studies and provides a helpful account of ways in which learning and teaching strategies used by IWLPs can be (re)located within the HE graduate skills agenda.

> ▶ You are engaged in writing a review document for your language
> provision which caters for both specialist and non-specialist learners.
> Try to map your provision onto the above or another relevant frame-
> work. How would your mapping take account of your institution's
> increasing interest in the joint teaching of specialist and non-
> specialist language learners?

Notes

1   TransLang remains the largest relevant survey to date. It defined non-specialist learners as 'students whose degree titles do not include Modern Languages, a named foreign language, or the words "European" or "International". Language provision for such students represents up to 25 per cent of the total study programme for their award' (Pilkington 1997: Introduction). However, while the TransLang distinction serves as a useful rule of thumb there is evidence that specialist and non-specialist provision may be converging to the point of merger in some institutions (Phillips 2000).

2   The debate about the 'degree worthiness' of sub-A level IWLP modules has still not been entirely resolved. See Fay and Ferney (2000: Introduction) for a discussion of this tension.

3   For an interesting insight into more profound differences between GP and LSP provision, see Howarth (1995).

4   A 'straw poll' published by the Association of University Language Centres (AULC) in January 2004 revealed that the Language Centres in the 34 institutions surveyed were teaching a total of 47,538 students, 22,530 of whom were not following a credit-rated modular language programme, i.e. were studying a language as an optional extra.

5   See Huss (1994), Rothwell (1995), Leconte (1995), Lyne (1995), Woodin and Lewis (1995) and Little and Ushioda (1998: 39–40).

6   See Chapters 10 and 11 for an account of assessment issues. See Pilkington (2000: section 3) and Chapter 10 for the assessment of transferable skills.

7   Ife (1994) describes how one IWLP was mapped against the Council of Europe's Modern Languages Project, and Fay (1995) describes the articulation of an IWLP with the Languages Lead Body's National Language Standards.

Sources of information

ICT in language learning and teaching

WELL (Web Enhanced Language Learning). Online. Available at: www.well.ac.uk (accessed 23 April 2004).

ICT4LT (Information and Communications Technology for Language Teachers). Online. Available at: http://www.ict4lt.org (accessed 23 April 2004).

CILT portal to ICT websites. Online. Available at: www.cilt.org.uk/ICT/index.htm (accessed 23 April 2004).

Fund for the Development of Teaching and Learning projects

Teaching Quality Enhancement Fund Projects portal (includes links to SMILE and TransLang). Online. Available at: www.ncteam.ac.uk/projects/index.htm (accessed 23 April 2004).

Learning frameworks

European Council: Common European Framework. Online. Available at: www.coe.int/ T/E/Cultural_Cooperation/education/Languages/Language_Policy/Common_ Framework_of_Reference/default.asp (accessed 23 April 2004).

DfES, The Languages Ladder – Steps to Success. Online. Available at: www.dfes.gov.uk/ languages/DSP_languagesladder.cfm (accessed 23 April 2004).

15

Residence abroad

James A. Coleman

Introduction

Residence abroad – spending part of one's degree at a foreign university, as an English language assistant, or on an overseas work placement – is usually undertaken to improve foreign language proficiency. But it can bring other academic, personal and employability benefits. Best practice dictates, first, that the learning objectives should be clearly defined for – and with – each student; and second, that those objectives should underpin the preparation for residence abroad, its curriculum integration, the support, monitoring and academic work while abroad, the debriefing and follow-up on return, assessment and accreditation, and related staff development.

The term 'residence abroad' reflects the British practice of including within a Modern Languages or other degree an extended period of residence in a country whose language one wishes to learn. The phrase 'Study Abroad', widely used in the research literature, reflects North American practice, whereby students go abroad in groups, often accompanied by home-institution faculty (staff), and follow formal study – including language study – in the target-language (TL) country. Other labels (*séjour à l'étranger, Auslandsaufenthalt*) suggest a short and provisional immersion, whereas UK students typically have to deal with living for an extended period in circumstances akin to those of local native speakers.

Historical development

For most of the twentieth century, degrees in Modern Languages attracted an intellectual elite with a good command of the written TL, honed to provide an appreciation of great literary works in the original tongue. Practical, productive use of the TL was a by-product, but the intuition that surviving alone in the TL community would develop both oral proficiency and a first-hand insight into the target culture led to the development of assistantship programmes, on an exchange basis, which also brought native speakers to British schools and universities. Until the 1960s, the placement abroad was only as a language assistant. However, in the last third of the century, work and study placements also became available. The 'year abroad' had become a standard feature of UK language degrees long before EU programmes were devised to attract other European countries, often with less structured degree programmes, to promote the mobility of students.

Thanks to the EU's successive Joint Study Programme (1976), ERASMUS (1987) and SOCRATES (1995, renewed 2000–2006), over a million European students have now spent part of their degree in one of over 30 participating countries (see www.europa.eu.int/comm/education/programmes/socrates/erasmus/erasmus_en.html). Regular surveys by the University of Kassel (Teichler 1997, 2002) have provided insights into and evaluation of what has become the most widespread framework for residence abroad among students of Languages, Linguistics and Area Studies.

A 1994 survey of residence abroad by UK students (Coleman 1996: 60–63, 87–89, 190–93) shows the pattern at the height of residence abroad activity, before overall language student numbers dropped, fear of additional debt reduced the proportion going abroad, and skewed Government funding regulations nudged students towards SOCRATES-ERASMUS exchanges. A large majority of students had already visited the target country, often several times. More than half spent their year abroad on student exchanges, with up to a quarter going as assistants (especially from old universities) and most of the remainder on other work placements.

Research findings

Most research has focused on linguistic gains (for a review, see Coleman 1997). Generalizability of findings is reduced by the variety of residence abroad contexts, and while linguistic progress is, on average, faster than under home university tuition, there is considerable individual variation. Initially less proficient students make faster progress, and interacting intensively with native speakers is more productive than simply attending classes: this may be why work placements appear more beneficial than university exchanges (Coleman 1996), and why learner strategy training is worthwhile (Cohen 1998). Progress is most notable in fluency (Freed 1995), oral-aural and sociolinguistic skills and in vocabulary, and less marked in reading, writing and grammar – although recent studies do show the importance of living in a target-language country for acquiring intuitive control of complex grammatical features. The work of

Byram and Zarate within the Council of Europe (Byram and Zarate 1997) has highlighted the need to acquire intercultural communicative competence.

As yet unpublished findings (Coleman, in preparation) confirm the employment value of the skills acquired through residence abroad, both in obtaining first and subsequent jobs and in daily work (cf. Jahr and Teichler 2002). Virtually all 1,117 respondents felt the investment in residence abroad was worthwhile. Indeed, for most language graduates – and especially recent graduates – the experiential learning during a year abroad is more highly valued than the cognitive, content learning of three years in the UK university.

Good practices

The flawed but instructive Quality Assessment process of 1995/96 found that residence abroad was the area of UK university language provision that raised more problems than any other. Subsequently, three projects supported by the Fund for the Development of Learning and Teaching from 1997 to 2001 sought to identify, evaluate and promote best practices. They were Learning and Residence Abroad (LARA), Lancaster's Interculture Project and the Residence Abroad Project (coordinated from Portsmouth University, hence the acronym RAPPORT). The projects worked with the profession to assemble a wealth of material capable of optimizing the success of the huge range of residence abroad schemes. Originally shared through seminars and workshops, the communal wisdom remains accessible on the project websites, while two specific approaches to staff development are described in Coleman and Parker (2001).

Learning objectives

RAPPORT developed an alphabetical taxonomy of learning objectives, applicable to residence abroad of any duration, in any country, in any subject discipline, and described in full in Coleman and Parker (2001: 137–41):

Academic

- course at a foreign university, which may have a defined curriculum, core plus options or a free choice;
- dissertation, project and/or language work for the home institution;
- preparation for final year including reading and researching.

Cultural

- insight into institutions, way of life;
- can overlap with academic outcomes.

Intercultural

- amalgam of knowledge, beliefs, attitudes, skills, behaviours;
- awareness of relativity of cultures – including one's own;
- recognition that culture is a social construct;
- cognitive *and* affective learning;
- ethnographic skills allowing observation without misunderstanding, objectivity free of ethnocentrism;
- interpersonal skills allowing adaptation to multiple cultural milieux, respecting local values without abandoning one's own;
- work-related: ability to function in new linguistic/cultural environment.

Linguistic

- speaking
- listening
- reading
- writing
- grammar
- vocabulary
- sociolinguistic (register)
- fluency
- language learning strategies.

Personal

- independence and self-reliance
- confidence
- self-awareness.

Professional

- transferable skills
- work experience
- intercultural competence
- awareness of target-country work conventions.

Preparation, support and assessment

Once established, the objectives or learning outcomes guide all other decisions. Preparation may focus on any or all of familiarization with target-culture institutions and education systems, research methods, practical advice, CVs and letters of application, language learning strategies, EFL teaching, briefings on assessment, etc. Since residence abroad represents highly autonomous learning, a self-directed or experiential approach to preparation can be more appropriate than traditional pedagogy, especially since affective as well as cognitive learning is involved, for example in laying the groundwork for intercultural learning. Most institutions hold a series of meetings from year 1 or the start of year 2 (careers advice, choice of assistantship, work placement of studentship) to the end of year 2 just months from departure (agreeing personal objectives, learning contract, check that work contract and insurance policy are in place). Regrettably, most also find that it is not only desirable to integrate the preparation with normal coursework, but also essential to make attendance compulsory: students who would not dream of undertaking competitive sports or even going clubbing without intensive preparation need convincing that residence abroad works better if they are ready for it. The credibility of preparation is enhanced if a major role is played by students still abroad or recently returned, by graduates, and by exchange students.

Though budgets for visiting students have shrunk, in these days of e-mail, instant messaging and webcams, it is inexcusable not to maintain contact with students abroad. 'The year abroad is all about students becoming independent' is an unacceptable excuse for neglecting them, especially now that fees are paid to the home university while students are away.

Equitable, valid, practical assessment of progress towards the six categories of objective is complex but essential. One widespread practice is for assessment to be based on personal objectives set by agreement before departure, embedded in a learning contract, tracked in regularly submitted learner diaries while abroad, and evaluated through a project report and oral debriefing on return. The learning contract will determine different percentages for academic, linguistic or professional outcomes depending on whether the student has been on an exchange or a placement.

Debriefing, whether or not part of assessment, is vital:

- to allow returners to contribute to the preparation of departers;
- to validate the students' experience by showing the importance the home university attaches to it;
- to help them begin the process of reflection and making sense of the experience they have lived;
- to provide them with strategies for maintaining the linguistic and other gains made;
- to enhance institutional arrangements for future cohorts.

▶ List three problems that you know your colleagues and students face with regard to residence abroad, and research the solutions offered by the Interculture, LARA and RAPPORT websites.

Two final observations are appropriate. First, in order to despatch its duty of care, the home institution must always take all reasonable steps to ensure the security of students abroad (including checking that they have adequate insurance). Second, that parents, in their role as investors, increasingly seek to involve themselves in residence abroad issues: it is worth remembering that the Data Protection Act prohibits you from discussing things with them, and that your best plan is to encourage them to support their offspring but to let the latter fight their own battles.

Sources of information

The British Council has a website for all assistants and anyone going abroad. Online. Available at: www.languageassistant.co.uk (accessed 19 June 2004); the linked Language Assistant website even contains materials and lesson plans. Online. Available at: www.2.britishcouncil. org/home/learning/languageassistants/languageassistants-ela.htm (accessed 19 June 2004).

FDTL projects

Although completed in 2001, these three projects still provide a wealth of information on good practices in support of student residence abroad.

The Interculture Project. Online. Available at: www.lancs.ac.uk/users/interculture/ (accessed 19 June 2004).

Learning and Residence Abroad. Online. Available at: www.lang.ltsn.ac.uk/lara (accessed 19 June 2004).

The Residence Abroad Project has partly moved to the Subject Centre as Work and Study Abroad. Online. Available at: www.lang.ltsn.ac.uk/resources/materialsbank.aspx?resource id=626 (accessed 19 June 2004). The original website is also still live (though not maintained and with some broken links). Online. Available at: at www.hum.port.ac.uk/slas/rapport (accessed 19 June 2004).

Generally relevant and useful

UNESCO's rich and helpful site. Online. Available at: www.unesco.org/education/ studyingabroad/index.shtml (accessed 19 June 2004).

Council for International Education, primarily designed for students wishing to study in the UK. Online. Available at: www.ukcosa.org.uk (accessed 19 June 2004).

StudyAbroad.com, a commercial, US-based but global operation. Online. Available at: www.studyabroad.com (accessed 19 June 2004).

Advice on safe travel and a lot more

Suzy Lamplugh Trust. Online. Available at: www.suzylamplugh.org/worldwise/index.shtml (accessed 19 June 2004).

Foreign and Commonwealth Office. Online. Available at: www.fco.gov.uk (accessed 19 June 2004).

Lonely Planet. Online. Available at: www.lonelyplanet.com (accessed 19 June 2004).

Rough Guides. Online. Available at: www.travel.roughguides.com (accessed 19 June 2004).

Education systems

HERO portal for information on the UK Higher Education system. Online. Available at: www.hero.ac.uk/about_hero/index.cfm (accessed 19 June 2004).

Eurydice has extensive data on education systems in Europe. Online. Available at: www.eurydice.org (accessed 19 June 2004). INCA covers more countries, but only up to the end of secondary. Online. Available at: www.inca.org.uk (accessed 19 June 2004).

The National Centre for Languages has, as ever, much relevant information. Online. Available at: www.cilt.org.uk (accessed 19 June 2004).

16

Independent learning

Vicky Wright

Introduction

> Independent learning is part of an ongoing, lifelong process of education that stimulates greater thoughtfulness and reflection and promotes the continuing growth of students' capabilities and powers. More than the rote learning of facts and skills, this approach to learning encourages students to make meaning for themselves, based on their understanding of why and how new knowledge is related to their own experiences, interests and needs.
>
> Saskatchewan Education (1988)

Independent learning is a term in common use in relation to teaching and learning in higher education. In fact, the word 'independent' occurs at least eight times in the UK Subject Benchmarking statement for Languages and Related Studies (QAA 2002) where it is associated with terms such as 'learner autonomy', 'responsibility', 'effective' and 'self-aware' and is said to be 'usually undertaken in close relationship with classroom-based learning'. However, there still seems to be some confusion as to what we mean by independent learning; it is sometimes used to describe a major educational objective, as in the quotation above, or it is used to refer to all work carried out beyond the classroom or lecture theatre. Sometimes it is another term for self-instruction. This chapter aims to introduce some of the current thinking in the area of independent learning/learner independence and to discuss practical implications for the language teacher. It refers to and builds on the work of the CIEL (Curriculum and IndEpendence for the Learner) project (see www.ncteam.ac.uk/projects/fdtl/fdtl2/index.htm) which was funded between 1997 and 2001 under the second phase of the UK's Fund for the Development of Teaching and Learning to support the integration of independent language learning with the curriculum and to achieve more effective use of university self-access centres.

Definitions and approaches

▶ There are a number of overlapping terms in the area of learner independence and learner autonomy. Sometimes different terms refer to a single concept and sometimes one term seems to refer to differing concepts. Consider the terms below and decide which are in common use in your own context and how they are used. Are there any other terms that could be added to the list?

autonomous learning	differentiation
distance learning	directed study
flexible learning	individualization
independent learning	learning to learn
open learning	self-access
resource-based learning	self-instruction
self-directed learning	supported self-study
self-paced learning	

A number of writers in the field have tried to disentangle this maze (e.g. Broady and Kenning 1996, Pemberton 1996, Gardner and Miller 1999) in order to move forward discussion of practice. All agree that these terms share one element; they reflect a move towards learner-centred approaches which view learners as individuals with individual needs and rights. 'Autonomy' may define an entitlement, a capacity or a behaviour, and is often taken to refer to significant learner responsibility and involvement in decision-making (see Tudor 1996, Benson and Voller 1997, Benson 2001, Little 1991 and 2003a for discussion); 'independent learning' may be no more than set homework. For the present chapter, referring to the higher education context, the terms will be assumed to be virtually synonymous. Both indicate (see CIEL Project 2000a) a number of dimensions in which learners move away from dependence on the teacher and:

- take responsibility for their own learning and learn to learn;
- develop transferable skills (e.g. study, time-management, ICT, interpersonal skills, etc., see also Chapters 10 and 14);
- actively manage their learning; seeking out learning opportunities and using appropriate learning strategies;
- involve themselves in an iterative process in which they set short- and long-term learning objectives, reflect on and evaluate progress.

Independent learning is thus an approach to learning which, even if it takes place largely outside the structured contact of the classroom, is not a replacement for formal teaching but an integral part of the learning and teaching process; it provides an opportunity for learners to extend their learning and to develop lifelong skills.

Roles and responsibilities

Dam (2003) suggests that we have been slow in recognizing the role of the teacher in getting learners to play an active part in their own learning. It is not sufficient to expect learners to take responsibility (and to complain when they do not); the teacher needs to prepare them to take charge of their own learning and to establish suitable learning opportunities including the setting of appropriate tasks and activities. This implies a shift in role for the teacher away from that of traditional classroom manager towards one that focuses on facilitating learning and involves negotiation and dialogue with learners. As Nunan (1996: 15) reminds us, learners also need time to develop their independence: 'It is usually well into a course before learners are in a position to make informed choices about what they want to learn and how they want to learn and it is not uncommon that learners are in such a position only at the end of the course.'

At institutional level, support for independent learning includes the responsibility to provide an appropriate learning environment beyond the classroom (such as a well-stocked self-access centre or the opportunity to meet with target-language speakers).

▶ Conduct a small piece of action research. Select five language learners working in your self-access centre or library and use the following questions to establish how teacher-directed/independent they are in their choice of activity or goal. Note learners working collaboratively, since those using effective learning strategies are not necessarily working on their own.

1 What are you doing? What language/level/activity?
2 Why did you come? Did you choose to do this activity?
3 How often do you come? How long do you spend on self-access every week? Do you work on your own or with other students?
4 How does your self-access work compare to work done in the classroom (more/less valuable)?

Embedding independent language learning

Experience gained by the CIEL project shows that it is important to address a number of key elements if independent language learning is to be successfully embedded in a given context, since any one addressed on its own may not be effective. The six overlapping areas are:

- policy-making
- management
- staff development
- learner training and support
- learning resources
- curriculum design.

Each is discussed separately below.

Policy-making

If one does not already exist, the development of a policy statement that addresses the role of independent language learning and the provision and use of learning resources will serve a number of purposes. The process of hammering out the detail of a framework that addresses implementation and resourcing issues is likely to bring ownership and commitment from the staff and other stakeholders involved. Without such a statement, it will be more difficult to implement independent learning in a coherent way and to attract institutional, faculty or departmental support. The policy might form part of a departmental teaching and learning strategy or it might be a statement from a group of committed colleagues. It is likely to include definitions of terms, details of the goals to be achieved and the strategies needed to reach them. Key actions and deadlines might also be added. An example of how such a policy might be developed can be seen in the case study below.

Case study: extracts from the University of Manchester (2002) policy on independent language learning

Proposal
- That the School of Modern Languages (SML) actively encourage students to become independent language learners
- That the main vehicle to achieve this aim be the implementation across SML of Independent Language Learning Programmes, as defined below
  . . .

Definition of an Independent Language Learning Programme (ILLP)
- The ILLP is specifically intended to complement and enhance the learning experience and not to replace contact hours, directed work (homework tasks/assignments) or formal assessment procedures

- Learners are in receipt of guidance and support, particularly in their first year of study and/or as part of the first language course unit on which they are enrolled in the School . . .
- Learners define their strengths and weaknesses, and generate their own action plans for language learning . . .
- Learners maintain a file of work in all four skill areas (listening, reading, speaking and writing), plus vocabulary and grammar, to support their own learning process and assist in reflection on progress and on learning strategies . . .

Recommended requirements for successful implementation
- Integration into the learning culture of the School, owned collectively by staff (personal tutors, language tutors, lectors) and students
- Clear expectations to be communicated through course unit documentation/programme handbooks, reinforced through the Progress File and tutorial system as well as through language classes
- The timely and regular submission of reflective questionnaires and portfolios of evidence by students during the academic year and not solely at the end of the course unit . . .
- Guidance on approaches and strategies that can be adopted by the student
- A readily available range of resources to respond to the diverse requirements of individual learners . . .

Management

One of the key areas of management for institution-based independent learning is within the self-access centre (wherever it is positioned or whatever it is called). Successful management will mean taking into account a range of factors when planning and reviewing provision. These include:

- the type of learner (e.g. full- or part-time, international students, staff, members of the community), the languages they are learning and their level;
- integration with the language curriculum;
- development, purchase and maintenance of learning resources;
- the facilities provided and location of the centre;
- monitoring of use and assessment of work done;
- the individual needs, interests and expectations of the learners (and teaching staff);
- learner/staff training and support;
- staffing levels;
- management structures within the centre;
- finances;
- responsiveness to change.

Details such as the availability of loan facilities, opening hours, staff available to advise new and familiar 'faces' and an easy-to-find location also need addressing. However, primary consideration must be given to the relationship between learning carried out in the self-access centre and the focus of the language curriculum, as well as the relationship between the centre and all language providers within the institution. If one does not take account of the other/s, any independent learning policy is unlikely to be effective.

Staff development

Benson and Voller (1997) remind us that 'teacher training tends to prescribe a leading intellectual and managerial role for teachers and ill prepares for the demands of learner autonomy'. Staff may need support and guidance as they address any changes in the focus of the curriculum and the development of learner independence. Staff development sessions and the sharing of good practice (for instance during staff meetings or through peer observation) are helpful and encourage collaboration, but the needs of the many part-time language staff should not be forgotten. Central staff development units can often provide specific training needed (e.g. in the use of particular technologies). Staff who act in an advisory capacity to learners may need focused training and support as Sturtridge (1997) points out: we need 'to help teachers become aware of their new role as facilitators when working in the [self-access] centre; teachers need to be trained to *stop teaching* students' (see also Davies *et al.* 2001).

> ▶ To what extent are you as a teacher able to be autonomous in your
> actions? What specific changes in the way you work or in your work-
> ing environment would help you become a more effective 'teacher-
> facilitator', more able to understand and address students' needs? On
> the basis of this, draw up a two-year professional development plan
> for yourself (this might involve attendance at courses, working with
> colleagues, reading up on aspects of independent learning, etc.).

Learner training and support

To be effective, learner training needs to be a well-planned and considered process that is implemented across the curriculum (see case study below) and supported by appropriate materials, activities and staff. Within the classroom, learning can be made more transparent with the discussion and setting of class and personal goals, reflection on learning styles and with activities that practise different strategies (see, for example, Wenden 1991, Oxford 1990, O'Malley and Chamot 1990). Tools to facilitate this include learning logs, learner diaries, personal development plans (PDPs) and portfolios, such as the

European Language Portfolio (see Chapter 11), but, as Forshaw (2000) warns: 'one of the challenges in training and supporting independent learners is to help them to develop the skills they need without overwhelming them with theory or paperwork. The trick is to get the balance right.'

Within the self-access centre, there need to be support mechanisms in place which include induction and help in the use of the materials and facilities. Learner workshops and a one-to-one advisory service (see Mozzon-McPherson 2002) are useful to orient, support and guide learners. A structure to support tandem learning (see Chapter 20) will encourage collaborative learning and meaningful use of the target language. Peer support in other forms (e.g. through group tasks and buddy systems) will be equally useful. Support materials in the centre may include self-assessment and needs analysis questionnaires, familiarization exercises, access and study guides and guides to available materials. Increasingly, however, learners will be able to access support in the way of materials and tutors online.

Case study: description of the University of Southampton language skills training workshops

Skills sessions are timetabled every two weeks in semester 1 for all first-year language students. Sessions are in English, are not language-specific and were planned to give even reluctant students the benefit of training. They are followed up in language classes with materials available on BlackBoard (the University's virtual learning environment). Further workshops and the language advisory service are available throughout the year.

Programme

Session 1: Needs analysis, reflection and time management (short action plan in the target language, focus on communication not accuracy)

Session 2: Dictionary use and vocabulary learning (vocabulary/dictionary exercise in target language)

Session 3: From receptive to active skills: listening/reading (listen to news, fill in gaps of understanding by reading the front page of an online newspaper, write a commentary on a news item or a follow-up story)

Session 4: More action: speaking/writing (spoken/written task)

Session 5: Revision, learning from and reacting to feedback (students work on a piece of homework)

Assessment takes the form of a portfolio of completed tasks and a reflective report. The assessment makes up one of the coursework elements and counts for 10 per cent.

Learning resources

The language learning resources within an institution, whether in a library, self-access centre, classroom or cupboard, are likely to serve learners with a number of different needs and learning objectives. The materials should complement and extend work done in the classroom, thus giving opportunities for independent learning, but may be the primary learning resource for self-directed language learners. Materials will have to be carefully chosen (Gardner and Miller 1999) or designed (Sheerin 1989, Littlejohn 1998, Tomlinson 2000, CIEL Project 2000b), well presented and easily accessible. In some self-access centres, pathways through the learning resources have been developed to guide learners. These can be paper-based or electronic but the time when all re-usable, digital learning objects, or 'chunks of learning', are easily retrieved from a worldwide content management system is still a technologist's dream at the time of writing.

Materials will normally have to support the development of all language skills and will be available in a range of media – increasingly this will mean access via a computer as digital sound and video replaces analogue. However, despite the vast range of resources now available online over the internet, through virtual learning environments or via locally provided software (see Chapters 18 and 19), it is likely that most learners will still want to use hard copy materials as well.

Curriculum design

Of the six key elements that make for successful independent learning, it is the integration of independent learning with the curriculum that is the most important. A curriculum that values the development of learner independence and makes time and space for it in the academic timetable is most likely to be successful. If not, only the most dedicated of learners will prioritize it and succeed in taking charge of their own learning.

Many curricular issues that need to be considered (e.g. learner training) have been discussed briefly above under other headings. Further considerations are: the content of the syllabus; tasks and activities in the classroom and outside; the ratio of classroom contact time to independent learning time; the role of the teacher and the learners; and the place of assessment. Formative assessment will provide feedback for learners on progress but summative assessment, or work that 'counts', may well play its part in motivating them and setting them more firmly on the path to independence.

Conclusions: benefits and challenges

Independent learning can bring numerous benefits. It:

- extends learning beyond the classroom;
- offers flexibility;

- encourages and develops key transferable skills;
- gives students greater responsibility for their learning;
- increases motivation;
- caters for different learning styles.

But there are distinct challenges to be faced:

- time and expertise are needed to develop appropriate materials and activities and to train and support learners;
- the cost and space implications of setting up and maintaining an up-to-date self-access centre are not inconsiderable;
- there is always resistance to change and there are likely to be both teachers and learners (especially weaker students) who are not comfortable with student-centred approaches.

Sources of information

CIEL Project (2000) CIEL Project Handbooks:

1 Integrating independent learning with the curriculum
2 Managing independent language learning: management and policy considerations
3 Resources for independent language learning: design and use
4 Assessment and independent language learning
5 Supporting independent language learning: development for learners and teachers
6 Making independent language learning accessible

All accessible via the HEA Subject Centre for Languages, Linguistics and Area Studies *Good Practice Guide*. Online. Available at: www.lang.ltsn.ac.uk/resources/guidecontents. aspx (accessed 20 June 2004).

For anyone interested in following up their interest in learner independence, there are several useful websites that act as starting points. These include:

- the website of the AILA (Association Internationale de Linguistique Appliqueé) Scientific Commission on Learner Autonomy. Online. Available at: www.lc.ust.hk/~ ailasc (accessed 20 June 2004).
- the Autonomy in Language Learning website maintained by Phil Benson, which has over 1,000 entries in its bibliography section. Online. Available at: www.ec.hku.hk/ autonomy (accessed 20 June 2004).
- the Authentik teacher development series, which has a number of titles focusing on learner autonomy and provides a useful reference point for those interested in the interface between practice and research. Online. Available at: www.authentik.com/ developm.htm (accessed 20 June 2004).

17

Distance learning in Modern Languages

Stella Hurd

Introduction

What are the implications for learning and teaching languages using a distance teaching model? Which particular factors need to be addressed to ensure optimum conditions for learner success and how best can we incorporate reflective practice and ensure the continued development of an effective learning and teaching environment? Using the Open University UK (OU) as a model, this chapter addresses these questions through an investigation of the principles underlying open and distance language learning, including course design and assessment, learner support strategies and course evaluation mechanisms (cf. White 2003).

> ▶ List what you regard as the main differences between face-to-face and distance language teaching. What would you consider to be the key issues for tutors?

Distance language learning: generic principles

It is generally accepted that learning a language is different from learning other subjects, both because of the highly complex nature of its structures and systems and because it involves a significant social dimension (Victori 1992, White

1994, Dörnyei 2003). In the distance context, these aspects come into sharper focus, not only because learners are denied the classroom situation where speaking practice, sharing difficulties and giving immediate support can be easily incorporated into lessons, but also because of the inherently non-social nature of this mode of learning, which militates against the interdependence that many language experts would consider fundamental to successful language learning.

Distance language providers thus have a major challenge: to provide the means by which students can acquire good language skills, without the support, practice opportunities and facility to monitor progress that are provided in a more conventional setting. A pedagogical approach that incorporates learner support, an emphasis on the development of autonomy, high-quality tutor feedback and the encouragement of reflective practice are all key principles underlying good distance language provision. How does the Open University attempt to incorporate these principles into its course design and production?

The Open University language learning and teaching context

The Open University's Department of Languages, established in 1991, offers courses in French, German and Spanish from beginners to degree level to around 8,000 students a year, which makes it the UK's largest higher education language provider. Students register for a course and can accumulate credit points from courses to count towards an award of their choice at Certificate, Diploma or degree level. They may target the BA (Hons) Modern Language Studies or other named qualifications such as the Diploma in Law and Languages, the BA/BSc (Hons) in European Studies or International Studies, or the BA (Hons) Humanities. Language provision is 'open' in that there are no prerequisites to any language courses. Students may, if they wish, take advantage of the self-assessment tests which are offered in all three languages, to help them determine their initial level of proficiency.

To give some idea of the time required to gain an award, students following a 30-credit course are expected to devote around eight hours a week to their studies. To achieve the Diploma, students must study around 16 hours weekly over two years, and attend a one-week-long compulsory Residential Summer School in France, Spain or Germany. Given that the majority of OU students are in work and have family commitments, this represents a not inconsiderable workload. How do they cope and what help is available?

Students may seek general guidance from Student Services who operate regionally and have staff who are trained to advise on a range of issues concerning academic study. There are also print support materials in the form of course and study guides, transcripts, study charts and supplementary notes.

Web-based guides (Open University 2002, 2003) give general information, advice on choosing a course or qualification, career planning, services for disabled students and study skills. Each student is assigned a tutor (associate lecturer) who conducts tutorials at regular intervals throughout the course, either face-to-face in a regional centre or online. There are between 18 and 21 tutorial hours depending on level, and students can choose whether to participate or not. Most regions also offer the occasional day school at a local centre. Online tuition is carried out using Lyceum, an OU-developed synchronous online conferencing system that offers multi-way voice communication, as well as text chat and visual resources such as an online whiteboard, diagrammatic concept maps, web browser and text documents. All Open University language students are now offered a choice of tuition mode – face-to-face or online – which has considerably reduced the impact of geographical location on access to personal support. In addition, all OU learners have access to the OU's First Class electronic conferencing system where they can contact other students on their course to exchange information and for mutual support. Other support is available through the Open University Students Association (OUSA) and *Sesame*, a newspaper produced bi-monthly by the Publications Team of the OU and issued free to all students and staff.

The design and planning of OU language courses

The development of an OU language course normally takes three years, encompassing draft syllabus and audiovisual specification, location recording and editing on to CD, successive drafts of course books by teams of authors, design and printing, and implementation of integrated-skills assessment. The production of a course is a complex process and has huge resource implications. Changes are therefore kept to a minimum for the duration of its life, which is normally eight years, incorporating a mid-life review and updating.

Pedagogical approach

The aim of course writers is to provide for the learning needs of students, while at the same time encouraging learners to develop an autonomous approach to learning. This involves treading a fine line between giving appropriate guidance and support on the one hand and being over-prescriptive and patronizing on the other. The process is further complicated by the fact that distance learners, like all learners, are not homogeneous, and course writers must try to cater for as many different learner variables as possible. The format is, of necessity, highly structured, with course guides, study charts, 'organizers' indicating the nature and purpose of each activity, navigational aids, and fixed assessment points. The materials play a central role as the teaching voice, the link between teacher and learner. In other words, they carry out all the functions of a teacher in a more conventional setting: 'guiding, motivating, intriguing, expounding, explaining, provoking, reminding, asking questions, discussing alternative answers, appraising each learner's progress, and giving appropriate remedial help' (Rowntree 1990: 11). Activities are carefully sequenced to provide steady progression and ensure variety. Grammar explanations and sections on improving style based on examples from source material are included at intervals throughout the courses. Video, audio, CD-ROM or online materials are 'carefully designed to integrate with other elements of the course, so that the finished product is a coherent whole with a transparent structure' (Hurd 2001: 136).

Developing autonomy

The highly structured nature of OU language courses does not preclude learner independence. Structure has elements of both control and liberation, as Van Lier (1996: 21) points out: 'On the one hand the structure limits or constrains the kind of things that can be done, and on the other it provides opportunities and resources for doing things.' While learners are not at liberty to negotiate their own syllabus or select their own source materials, they are autonomous in the sense that they can decide when and where to learn, and whether to follow the advised learning paths or find their own way through the materials. All beginner language courses include a set book containing guidance in language learning strategies, study skills and effective use of resources, which students are expected to use as an integral part of their studies. To help students at all levels to develop their own approaches, 'specific strategies are presented at specific times in order to address particular difficulties, thus providing practical and focused advice at regular intervals' (Hurd *et al.* 2001). The strategy development embedded in the OU course materials offers more than just the basic tools, and is constantly being improved and extended. Designated learning strategy sections throughout the courses offer a range of ideas to try out. There are also suggestions for further practice, and opportunities for transfer to individual contexts. Language awareness activities encourage students to reflect on what they already know and make connections. In all courses, students are encouraged to experiment and reflect, in order to determine which strategies work best for them.

Assessment and feedback

Students complete tutor-marked assignments (TMAs) which they submit to their tutor at regular intervals. The number of TMAs varies according to the credit-point rating of the course. Productive and receptive skills are tested through a mix of writing and speaking assignments, and include some that are formative. An end-of-course examination containing a writing and a speaking test completes the assessment pattern.

Feedback is an integral part of the teaching and learning cycle, and 'the right kind of feedback is crucial if students are to maintain their motivation throughout the course' (Open University Institute of Educational Technology 1999: 44). In addition to awarding marks using band descriptors under specified criterion headings, tutors are expected to give individualized comprehensive and constructive feedback in print (writing TMAs) and on audio (speaking TMAs), which not only addresses errors, but also gives practical guidance for improving learning and language skills. To help them develop this essential skill, all associate lecturers are offered staff development sessions and provided with handbooks on good practice. These include the OU/CILT publication *Supporting Lifelong Language Learning* (Arthur and Hurd 2001), the handbook for associate language lecturers *Supporting Language Learning* (Open University 1998) and the *Open Teaching Toolkits*, an ongoing series produced for associate lecturers of the Open University by the Staff Development Team, which covers a variety of topics such as 'Learning how to learn', 'Revision and examinations', and 'Tutoring online'. Associate lecturers are also monitored by OU central and regional academics, at frequent intervals to start with, and less frequently as they gain in competence.

Developing reflective practice

Learners, tutors and course writers all need to engage in reflective practice for personal development and to ensure that learning and teaching are taking place as effectively as possible. This is especially true of the distance learning environment, where there are few opportunities for spontaneous interaction and informal exchange, which are often the catalyst for shifts in practice to fit changing priorities and needs.

One of the features of an autonomous learner is the ability to reflect on learning, in order to monitor progress, identify gaps and solve problems, as part of the process of taking control. In the OU language courses, opportunities for self-monitoring are provided through the use of answer keys to all activities. Students are also encouraged to re-draft texts and re-work oral presentations by using 'models' provided in the course books or tutor examples given through feedback. Student-marked assignments (SMAs) allow learners to assess grammatical and semantic knowledge as they progress through the course, and give detailed feedback that enables students to analyse the origin of their mistakes. Such tasks are 'not only about monitoring progress, but also about extending knowledge and competence by setting further targets' (Hunt 2001: 160).

For tutors and course writers, reflection means subjecting all aspects of their work to ongoing rigorous scrutiny, which can happen through self-evaluation activities, feedback from students through questionnaires, peer observation, research projects and regular review. All OU students are asked to complete a survey at the end of their course, which covers all aspects of their learning. Results are collated by the OU Institute of Educational Technology (IET) and made available to course teams.

Sources of information

Information on distance learning courses and qualifications at the Open University. Online. Available at: www3.open.ac.uk/stepforward/index.asp (accessed 20 June 2004).

The refereed journal *Open Learning* covers a range of issues to do with open and distance learning. Online. Available at: www.tandf.co.uk/journals/titles/02680513.asp (accessed 20 June 2004).

The refereed online journal *Language Learning and Technology* special issue on distance language learning. Online. Available at: www.llt.msu.edu/vol7num3/default.html (accessed 20 June 2004).

The web page of Cynthia White who has written widely on distance language learning issues. Online. Available at: www.language.massey.ac.nz/staff/CW.shtml (accessed 20 June 2004).

To join the autonomy in language learning mailbase, e-mail auto-l@york.cuny.edu.

18

Computer-assisted language learning (CALL)

June Thompson

Given the increasing emphasis on the use of technology in all areas of education, and the development of pedagogic approaches and methodologies in which the computer functions as a tool rather than a 'teaching machine', the term CALL has, in recent years, become synonymous with TELL (Technology Enhanced Language Learning). This encompasses a wide range of pedagogic approaches and activities such as exploitation of internet resources, the development and use of Virtual Learning Environments (VLEs), speech recognition and language processing. With the advent of the internet and particularly e-mail, the use of computers is becoming second nature to teachers and learners alike and is thus an obvious resource for use in language learning. However, just as we do not assume that anyone who can speak a language can also teach it, we must not assume that the availability of technology will guarantee improvements in language learning: careful integration and a clear focus on precise language learning needs are essential.

For many years CALL was synonymous with the 'drill and practice' approach: activities such as gap-filling or text manipulation exercises to reinforce vocabulary or grammatical points initially taught in the classroom were developed in a variety of languages, often incorporating simple authoring tools to enable teachers to produce their own tailor-made exercises, at an appropriate level and with appropriate subject matter. The academic debate as to the real language learning value of such activities has continued over the years (see Decoo 1994, McCarthy 1996). Yet, interestingly, despite the introduction of multimedia CD-ROMs, closely followed in the mid-1990s by a proliferation of web-based materials, the tried-and-tested programs such as *Gapkit* (2004), *Fun With Texts* (2004), the *Wida Authoring Suite* (2004) and *GramEx* (2002) are still being bought and used in UK schools, colleges and universities, and are still regarded by teachers and learners as a useful part of the language learning experience.

> ▶ Take a moment to consider three practical benefits of using CALL in your language teaching.

A frequently asked question is 'What can CALL provide that pencil-and-paper exercises can't?' Perhaps the most important answer is 'flexibility'. There is flexibility for students in that they may work in their own time, on the specific topics they need, for as long as they need, obtaining instant feedback as they go along. They can also, for example, use a CD-ROM to practise listening and speaking through role-play scenarios, checking vocabulary and grammatical points as required, in privacy, without the inhibitions which might accompany a similar activity in the classroom. For the teacher there is flexibility in that they may make the best possible use of their face-to-face contact hours with students by focusing on key issues and new concepts rather than on supervising practice sessions, and there can be the very real advantage of reducing the time spent on marking.

A good starting point for teachers who are new to CALL is EUROCALL (2004), the European Association for Computer Assisted Language Learning. Apart from bringing together researchers and practitioners and providing information and resources via its discussion list and web pages, this association, through its journal, *ReCALL*, has been instrumental in developing a credible research base that underpins teaching and learning in this area. EUROCALL's annual conferences provide an ideal context in which collaborators in language teaching from various countries can develop and display CALL projects that are of real value to other teachers and learners.

One such project is the BP–BLTM (Best Practice – Best Language Teaching Methods) project with partners from the Basque country, Belgium, Denmark, Germany, the Netherlands, Romania, Scotland and Spain. The objectives of the project are to demonstrate five communicative language learning methods with freely distributable, ready-to-use materials developed for each method. The first of these methods is CALLiC (Computer Assisted Language Learning in Context). The material comprises web-quests and a text with video (at two language levels, basic and intermediate) showing how to wire a standard British plug. The text is hyperlinked to the eight project languages so any sequence can be translated and watched or listened to in eight languages. The text/video is followed by a sequence of exercises. The manual describing CALLiC and the accompanying material can be downloaded from the project website (BP–BLTM 2004) in English, German, Romanian and Spanish.

The selection and evaluation of CALL materials can be complex and time-consuming, particularly in the context of higher education. Much of the commercially produced material is designed for use in secondary schools, and there is a dearth of good material for languages other than French. The selection of software is often subjective, depending on the perceived needs of students and the context in which the teacher wishes to use the software. The best way to select appropriate software is to try out various programs and make a comparative evaluation. Useful questions a teacher might ask when evaluating software are:

- What is the intended use/area of application?
- What learning problems does the program address and how are the problems manifested in performance?
- What do learners have to do to overcome these problems and how does the program help them to do that?
- What else will they need? Books? Internet access?
- Do the learners need any special skills (e.g. word processing) or will they need prior briefing or training?
- Does the program make it clear what learners are expected to do, and why?
- Does every screen let you know how to exit the program, how to get to the next screen, how to get back?
- Is the text easy to read, and the colour scheme easy on the eye, or is the screen 'cluttered' with too many icons, etc.?
- Does the program include what you would expect, from reading its stated aims?
- Is the language content at the right level?
- Are there many errors in the language content?
- Is the feedback given to the learners relevant and useful?
- Will the program help your students?
- Does the program give learners a score? Can their errors be tracked?
- Is the manual/workbook/online help relevant, clear and useful, or can the learner use the program without reference to a manual?
- How would you integrate this into your teaching?

▶ Choose a CALL materials package that you have not yet used on a regular basis in your teaching. Employing the above list of criteria, assess its value and decide whether and how you could use it with any of the groups you teach.

Some teachers prefer to prepare their own CALL materials using a dedicated authoring tool, but for many this can prove daunting in terms of the time required to acquire the necessary expertise. Nowadays, this is less likely to be a question of 'technical' ability, than the ability to 'conceptualize' CALL, as coined by Levy (1997): in practice, to adapt familiar approaches to the selection of appropriate examples, to predict students' likely responses and to provide helpful feedback, always within the limitations of whatever framework the authoring tool provides. Above all, teachers need to understand what can realistically be done with a computer and what is best tackled in some other way. These are all aspects of CALL that are rarely the subject of training for language teachers.

A particularly valuable European-funded project was designed to go some way towards closing this training gap by providing a wide range of online modules for language teachers. The ICT4LT (Information and Communication Technologies for Language Teachers) project drafted in a number of experts to write modules at Basic, Intermediate and Advanced levels in topics ranging from 'Using text tools in the modern foreign languages classroom' and 'Introduction to multimedia CALL' to 'Managing a multimedia language centre', 'CALL software design and implementation' and 'Computer Aided Assessment (CAA) and language learning'. Each module contains links to extensive resources and provides trainees with online tasks to reinforce their learning (ICT4LT 2000).

The importance of the careful integration of CALL into the language learning curriculum has long been accepted in the published literature in this area (e.g. Hardisty and Windeatt 1989, Garrett 1991, Brett 1994, Warschauer 1995, McCarthy 1996). Commentators such as Levy (1997) and Esch and Zähner (2000) have articulated the benefits of involving teachers and learners in all stages of the development of technology-based learning. Hémard and Cushion (2001) go so far as to say that: 'future CALL developments and, in particular, web-based language learning deliveries can only be successful on the basis of a close involvement between language teachers and learners'.

At the most basic, practical level, successful integration depends on a small number of key elements. The most important of these, and one that is often overlooked, perhaps because it is so obvious, is the relevance of CALL materials to learners' needs. Unless they are directed towards specific modules in specific programs, which relate in a meaningful way to their general language learning programme, learners will soon dismiss CALL as a waste of their time.

It cannot be over-emphasized that institutional and departmental support is crucial in the successful integration of CALL. The need for dedicated hardware for language learners must be recognized, as well as the provision of suitable rooms with a convenient layout for CALL activities. Organizational issues such as ensuring security and compliance with copyright law, as well as the all-important technical support, need careful consideration.

Finally, while some teachers may express their fears that they will be replaced by computers, it is more than ever true that, in future, the only redundant teachers are likely to be those who are unable to use CALL and other information and communication technologies in their teaching.

Sources of information

ICT4LT Online. Available at: www.ict4lt.org (accessed 12 February 2004).

Lingu@net (2001) Online. Available at: www.linguanet.org.uk (accessed 12 February 2004).

The EUROCALL Resources section provides a comprehensive bibliography. Online. Available at: www.eurocall-languages.org/resources/reading.htm (accessed 12 February 2004).

19

The internet and computer-mediated communication

Sophie Ioannou-Georgiou

The internet has now become an indispensable part of our lives. As a consequence, when preparing students for the future we not only have to prepare them in language proficiency, but also in dealing with information and electronic literacy. Ignoring this would disadvantage our students in the competitive societies they are joining. Not making our students electronically literate would be the same as if we were sending them out there illiterate (Lemke 1998 cited in Warschauer *et al.* 2000). Using the internet in our teaching is therefore not a question of *whether* but only a question of *how*.

The internet can benefit both the teacher and the learner and using it efficiently may enhance our teaching, our students' learning and our personal and professional development. Nevertheless, a first step towards using the internet in teaching may leave you confused and frustrated. The internet is so vast and technology develops so fast, it can be daunting. We should, therefore, capitalize on the knowledge and experience of other colleagues.

It is on this collective experience of colleagues that the techniques recommended in this chapter have been based. The focus here is on online instruction, which is widespread at lower proficiency levels and in North America, but bear in mind that the internet can also be used in more autonomous or self-directed approaches. The techniques presented here are divided into the following categories:

- using authentic websites for research;
- student publishing on the web;
- using computer-mediated communication (CMC).

General guidelines

1   Integration – The internet activities or projects you intend to use should be integrated with the rest of the syllabus and considered as an integral and essential part of the course and not as a mere add-on.
2   Pedagogy – Do not sacrifice pedagogy for the sake of technology. Activities should be meaningful and have a purpose. Tasks should be designed bearing in mind the guidelines for successful communicative tasks (see Candlin and Murphy 1987).
3   Change – Be prepared for your role to change. When on the internet you will find the students empowered and in control. Be prepared to leave the centre of the stage and step to the side.
4   Communication – One of the characteristics of the internet that cannot be simulated in the classroom is its ability to connect people from all over the world. Meeting and communicating with people is also highly motivating for students, so try to include the element of communication whenever possible.
5   Net-Savvy – Teach your students to be critical. The internet offers a huge amount of information; some good, some bad. One of the skills necessary for this new medium is critical thinking. They should never take anything they read for granted.
6   Safety – Just as we learn the safety rules of crossing the road or not leaving our car unlocked, we should teach students the safety rules of the internet such as never giving their real names and contact details to strangers on the net.

Using authentic websites for research

The primary use of the internet is as a rich and motivating source of information. Although most websites are in English, the number of sites in other languages is growing. Nevertheless, sometimes students might be tempted to use online translation engines or the English version of a particular site. In this case, you may try:

● pointing them to target language search engines that do not search English sites (yahoo.de, google.fr, etc.);
● choosing sites with no English version, sites that address a domestic audience or whose content is too ephemeral to be translated into English, such as newspapers and journals of the target language community which are freely available on the net;
● on the institution's PCs, disabling the translation option offered by certain search engines and adapting their preferences so that they access only target language websites.

Access to newspapers and journals offers a chance for close contact with the country and culture. You can ask students to monitor certain sites for events that interest them and ask them to report back regularly to the class. It is also a good idea to assign online reading to supplement the often out-of-date coursebook. In this way the internet allows you to stay current and tailor your lessons to your specific students by finding and using material that interests them and/or is directly related to them.

You can also have students search the internet to research topics for written tasks, presentations, simulation activities or role plays. A sample activity is presented below:

You and your friend want to spend a weekend in Barcelona. You only have £300.

a Search the internet to find flights and accommodation.
b Search the internet and organize a programme for the whole weekend (entertainment, sightseeing, etc.).

Make sure that your weekend doesn't cost you more than £300!

The above might be turned into a role play if the students carry out the task as travel agents following the instructions of their customers. They then have to present their findings to another group who will be acting as the customers and can choose the best weekend offered.

You could use a similar activity before the students' residence abroad. They can use the internet to get to know the place they are going to, find a place to stay, find means of transport and even make friends who will be waiting for them when they arrive. Having all this information beforehand makes the move a less stressful experience (see Weinmann 1996).

Finally, it should be emphasized that when students are using the internet for research, they should be trained in copyright issues, plagiarism and critical evaluation of website content.

Student publishing on the web

Current pedagogy supports communicative writing and adopts the method of process writing, which involves drafting and revising before a piece of writing is finalized (see White and Arndt 1991). Such a labour-intensive process is often not well received by students, especially if the teacher is the only one who will read the final paper.

If, however, the students know that their work will be published on the internet for a real audience, motivation rises and the students are willing to revise and spend much more time polishing their work than they would normally for a traditional piece of writing.

Student publishing can come in the form of a personal website or blog (see Appendix B), a group website, a class website, or it may even be the result of a joint effort between two different classes collaborating over the internet.

Making a website need not be very complicated and does not require highly specialized knowledge. You can save a Microsoft Word document as a web-page or you can use software to make the process easier (e.g. Netscape Composer or Dreamweaver). Don't let students get carried away by all the bells and whistles that are available on the net. What is important is not the jazzy appearance of the site but the content and the effort that went into it and whether the students achieved their original objectives (Doble 1999). You may also get lucky and have student web-wizards who are willing to take on the responsibility themselves!

Computer-mediated communication

CMC is either asynchronous or synchronous (or occasionally both). In synchronous communication, messages between the participants are exchanged almost instantaneously, whereas asynchronous communication is delayed. Forms of asynchronous CMC are newsgroups and e-mail, while examples of synchronous CMC are text-based chatting (e.g. IRC), MOOs (see Appendix B), audio- and videoconferencing.

E-mail is, perhaps, the most popular mode of CMC. If you are a beginner with technology as a learning tool, then it is a good idea to start with e-mail. Nevertheless, all the ideas presented below can be used with any CMC mode, with the exception of audio- and videoconferencing which are best used for interclass projects only.

Within class

E-mail can be used as a way of increasing student–teacher interaction for which we often do not have enough time during class. In addition to the lack of time, we sometimes have shy students who may avoid participating in class. Initiating communication via e-mail can help solve these problems. Announcements, reminders and assignment guidelines can be sent via e-mail. Students can communicate with you when they cannot make office hours and can submit assignments or weekly journals via e-mail.

Creating a class discussion list or bulletin board (see Appendix B) may also increase student interaction. Students can send their dialogue journals either privately to the teacher or to the class. 'Hot' issues may be discussed using the class discussion list.

Peer review can also be very effective online. Students may send their first drafts to the class discussion list, receive feedback from other students and then send their final version back to the list. Peer reviewing can also begin in smaller online groups (e.g. two or three students) for revisions of the first draft, or the first draft may be revised privately between the teacher and student. The second draft may then be sent to the whole class where further feedback can be obtained for the preparation of the final version of the paper.

Synchronous chat or MOO may be used for within-class or inter-class discussions to debate a topic they have already read about, to brainstorm ideas in preparation for a writing assignment, to discuss a reading assignment or to prepare for an oral debate or presentation. There are benefits in conducting text-based discussions online even though the students are physically present and belong to the same class. Some of the potential benefits are, for example, that:

- students can participate at the same time without having to wait for their turn, which maximizes participation rates (Ioannou-Georgiou and Michaelides 2001, Kern 1995, Warschauer 1996);
- students have to monitor their own discussions and consequently practise many more functions rather than just question–answer, which is often what happens in classrooms (Ioannou-Georgiou and Michaelides 2001, Chun 1994);
- students have time to think before they write and can produce more complex sentences, thus practising more advanced structures (Warschauer 1996);
- shy students can hide behind pseudonyms or avatars and communicate more freely (Ioannou-Georgiou 2000);
- students who may be worried about their pronunciation or who may be suffering from a lisp or other speech impairment are also liberated, and text-based CMC is also helpful with deaf (see Kreeft and French 1996) and blind students (see Grassroots MOO);
- cliques that may have been formed in class can be broken through the use of pseudonyms (Ioannou-Georgiou 2000, Kern 1995);
- students can take home the text of the interactions and study it for ideas expressed, vocabulary and structures used or mistakes made.

You must, however, be aware that the type of task you give to students is also of primary importance. If, for example, it is an informal problem-solving task, students may not produce complex utterances but language more typical of oral production.

Inter-class

Inter-class projects take advantage of the internet's power to bring people closer. All CMC tools can be used for those projects for which the major problem is to find a partner class or individual partner students. You can find help in various resources (see Appendix B), the most successful of which is, at the time of writing, e-pals.com. A search at this website for French-speaking students at college/university can give you up to 235 potential partners.

Some basic guidelines for a successful inter-class project are:

- ensure there is good communication between you and the teacher of your partner class;
- establish a common approach;
- establish common objectives;
- clarify aims, structure and details of the project before it begins;
- work with a partner class that shares the same or similar academic year;
- when students interact one-on-one with partner keypals, assign two keypals for each student.

Inter-class projects may use any combination of CMC tools. They may, for example, start off with an inter-class discussion list, later use private e-mails or chat rooms and finally present their work on a website (Vilmi 2000).

Some ideas for inter-class projects are:

- comparing information on cultural backgrounds;
- investigating various aspects of communities or personal histories;
- producing a joint website or electronic journal;
- acting out a simulation.

You may also use CMC to connect your students with target language speakers for additional practice and input in the target language. Their work can be monitored and assisted by you until they are able to continue on their own. Meeting target language speakers and creating relationships may be facilitated in a target language MOO. Also, tandem learning partnerships with target language speakers may be assisted by the International E-Mail Tandem Network (see Chapter 20 and Appendix B).

Conclusion

There is tremendous potential in using the internet and CMC for language learning both in that it enables you to bring real communication to the classroom and, not least, because of its great motivating power. Young generations are growing up with the internet as part of their lives. By bringing it into the classroom, we are building on their interests to teach them the target language, while at the same time we make their chosen language come alive.

Appendix A: Internet teaching survival tips

1   Try it out first. Go through the activity if possible. Get comfortable with the technology.
2   Start small. Gradually, as you become more experienced and more confident, you can expand your projects.
3   Have clear objectives about what the students should achieve.
4   Leave some time for your students to be trained to use the technology. Use computer-knowledgeable students as assistants.
5   Always have a back-up plan for an internet-based class. Anything can go wrong. If links are down or sites disappear, have alternative sites available or alternative activities ready. If all equipment or electricity is down, have a back-up, non-computer lesson ready.
6   When possible have the students work in groups. That way you achieve more interaction and also less traffic on your chosen sites. If all the students have to go to the same site, give them a selection of activities in different order on the handouts so they are not all on the same site at the same time.
7   Give clear instructions orally as well as a written handout and make sure they all understand and do not waste valuable time on the computer trying to find out what they are supposed to do. *When you need to talk to them, have them turn away from their computers. If this is not possible, have them turn off the computer monitors.*
8   Ask for the students' permission before you publish anything that belongs to them.

Appendix B: Glossary

Avatar: Usually found in MOOs. It is a fictional identity, i.e. a text-based or graphical representation of the user when he/she is interacting in a MOO.
Blog: Short for weblog, an informal online diary or frequently updated personal web page intended for public consumption. The author requires little or no technical knowledge.
Bulletin board: Allows messages to be posted and read. It can run on a local network or on the internet. Convenient because the messages are threaded by topic, but requires the user to connect to the network and visit the board to get the messages. It does not send messages to your mailbox.
Discussion list: A computer program that redistributes an e-mail message to all its subscribers. Once registered, you can send a message to a central computer for redistribution to all the other subscribers.

Instant messaging: A type of communications program that instantly sends messages from one computer to another by means of small pop-up windows. One of the advantages of instant messaging is its ability to create a 'buddy list' which alerts you when any of your contacts are online. Usually two-way, but some instant messagers offer a chat option in which conversations are open to larger groups.

IRC: Internet Relay Chat (IRC) is a program freely available on the net. It allows synchronous written communication between many participants.

MOO: Multi-User Domain Object Oriented (MOO) is a computer program that enables many participants to communicate with each other in a virtual world. Traditional MOOs are purely text-based but modern ones include two-dimensional or three-dimensional graphics. Many are available for free on the net. They include a strong element of role-playing.

Newsgroups: See Bulletin board.

Search engine: A program that searches the net based on keywords that are typed in by the user. It then displays the results of the search providing the user with links to the relevant sites that were found.

Tandem learning: Two learners of different native languages work together, helping each other to learn each other's language. Communication between the two partners usually takes place 50 per cent in one language and 50 per cent in the other (see Chapter 20).

Videoconferencing: A method of synchronous CMC that allows for video-, audio- and text-based communication.

Sources of information

Dudeney, G. (2000) *The Internet and the Language Classroom*, Cambridge: Cambridge University Press.

Pennington, M. C. (2004) 'Cycles of Innovation in the Adoption of Information Technology: a view for language teaching', *Computer Assisted Language Learning*, 17, 1: 7–33.

Sanchez, B. (1996) 'MOOving to a New Frontier in Language Teaching', in M. Warschauer (ed.) *Telecollaboration in Foreign Language Learning*, Hawaii: University of Hawaii at Manoa Second Language Teaching and Curriculum Center.

Schwienhorst, K. (2004) 'Native-speaker/Non-native Speaker Discourse in the MOO: topic negotiation and initiation in a synchronous text-based environment', *Computer Assisted Language Learning*, 17, 1: 35–50.

Shield L. (2002) 'Technology-mediated Learning', Subject Centre Good Practice Guide. Online. Available at: www.lang.ltsn.ac.uk/resources/goodpractice.aspx?resourceid=416 (accessed 31 May 2004).

Warschauer, M. (1995) *E-Mail for English Teaching*, TESOL Inc.

Warschauer, M. and Kern, R. (2000) *Networked-based Language Teaching: Concepts and Practice*, Cambridge: Cambridge University Press.

Windeatt, S., Hardisty, D. and Eastment, D. (2000) *The Internet*, Oxford: Oxford University Press.

Information and Communications Technology for Language Teachers (ICT4LT) – very useful site for both novice and experienced technology-using teachers. Online. Available at: www.ict4lt.org/en/index.htm (accessed 20 June 2004).

The Materials Bank of the Subject Centre for Languages, Linguistics and Area Studies has a large collection of useful resources. Online. Available at: www.lang.ltsn.ac.uk/resources/bankcontents.aspx (accessed 20 June 2004).

Media

French

Le Monde	www.lemonde.fr
Le Figaro	www.lefigaro.fr
Le Parisien	www.leparisien.fr
Le Figaro Etudiant	www.figaroetudiant.com
French e-magazines, searchable	www.loria.fr/~charoy/autozines.html

German

Stern	www.stern.de
Der Tagesspiegel	www.tagesspiegel.de
Die Welt	www.diewelt.de
Der Spiegel	www.spiegel.de

Italian

Il Corriere della Sera	www.corriere.it
Il Mondo	www.ilmondo.rcs.it
La Stampa	www.lastampa.it

Spanish

Diari de Barcelona	www.diaridebarcelona.com
El Pais	www.elpais.es
El Mundo	www.elmundo.es

More news

Global and local	onlinenewspapers.com
Electronic delivery of selected journals, or make your own newspaper	www.crayon.net

'GermNews' sends German News Bulletins to your or your students' mailbox. To subscribe, send an e-mail to listserv@listserv.gmd.de. In the body of the message type: SUB GERMNEWS yourfirstname yoursurname

Dictionaries

Basic and specialized	www.yourdictionary.com
Harper Collins bilingual	www.wordreference.com

MOOs

UNItopia (German)	www.unitopia.uni-stuttgart.de
Le MOO Francais	www.umsl.edu/~moosproj/moofrancais.html
Mundo Hispano	www.umsl.edu/~moosproj/mundo.html
Little Italy	www.kame.usr.dsi.unimi.it:4444
MOOsaico (multilingual)	www.terravista.pt/ancora/1833/moo-pt.html
Grassroots MOO	www.enabling.org/grassroots (also caters for people with disabilities)
SchMOOze (EFL, MOO tutorial)	www.schmooze.hunter.cuny.edu:8888

Finding partner classes or individual keypals

E-pals	www.epals.com
Connections	www.iecc.org
International Tandem Network	www.slf.ruhr-uni-bochum.de/email
Volterre	www.wfi.fr/volterre/francophone.html

Discussion lists for teachers

FLTEACH

Discussion list for foreign language teachers. Send a message to: LISTSERV@listserv.acsu.buffalo.edu. In the body of the message type: SUBSCRIBE FLTEACH yourfirstname yoursurname

NETEACH-L

Discussion list for teachers (mainly EFL) who are interested in using the net. Send a message to: listserv@hunter.listserv.cuny.edu. In the body of the message type: subscribe NETEACH-L yourfirstname yoursurname

WEBHEADS in Action – Community of Practice

www.geocities.com/vance_stevens/papers/evonline2002/webheads.htm. Much more than just a discussion list: a community of practice where members learn together about new developments on the internet; especially in the area of CMC.

Discussion lists for students

RIBO-L

German–English bilingual discussion list. Send a message to: LISTSERV@pete.uri.edu. In the body of the message type: SUBSCRIBE RIBO-L yourfirstname yoursurname

ENG-FRA

English–French bilingual discussion list run by the International E-mail Tandem Network (IETN). Send a message to: majordomo@ruhr-uni-bochum.de with SUBSCRIBE ENG-FRA in the body of the message. Similarly ENG-ESP, ENG-ITA, ENG-POL, ENG-NED, ENG-NIH (Japanese), etc.

Search engines

Google*	www.google.com
Altavista*	www.altavista.com
Excite	www.excite.com
Lycos	www.lycos.com
Yahoo!	www.yahoo.com
(* Translation can be disabled)	

Foreign language search engines

Ecila (French)	www.ecila.nomade.fr
Web.de (German)	www.web.de
Yahoo (in Spanish)	www.espanol.yahoo.com
Buscar (Spanish)	www.buscar.com
Google (multilingual, select language)	www.google.com

Tools on the net

Creating bulletin boards

Nicenet	www.nicenet.org
Blackboard	www.blackboard.com

Creating discussion lists

Yahoogroups   www.yahoogroups.com

Creating websites

Netscape Composer   www.netscape.com
Microsoft Front Page   www.microsoft.com/frontpage
Dreamweaver 3   www.dreamweaver.com

Creating weblogs

Blogger   www.blogger.com/start

20

The effective learning of languages in tandem

Tim Lewis

Introduction

In tandem learning, two people who are learning each other's language work together to help one another achieve their desired aims. These are normally:

- to improve their communicative ability in their partner's mother tongue;
- to get to know their partner better and learn about his or her cultural background;
- to benefit from their partner's knowledge and experience, e.g. in the areas of work, education and leisure (Brammerts 2003: 28–29).

Tandem learning has a considerable pedigree, having been practised since the 1960s by the *Deutsch-Französisches Jugendwerk/Office Franco-Allemand pour la Jeunesse*. In the 1990s the learning of languages in tandem was given new impetus by the advent of the internet. Ready access to electronic means of communication now made it possible to learn languages in tandem at distance. Tandem learning became potentially available to a far greater number of people. At the same time it underwent significant changes. Whereas face-to-face tandem learning involves synchronous spoken communication, e-tandem tends to be text-based and asynchronous. Both variants have advantages and disadvantages.

One strength of e-tandem is precisely its textuality, which enables the study and comparison of one's own and one's partner's production. In Little's words, 'written forms seem positively to invite the scrutiny and analysis that oral forms of their nature resist' (2003b: 43). The importance of such metalinguistic reflection in second language learning is widely acknowledged.

On the other hand, face-to-face tandem learners benefit from a multiplicity of paralinguistic cues (including non-verbal behaviour). What is more, if a speaker stops in mid-utterance, unable to complete a construction or find the right form, the partner can provide instant scaffolding. This is not the case in asynchronous e-mail, where correspondingly greater explicitness is required to maintain effective communication. This is time-consuming and can seem stilted.

Asynchronous e-mail, though the most widely used instrument for e-tandem, is not the only one. Practitioners of e-tandem learning have explored several means of alleviating the potentially alienating effects of working at distance with an unseen partner. They include the use of multi-user chat, audioconferencing, videoconferencing, and MOOs – the latter in an attempt to provide a virtual space in which tandem learners can meet and collaborate. It is quite possible – given adequate bandwidth – to envisage future tandem learners using synchronous or asynchronous video. E-tandem learning will continue to evolve with technological advance, possibly returning more closely to its roots. In the interim, those seeking to organize e-tandem learning may be well advised to use a mixture of modes.

▶ Make notes on how tandem learning might be integrated into your own teaching activity:

- Which of the classes you teach could benefit from tandem learning?
- Which is more suited to their needs: face-to-face tandem or e-tandem?
- Draw up a list of the steps you will need to take to make a tandem exchange happen.

Autonomy: an effective learning environment

It may seem odd to be advocating autonomy in a volume dedicated – at least in part – to effective teaching. But there is growing evidence that learning autonomously can be more enjoyable and more effective than being taught in more traditional ways, and – at the very least – usefully complements other approaches. Autonomy is a basic principle of tandem learning. At its simplest, for tandem learners, autonomy means that: 'Each of the two partners is responsible for their own learning. Each decides *what* they want to learn, *how* and *when*, and what sort of help is required from their partner' (Brammerts 2003: 29).

This may sound egocentric. But precisely because it relies so crucially on partnership, tandem learning is largely innocent of the charge of fostering 'individualization and even isolation in learning' which some critics have levelled at proponents of learner autonomy (Benson 1996: 33). Instead, it develops what has been referred to as 'social autonomy': 'Social autonomy recognizes that awareness raising and learning takes [*sic*] place through interaction and collaboration, as well as through individual reflection and experimentation' (Sinclair 2000: 11–12).

Moreover, the interaction at the heart of tandem learning is cognitive, as well as social. The advantages of collaboration as a mode of learning are considerable. In Little's words: 'group work in which learners collaborate to achieve an outcome which is at least partly of their own devising can yield a great deal more learning than individual performance of the same task' (Little 2000: 20).

To the social and cognitive benefits of autonomy based on interaction can be added its motivational strengths. Nunan (1996: 17) cites research into autonomous language learning which reports such benefits as stronger motivation, an improvement in accuracy, increased self-esteem and greater confidence.

It appears, too, that topics that are self-initiated may remain more memorable to learners than teacher-initiated ones. Nunan cites a Singaporean study as positing a connection between the degree of learner participation and measurable levels of language proficiency (Nunan 1996: 19).

Reciprocity: support and commitment

A second key principle of tandem learning is reciprocity. This is best explained by Brammerts:

> Both partners should contribute equally to their work together and benefit to the same extent. Learners should be prepared and able to do as much for their partner as they themselves expect from their partner. They should not only dedicate the same amount of time to each language: they should also invest the same amount of energy in preparation, in the interest they show in the learning success of their partner, and in their concern for their partner's success in speaking and understanding their language.
>
> (1996: 11)

Reciprocity does not imply that both partners have identical goals, nor that they must be equally proficient in their second language. Instead, it seeks to establish that, whatever their individual differences, both partners should provide each other with the same level of support and commitment.

The greater the differential in foreign language (FL) proficiency – especially where one partner is a near-beginner – the heavier the demands imposed on the partnership. They will be borne more obviously, but not solely, by the more proficient partner. Extra care and skill will be required to make input and interaction comprehensible. It will help if partners possess well-developed explanatory skills. Qualities such as tact, patience and perseverance will also be necessary. But both learners will need to be reflective and the less proficient learner will need somehow to ensure a balance in the amount of support afforded to the more advanced partner. This may take the form, for example, of preparing materials to help the latter attain specific objectives. Working with a less proficient partner can be extremely rewarding linguistically, precisely by virtue of the greater amount of the FL the learner is likely to be called upon to understand and use.

There is no magic recipe for a successful partnership. There is equally no means of calibrating precisely whether a differential is bridgeable. It can only be weighed against the degree of commitment and level of skill of the two partners. Organizers of tandem learning are regularly surprised to discover that partnerships they regarded as fragile have proved to be outstandingly successful.

Organizing tandem learning

Arranging partners, analysing needs, setting goals

One of the first tasks for organizers of tandem learning is that of matching up partners. Partners can be paired at random, if it is clear that all will have something in common. But experience suggests that it is important to avoid mismatching by identifying a few basic preferences. This can be quite a simple process, but should deal with what experience suggests are the key criteria:

- mother tongue
- target language
- level of FL proficiency
- learning objectives
- age
- gender
- profession/interests and hobbies.

Depending on the context, this information can be elicited with more or less sophistication. The most efficient way of doing so, especially with large numbers, is by means of a self-assessment questionnaire or grid. These can also be used to start the planning process, which is essential to productive autonomous learning. At the University of Sheffield, as part of their initial needs analysis, learners on the Tandem Module complete three grids, in which they successively:

- identify, on a scale of 1–5, their present level of proficiency in a range of areas (e.g. listening skills, cultural knowledge, techniques for language learning);

- rank these in terms of their greatest learning need or priority;
- set three or four realistic learning goals for the semester ahead.

> ▶ Draw up a questionnaire to enable your language learners to identify their current strengths and weaknesses.

Designing learning activities and materials

Tandem partners are expected to divide their working time more or less equally between the two languages of the partnership. They should agree at the outset how to do this. Some partners opt for separate sessions, each of which is held entirely in one language. Others divide each session into two halves.

It is sensible to provide learners with at least a 'Getting to know you' activity, which, like all tandem activities, will need to be dual-language. The most popular activities are currently archived at www.slf.ruhr-uni-bochum.de/tandem/tasks-en.html. Some partners may need to be supplied with worksheets for the duration of the course. Others – especially the more practised – will be able to plan and manage their own learning after working together for a few weeks.

One of the advantages of tandem learning is its sheer flexibility. Its only major limitation is that it is not best suited to *ab initio* language learning. That apart, it can be integrated into almost any course of study. But those responsible for providing support cannot produce learning materials for every eventuality. Learners with highly specific objectives will therefore need to assume responsibility for designing their own learning activities. In practice, most learners choose to devise their own learning materials after a few weeks.

> ▶ Devise an ice-breaking activity for your learners to do with their intended tandem partners. It will need to be in the two languages of the partnership.

Given the flexibility available to tandem learners, the Tandem Learner Diary, developed at the University of Sheffield (Walker 2003), is an extremely useful tool for guiding them through the learning process. It offers a framework in which learners can:

- analyse needs;
- prioritize learning objectives;
- record and review progress;
- plan next steps.

In the diary's assessment section learners are expected to:

- evaluate their own development as learners;
- assess their language proficiency and that of their partner;
- write a reflective account of their experience as tandem learners.

The first two of these are achieved by means of self-assessment tables, in which learners rate their own (and their partner's) performance against a set of clear and explicit descriptors, using whatever scale has been adopted by the institution. All three elements receive a weighting in the final grade for the University's tandem module. Would-be organizers of tandem learning can obtain a copy of the diary, for a small fee, from Lesley Walker at the University's Modern Languages Teaching Centre.

Error correction

As part of their learning contract, tandem partners correct and give feedback on the errors made by their partner. This distinguishes tandem learning from other forms of language partnership such as correspondence exchanges. Error correction is not entirely straightforward. Cultural differences may dictate the directness or indirectness with which the task is addressed, which can be a source of tension (Stickler in press). Learners from national educational systems where grammar is still taught will freely use metalinguistic terminology to explain their partner's errors. Learners from other backgrounds may have difficulty with this. Differences or difficulties can be resolved at the outset by explicitly agreeing what one would like corrected and how.

Evaluation and assessment

Autonomy includes the ability on the part of language learners to evaluate what they have acquired. Tandem learners are no exception. The Tandem Learner Diary (see above) offers one way of enabling them to assess their own progress and that of their peers. Organizers of tandem learning will need to consider how heavily to weight students' grades in the overall scheme. Though systematic research is thin on the ground, there is no strong evidence that learner participation in the assessment process leads to grade inflation. However, gender-related disparities in peer assessment should raise some concern, not least because a small-scale study of tandem learners, conducted in 1998, suggests that 'female students award higher grades to their male peers than the latter are prepared to award them' (Stickler et al. 1999: 281).

Tutor support: language advice and learner counselling

Learning autonomously may imply an absence of formal tuition. But the development of autonomy is unlikely to occur without support. Tandem partners have more sources of support than most autonomous learners. The first is each other, which is one of the great strengths of the method. However, support from outside the pair is also indispensable, not least in the event of problems with the partnership itself. This is of two kinds. Language advice sessions can deal with such matters as goal-setting and reviewing, locating and using resources, language-related problems, using effective learning strategies. At least one such session should be programmed for the start of the course. Learner counselling addresses the affective dimension of learning, including: motivation and the sense of progress; the functioning of the partnership; negotiating effectively with one's partner. The most fruitful approaches to counselling for language advisors are likely to be person-centred, transcultural and focused on helping (see Stickler 2001: 44–47). A counselling session might best be scheduled for the mid-point of any course. By then, any problems should have surfaced and there will be time to remedy them. It is important for learners to be able to consult an advisor/counsellor, on appointment.

Conclusion

Tandem learning is an effective and enjoyable way of learning or maintaining a second language for those at intermediate level or above. It is very well suited to the development of intercultural awareness, especially since this is channelled through interpersonal interaction. But it can also be targeted to highly specific linguistic aims. It is essential that tandem pairs be supported by a learning advisor with both pedagogic and counselling expertise. Learner training in such skills as goal-setting, time-management and error correction is also highly desirable, if not indispensable. E-tandem learning entails a higher risk of failure than the face-to-face variant and those venturing upon it would be well advised to use a mixture of modes. Face-to-face tandem learning is almost invariably successful and may lead to lasting friendships.

In the absence of any formal organization for providers of tandem learning, it is difficult to calculate exactly how widespread the method has become, except in terms of demonstrable minima. An internet search reveals that, in the UK alone, at least 22 universities or higher education institutions currently offer tandem learning in some form to their students, while the project partners of the International E-mail Tandem Network developed worksheets in 14 languages and made e-mail tandem learning available to 2,000 university students from 20 European countries. This takes no account, however, of the development of tandem learning in Japan, Russia, or the US, where active partners were prevented from formal participation in the project by funding restrictions. At secondary level, a subsequent project initiated tandem learning in 17 schools in five EU states.

Sources of information

The best sources of information on tandem learning are the handbooks that have been produced as a result of successive international collaborative projects. The English language versions of these are:

Lewis, T. and Walker, L. (eds) (2003) *Autonomous Language Learning in Tandem*, Sheffield: Academy Electronic Publications.

Little, D. and Brammerts, H. (eds) (1996) *A Guide to Language Learning in Tandem via the Internet*, Dublin: Centre for Language and Communication Studies, Trinity College Dublin.

Both handbooks have been produced in a number of European languages. Details of the various versions, plus a large amount of practical information about tandem learning (including worksheets) are available from the E-Tandem Agency website, currently hosted by the *Selbstlernzentrum* of the *Seminar für Sprachlehrforschung* of *Ruhr-Universität Bochum*. Online. Available at: www.slf.ruhr-uni-bochum.de/etandem/etindex-en.html (accessed 20 June 2004).

On language advising:

Mozzon-McPherson, M. and Vismans, R. (eds) (2001) *Beyond Language Teaching: towards language advising*, London: Centre for Information on Language Teaching and Research.

Corpora and concordances

Marie-Madeleine Kenning

Concordancers are search and retrieval software programs that enable the user to recover from a body of (electronic) text or corpus (pl. corpora) all instances of a given item in their immediate linguistic context. The search produces a list of citations or a concordance, which can take a number of forms. In the most common form, known as a Keyword-in-Context or KWIC concordance, the search item (keyword) is displayed in the centre of the page surrounded by parts of the context in which it occurs, as in the following concordance on 'display' from *The Times*, February 1995:

```
4   a. It promises in its full-page display advertisement:
    "Lose Weight! Lose 2
5   ted by producing a high-quality display after unluckily
    losing the first fr
6   emony includes a military-model display and inmates singing
    the American
7   s Ridd says: "We plan to have a display and stage area in
    the middle of t
8   ments such as the legibility of display and the audibility
    of prompts. Nass
9   d to put the treasure on public display, and to accept help
    in restoring wh
10  ult on the ears with a fireworks display and, for good
    measure, the lead s
11  nces. Royle described Elleray's display as "the most
    insensitive I've witne
12  goal the highlight of a vibrant display as Blackburn ran
    riot in midfield,
```

13   nt to put such vacuous works on <u>display</u>, asks Waldemar
     Januszczak.
14   k, however, we have witnessed a <u>display</u>, at least by Ulster
     standards, of
15   t to Picasso, is about to go on <u>display</u> at the Hermitage.
     These are not onl
16   where, her things were still on <u>display</u>. Boxes of
     chocolates mouldering, ha
17   hot behind. It was a remarkable <u>display</u> by Sandelin, 27,
     who trailed Ball
18   were undone by an eye-catching <u>display</u> by Andy Jones, a
     home-grown Island

Concordancers can be used to recover all kinds of strings: particular words, as
in the example above, parts of words (e.g. a prefix) or sequences of words
(e.g. 'race relations'). In order to gain some insights into the results of different
kinds of searches, you might like to experiment with one of the free concordance software packages available on-line. Here is one possible activity based
on the *Web Concordancer* of the Virtual Language Centre of Hong Kong (2004):

Stage 1

1   Click on 'simple search' under 'English'.
2   Enter 'riot' (without the quotation marks) in the blank search string
    box.
3   Select *The Times* March 95 from the list in the select corpus box.
4   Click the Search for concordances box.

Stage 2

5   Having looked at the concordance, go back to the previous screen
    (using the back arrow).
6   Click in turn on the various options offered in the search string box,
    and observe the differences in output.
7   Do the same with the options in the Sort type box.

Corpora are usually designed to offer a representative sample of a particular
language or language variety and therefore tend to be quite large. For example,
the British National Corpus (1997), which aims to represent a wide range of
modern British English, both spoken and written, contains over 100 million
words. Even the relatively small corpus used for the above concordance on
'display' contains more than three million words.

In addition to monolingual corpora, there are corpora consisting of collections of texts in two or more languages. Multilingual corpora fall into two categories. The first, known as comparable corpora, consists of sets of texts in different languages which have been collected using the same selection procedures and categories but are not translations of each other. The second type, called parallel corpora, comprises translations of the same texts. Here is an extract from a concordance on 'before' produced with Multiconcord, a Windows-based multilingual parallel concordancer (www.copycatchgold. com/multicon.htm):

Art galleries and antique dealers are generally not open *before* 10.30am	Les magasins d'antiquités ainsi que les galeries d'art n'ouvrent généralement pas avant 10h 30 le matin
Finally you will arrive *before* the town of Rostock	Enfin tu arriveras devant la ville de Rostock
Before her was another long passage	Devant elle s'étendait un autre couloir
Nearly a century passed *before* this idea was taken seriously	Presque un siècle s'écoula avant que cette hypothèse ne soit prise au sérieux
After around twenty years in Bruges, the director of the Medici's offshoot had become adviser to Prince Charles *before* the prince became a duke	Après une vingtaine d'années à Bruges, le directeur de la filiale des Médicis était devenu le conseiller du prince Charles avant que ce dernier ne devînt duc
Arthur Rimbaud had never seen the sea *before* composing 'Le Bateau ivre'	Arthur Rimbaud n'avait jamais vu la mer avant de composer 'Le Bateau ivre'
For his part, Claude Debussy first benefited from contact with the sea in Cannes *before* staying in Russia at the home of the Tchaikovsky's patroness	Claude Debussy, de son côté, bénéficia d'abord d'un contact avec la mer, à Cannes, avant de séjourner en Russie chez la protectrice de Tchaïkovski
She thought it over *before* she made her next remark	Elle y réfléchit un moment avant de demander

Corpora and concordancers are used in lexical studies (typically in the compilation of dictionaries), in research on grammar or syntax, in socio-linguistics (e.g. in relation to gender studies, to trace the evolution of political correctness, etc.), as well as in literary studies.

Concordancing also lends itself to a range of pedagogical applications in the area of language learning. In particular, concordances can be used to:

- find authentic examples to illustrate points of grammar, vocabulary use, common collocations;
- inform syllabus development by providing data on usage and use (for example the relative frequency of particular items or structures) or, with multilingual corpora, on similarities and differences between the native and target language (Kenning 2000a);
- generate activities and exercises;
- promote language awareness, develop analytical powers, and encourage autonomous learning.

One of the first to advocate the use of data from linguistic corpora for language teaching and language learning was Tim Johns, the developer of an approach known as Data-Driven Learning (DDL). Johns, who sees concordance data as offering a unique way of stimulating inductive learning strategies by giving learners opportunities to discover things for themselves, to notice patterns and form and test hypotheses, has discussed extensively both the merits of DDL and how it can be implemented (see, for example, Johns and King 1991).

At one end of the spectrum concordance software can be used on-line by experienced learners to answer their own queries; with less advanced learners it is generally advisable to work with edited output in the form of handouts or guided activities. There are many samples of concordance-based teaching and learning materials in a range of languages on the internet. The example that follows is adapted from Rézeau (2004):

Match each of the following words with one of the blocks of citations: allegations, claim, evidence:

1

had drunk a similar amount. There is also alarming ____ that more girls are smoking cigarettes, despite

of which concluded after examining available ____ that exposure to passive smoking was a "health hazard"

health education unit offers the first detailed ____ that drinking by children under 11 is now widespread

undo a great deal of the damage. "There is growing ____ that heart disease is reversible and that blockages in

---

which has taken $12m. The greatest single piece of ____ that the Academy is opening its heart to a different

2

Federal Reserve Board for a hearing to dismiss ____ that he breached banking laws. The Fed froze the assets

to the US of two British women who face ____ that they were part of a cult murder plot. Last week, a

the government announced an informal enquiry into ____ that computer games are a health hazard yesterday,

officers do have the power to investigate ____ that duty paid goods such as wine and beer bought on the

had bombed and gassed in the past. He rejected ____ that the raids were illegal, saying that such action had

3

All rights reserved. Despite Eastman Kodak's ____ that they unfairly keep competitors out of the complex

his defense witness questioned the prosecution's ____ that they were made by a knife during the murders.

Calls for Action, Not Words. The Bosnian Serb ____ that the UN safe haven had been secured by them has

discuss his physical limitations. To refute the ____ that Ron Goldman was somehow overpowered by O. J. Simpson

that the defense was promising to substantiate the ____ that O. J. Simpson was chipping golf balls out on his lawn

Finally, concordance output can help identify potential parsing difficulties that tend to go unnoticed by expert language users. These possible language processing problems often come as a surprise and, as illustrated by the next activity, invite teachers to reflect on the way in which they approach certain areas (Kenning 2000b). The activity also demonstrates how results can vary from corpus to corpus and shows the benefits of a reasonably large sample.

Stage 1

1 Access the Web Concordancer of the Virtual Language Centre of Hong Kong: www.edict.com.hk/concordance/default.htm
2 Click on 'simple search' under 'English'
3 Enter 'race for' (without the quotation marks) in the blank search string box

4 Select SCMP articles from the list in the select corpus box
5 Click the Search for concordances box and look at the results

Stage 2
Repeat using, in turn, *The Times* February 95, *The Times* March 95, and *The Times* January 95

Stage 3
How might these results influence:

● the way in which you present and teach the use of 'for' to introduce the goal following 'race' (as in the citation: a 'real contender in the race for the White House')?
● your general approach?

Sources of information

A clear and comprehensive treatment of concordances in the modern foreign languages classroom, including useful information on on-line corpora and a wealth of practical illustrations and activities, can be found in Lamy and Klarskov Mortensen (2002).

Part IV

A diverse discipline

22

Cultural Studies

Michael Kelly

What is Cultural Studies?

Cultural Studies has come to occupy an important place in Modern Languages programmes for two main reasons. First, the study of a language necessarily requires students to engage with a wide range of texts written in the language. Where authentic texts are used, without heavy editing for the purposes of teaching, they are likely to carry a rich cargo of references to the broader culture of the country concerned. They will also be accompanied by images and artefacts, and are often presented by teachers who are living embodiments of that country's culture. If students spend a period of residence abroad to improve their language, they will necessarily engage with the culture in direct and immediate ways. Second, where students are specializing in the language and culture of a particular country or group of countries, they need the conceptual and analytical tools to understand how different facets of the culture work. Traditionally, the study of literary and philosophical texts was the privileged route to understanding the culture, but in the last 20 or 30 years, most programmes have widened to accommodate film in the canon of cultural texts, and many have opened further to encompass a diverse range of cultural activities, including the creative and performing arts, television, comics, popular fiction, architecture, websites and the anthropology of everyday life (cafés, festivals, food, fashion, etc.).

The point of studying the broad cultural field in Modern Languages is to enable students to experience their language learning as a living, embodied activity, which enriches them personally, and to enable them to understand more deeply what it is like to live and work in another culture (Phipps and Gonzalez 2004). This aim reflects the shifting nature and role of culture in the contemporary world, and also the development of theoretical frameworks and conceptual tools. At its most general level, Cultural Studies draws on theories of society, ideology, identity and communication to elucidate the meanings and contexts of culture in its broadest sense. English writers such as Raymond Williams, Richard Hoggart and Stuart Hall are generally credited with launching Cultural Studies in the academic world in the 1960s and 1970s, though it really gained widespread acceptance in the 1990s (Grossberg *et al.* 1992, Easthope and McGowan 1992, During 1993, Featherstone 1995). Many other writers have contributed to its conceptual resources, including French theorists such as Roland Barthes and Pierre Bourdieu, American academics like Fredric Jameson and Homi Bhabha, German social theorists of the Frankfurt School (Adorno, Habermas, Benjamin), the Russian writer Mikhail Bakhtin and numerous others. Many of these writers are complex and challenging, and often require readers to bring considerable philosophical or sociological sophistication to their reading. Their ideas will need to be presented to students with care. First- and second-year undergraduates are likely to benefit from more accessible commentaries and volumes of collected readings, and from carefully worked applications of the ideas to specific examples.

Example: Roland Barthes, Mythologies (Barthes 1957, 1973)

A useful website is available at: www.orac.sund.ac.uk/~os0tmc/myth.htm.

The first part of *Mythologies* consists of 54 short journalistic discussions of a variety of topics drawn from French life in the mid-1950s, when they were written. Only 28 of them are included in the English translation. The topics range widely, including for example advertising, court cases, sports and public events (like the coronation of Elizabeth II) as they are presented in the media. The second part is a theoretical essay on 'Myth today', offering an analysis of how cultural meanings are constructed and of communication, inspired by Saussure's theory of the linguistic sign.

Work set for the first of three seminars on the text:
All the class should have read at least the first piece, 'Le monde où l'on catche' (The world of wrestling), and preferably should have watched an all-in wrestling match (such as WWF) in the recent past.

Tutorial presenters (two students nominated earlier in the course) should prepare a ten-minute presentation on the following questions:

● What is the distinction between sport and spectacle?
● What is the role of excess?
● What is the role of the body?
● What are the rules?
● How does wrestling make justice intelligible?

- How does Barthes's account of wrestling accord with wrestling matches you have seen?

A tutorial discussion follows the presentation, in which students are also encouraged to make comparisons with other sports, especially ones that Barthes discusses in other parts of his book, notably cycling.

Designing a Cultural Studies course

There are numerous books now offering a Cultural Studies approach to particular languages and cultures. The OUP books of the mid-1990s remain useful works of synthesis (Forbes and Kelly 1995, Burns 1995) and have been followed by numerous edited volumes, glossaries and encyclopedias providing rich resources for the study of particular cultures, and inspiration for teachers wishing to design courses.

Cultural Studies approaches to Modern Languages can be introduced in a number of ways. They often feature as part of a language-learning unit, as part of a methodological unit (e.g. 'Reading Culture' for first year undergraduates), or as part of an introductory unit to studying a particular country or culture. They may be offered as full units within a programme of study, amounting to between a tenth and a quarter of a year's study. There are also examples of whole programmes, especially postgraduate Masters degrees.

Looking at the level of full units, there are two popular ways of designing Cultural Studies approaches, often found in the second and final years of undergraduate programmes. The first is to study a particular cultural form. Many Modern Languages degrees include courses on film, with such topics as contemporary Spanish (or French or Italian, etc.) cinema. These are growing in popularity, and increasingly being offered in conjunction with specialist degrees in film and media studies. But many degrees will also offer courses in less mainstream academic genres such as popular song, sport, television, photography, detective fiction, or comics (e.g. French *bande dessinée*). The advantage of genre-based courses such as these is that they give students an opportunity to acquire the specialist skills needed to understand how a particular cultural form works and to develop a set of critical concepts necessary to understand a particular example (or 'text').

The second popular approach is to take a particular place, topic or period, which is then studied from a number of points of view, typically drawing on literary texts, journalism, popular music, films and other media to throw light on it. Major cities are a favourite focus of these kinds of courses. Paris, Berlin, Rome, Barcelona, Moscow, for example, have been the focus or the setting for vast numbers of books, films, television reportages, paintings, photographs and suchlike, spanning a wide historical period. Students and teachers are likely to be able to bring their own experiences to bear. The architecture, historical monuments and streets are often familiar sights, though students rarely come with extensive knowledge of their complexity and contexts, and they thus enjoy the experience of discovering new depths. The same approach can be taken with more general topics such as the Body, War, Love and Death, Migration and Diaspora, etc. It can also be applied to particular periods in the recent or more distant past of the country, ranging from a single month (e.g. May 1968 in France) or a year (e.g. 1989 in Germany) to a decade or more (e.g. the interwar period 1918–1939). The presence of mature students in such courses can add an additional dimension of eyewitness accounts to the classroom experience. This type of course has the advantage of enabling students to develop knowledge of how different cultural forms work, though they will not usually have time within the course to develop an extensive critical apparatus for studying, for example, film or popular song. They will typically focus rather on how the works they study might shed light on the topic or theme of the course.

Example: 'Everyday life in the 1950s.' A final year special subject course in French

Outline of the subject

During the years 1954–1964, France self-consciously entered the modern world. Alongside the polarizations of the Cold War and the crisis of decolonization, the 'economic miracle' brought radical changes to traditional French values and lifestyle.

The aim of this course is to examine some of the effects of modernity on daily life, as reflected in the popular culture of the time, and to explore some of the ideas developed to understand the process.

Objectives

By the end of the course, you may expect to have acquired:

1 *Knowledge* of the historical context, and aspects of cultural and intellectual activity in France during the 1950s, including a range of written and audiovisual material produced in the period.

2 *Understanding* of a number of concepts and debates that were developed during the period, including how and why they were significant at the time, and how they might relate to your own experience.

3 *Skills* in analysing a diverse range of cultural materials, in perceiving relationships both between different cultural phenomena and between them and their social context, and in presenting information and arguments in both oral and written form.

4   *Interest* in finding out more about the culture of the period and in exploring a wider application of the ideas and values you have encountered in these studies.

Prescribed material
Roland Barthes, *Mythologies* (Seuil)
Henri Lefebvre, *Critique de la vie quotidienne, 1. Introduction*, 2nd edition (L'Arche)
Elsa Triolet, *Roses à crédit* (Folio)
Françoise Sagan, *Bonjour Tristesse* (Julliard/Pocket)
Hergé, *L'Affaire Tournesol* (Casterman)
Jacques Tati, *Les vacances de Monsieur Hulot* (film)
Jacques Tati, *Mon oncle* (film)
Roger Vadim, *Et Dieu créa la femme* (film)
Georges Brassens, vol. 3 (Polygram Master Série)
Jacques Brel, vol. 1 (Polygram Master Série)

Assessing learning in Cultural Studies

Since Cultural Studies is a strongly interdisciplinary field, it is particularly important that teachers should clearly set out the basis on which students are assessed. This should preferably correspond to the focus of the course, so that students are aware, for example, how far they are expected to display their ability to manipulate critical concepts specific to a genre (e.g. camera angles, use of lighting or soundtrack in films), how far they are expected to show knowledge of the social and political development of a period, or how far they are expected to deploy a particular theoretical framework. (See also Chapter 10 on general assessment issues.)

Developing and supporting Cultural Studies

The range and variety of Cultural Studies means that it is highly dependent on a range of support that has not generally been available in traditional university libraries. A good deal of material is non-academic (e.g. children's comic books), likely to be ephemeral (e.g. newspapers, websites) or difficult to recover (e.g. live performances, broadcast material), often found in shops rather than libraries, or else lodged in specialist collections of, for example, film, music, art, design or photography, where Modern Languages students are less frequent visitors. However, modern university libraries are becoming accustomed to making provision for the wider range of materials. And, in practice, language resources centres often have significant holdings of relevant materials, such as recent newspapers and magazines, or off-air recordings. The growth in co-operation between libraries and learning resources centres is particularly encouraging for this kind of study, but it is important for teachers to take account of the learning resource needs of a course well in advance of offering it to students.

Perhaps the best part of teaching Cultural Studies is that it gives both teachers and students a constant source of delight and personal reflection. Part of the motivation of teaching the films of Almadóvar is that you thoroughly enjoy them, and that teaching them deepens your enjoyment. And the experience of applying critical theory to everyday life (football, soaps, the city) brings in its train a heightened awareness of the signifying practices that surround us everywhere. At its best, Cultural Studies also leads us to reflect on the meanings that we, as teachers, put into circulation and offer to our students, and on the negotiation of meanings that ensues in our dialogue with them.

23

Languages and Business Studies

David Head

Do you speak any foreign languages and what importance do you place on such skills?

I speak some French and some German. I think we are arrogant about not making an effort or an attempt to speak other people's languages in the UK. It's important from a business perspective that we do open our minds more to what's out there in Europe, and we've got to begin to do it on their terms instead of insisting it is done on our terms.

Rebecca Thomas, Chief Executive of
LeggMason Investors (2001)

In the era of globalization and the European Single Market, you will not be surprised to find that foreign–language study is firmly established in university Business Studies courses, not least because it offers students competitive advantage in the search for a job after graduation. Many Business Studies students are drawn to Modern Languages because they have enjoyed studying them at secondary school and do not want to abandon them, yet wish also to take a course which they perceive to have a clear vocational outcome. Those who aspire to be effective managers in the international business context also see the sense of broadening or improving further their communication and intercultural skills through foreign–language study. Some of these students will be motivated by the desire to make up for a decision taken at school to abandon language study in favour of other subjects. Your situation as a language specialist contributing to the Business curriculum is, thus, quite an enviable one, as your Business Studies students will invariably be motivated language learners.

If, however, you should find yourself having to provide encouragement, try mentioning to your class that in the European Union already, 75 per cent of all web content is in languages other than English. This should prove to be a salutary thought for any would-be international manager, as is the prediction that English will lose its global status as 'the default language of the web' before very long (Sage and Stanbridge 2000).

Many academic modern linguists are the products of an education that places little or no emphasis on knowing about the contemporary business or economic environment of other countries. You may well have such a background yourself. If so, you may find that you are the mirror image of those Business Studies lecturers who have little interest in truly international themes, but who place emphasis on business basics from an Anglo-American perspective. You may even find yourself deploring the fact that Business Studies students whom you are required to teach have had inadequate exposure to authors or ideas or to cultural issues that may well be the currency of conversation in, say, French, German or Spanish business circles. In some cases, the curriculum you are being asked to deliver may appear not to offer the possibility of filling these gaps. The chances are that your brief is simply to 'teach them the lingo', which, as you know, is simplistic. Try not to forget that you are doing much more than enabling students to master the niceties of grammar and usage when you take a language class. As a prominent British academic has put it: 'Learn a language and you have a chance to read literatures you can't otherwise access, to understand different mindsets, to move beyond the cosiness of familiarity, to learn to negotiate difference' (Bassnett 2000).

Here are some suggestions for enriching your Language for Business classes:

- Turn them into a vehicle for introducing information and themes that may not, strictly speaking, be on the class menu, but which are important aspects of the cultural, economic, social or political context of the language concerned. I have even used switching on the light in a German class as a pretext for asking the question: 'Whose dying words were "Mehr Licht"?' This, in turn, has given me the chance briefly to make the class aware that the German in question, Goethe, is the most famous son of the city that now houses the European Central Bank. If someone in the class knows either of these facts about Frankfurt am Main, there is fruitful ground for a degree of competitive tension in the class. At the very least, even before the class gets down to the task in hand, an introductory pattern has been set for future weeks. Next time, the topic of the day could be the location of other major cities (you cannot assume that your students will be fully conversant with the map of the country or countries to which your specialist language applies). In this particular instance, I also have scope for asking why Frankfurt is the home of the European Central Bank or why one of its nicknames is 'Bankfurt'.

- If a major story relating to 'your' country is coming up in the intervening week, get the class to look out for relevant media coverage, the world wide web included, especially if this coverage is in the relevant language and is germane to the broader context that you are seeking to develop. You could also get students to find a news report that exemplifies some aspect of grammar or usage you are covering. In my experience, there are always students in the class who welcome the opportunity to look around for some business news item relating to the foreign country they are primarily interested in or a relevant example of business terminology to bring to the next session and who will take pleasure in offering what they have found to everyone else. These students highlight another important feature of teaching languages to business students: the language class is something they look forward to because it is 'different' and even 'fun'. Furthermore, they will be keen to impress you with evidence of their progress as business specialists.

- Of course, you are teaching a foreign language for a special purpose, i.e. to facilitate or enhance effectiveness in the relevant foreign-language business environment. This means that you will be concentrating on grammar, usage and vocabulary, always with one eye on applications to potential business situations, from the basics of business travel and correspondence to major challenges such as negotiation, writing business reports and selling in the relevant foreign language. The texts or recordings you use in class and the materials you recommend for independent learning should, therefore, ideally focus on business-related issues, settings and situations. Unless you are into reinventing wheels, it would pay you to look around for textbooks and other ready-made materials that embody the balanced approach required by the specific purpose you have in mind and to use these to structure your courses.

- If you are wondering where to look first, start with a tried-and-tested publisher, such as Hodder and Stoughton, whose Languages catalogue contains some potentially useful titles under 'vocational languages'. For instance, if you are teaching *ab initio* students, Hodder and Stoughton's Absolute Beginners' Business Languages series is well worth exploring. It covers French, German, Italian and Spanish. Its *French for Business*, on the other hand, is aimed at the more advanced student, while its series on Languages for Leisure and Tourism addresses the needs of students specializing in an area of growing importance within Business Studies. Routledge's range of business language textbooks, which covers French, German and Spanish and includes business correspondence and spoken language guides to business situations, as well as comprehensive manuals, should also be on your shopping list. For online help with business language materials, you would be well advised to try the information sheets available from CILT, The National Centre for Languages (see www.cilt.org.uk/infos/cilt_infos.htm). Another online address that you should check out is www.bbc.co.uk/languages, where, among other things, you will find potentially useful words, phrases and activities aimed at people wanting to work or conduct business in French, German, Italian, Spanish and Welsh. Your final choice of books and materials will inevitably be guided by the objectives of the module or course concerned. For instance, the Languages for Business Qualifications offered by the London Chamber of Commerce and Industry give a clear indication of the syllabus topics to be covered.

- Make imaginative use of the information and communication technology (ICT) that is available to you, but be judicious about the amount of time you invest in developing your own computer-based material. A survey of UK Business Schools has made the point that this is an area where higher education institutions find themselves competing not only with one another, 'but increasingly with commercial providers of information and educational services very similar to their own' (Business Education Support Team 2000). In other words, any original use you make of ICT will be judged by a challenging benchmark.

In addition, there is something you can do to enrich the Business Studies syllabus to which you are contributing: suggest exciting new Business course components that only a linguist can teach well. This means above all taking a fresh look at your classes on Area Studies or even Cultural Studies themes and making them relevant and accessible to undergraduate Business students. In this regard, you should take heart from the fact that the Harvard Business School is now using 'great literature' (Shakespeare, Tolstoy, Chandler) to teach leadership and has an online 'working knowledge' information service that has recommended a book on the theme of women, culture and commerce. In other words, adapting your know-how and interests to the needs of Business Studies students does not mean having to say goodbye to knowledge-based courses that may be directly linked to your research interests.

Think also about exploiting the fact that language specialists are well placed to develop and offer the kind of courses or modules in International Communication, Cross-Cultural Competence, and Managing Cultural Diversity that are growing rapidly in importance within Business Studies. One of the pioneers of cross-cultural awareness in the business context, Geert Hofstede, states:

> Communication in trade languages or pidgin limits communications to those issues for which these simplified languages have words. To establish a more fundamental intercultural understanding, the foreign partner must acquire the host culture language. Having to express oneself in another language means learning to adopt someone else's reference frame. It is doubtful whether one can be bicultural without being bilingual . . . words of a language are . . . the vehicles of culture transfer.
>
> (Hofstede 1991)

This might sound very obvious to a linguist. But not enough linguists have brought this kind of message to bear on planning decisions affecting International Business courses.

Recently, two other influential figures in the field of intercultural competence, Charles Hampden-Turner and Fons Trompenaars, published a book on the tangible benefits – wealth-generation included – that accrue from the open-minded interaction of cultural opposites. Their book is replete with cultural references that will immediately appeal to the progressive linguist, among them analyses of films by Akira Kurosawa and Ingmar Bergman. The authors state: 'We finally noticed that foreign cultures are not arbitrarily or randomly different from one another. They are instead *mirror images* of one another's values, reversals of the order and sequence of looking and learning' (Hampden-Turner and Trompenaars 2000).

Such a cross-cultural insight is the kind of potential catalyst without which the Business Studies curriculum cannot effectively internationalize itself or globalize the minds of its students. It should also remind you that, as an academic linguist, you can really make a difference in the Business Studies context, while at the same time developing your special interests in new and exciting ways.

Sources of information

CILT, the National Centre for Languages, London. Online. Available at: www.cilt. org.uk/infos/cilt_infos.htm (accessed 20 May 2004).

24

Linguistics

Rosalind Temple

Linguistics is a diverse discipline and, indeed, linguists have long debated which subdisciplines should properly be included under the heading. It is still argued by some that linguistics proper should be restricted to the subdisciplines of phonology (which studies sound structure), morphology (word structure), syntax (sentence structure) and semantics (meaning), but it is generally accepted that phonetics (the acoustic, articulatory and auditory properties of speech sounds) and variationist sociolinguistics (structured variation in language) are essential components of any higher education course in linguistics. To these may be added discourse analysis (text structure), pragmatics (meaning in context), conversation analysis, applied linguistics (itself a diverse field) and the many areas of interest that can be loosely grouped under the heading 'sociolinguistics': language planning, societal bilingualism and multilingualism, language attitudes, standardization, and so on. All these areas (and the list above is far from exhaustive) can be shown to be relevant to the study of Modern Languages, but we shall focus here on applications of some core areas to language teaching before considering the place of linguistics courses in Modern Languages programmes.

Linguistics in language teaching

Phonetics and phonology

There exist many pronunciation manuals for learners of foreign languages, usually with accompanying cassettes or CDs, and these have been supplemented in recent years by computer packages and a plethora of websites which offer online sound files at the click of a button. However, many of these either offer examples with no explanation or use somewhat idiosyncratic descriptions of sounds (e.g. it is not obvious what it means to say that 'l' is 'lighter' in one language than another). Students can be given a huge headstart by being taught the basics of articulatory phonetics with reference to the internationally accepted standard descriptive terminology of the IPA, the International Phonetic Alphabet (International Phonetic Association 1999), and thus how consciously to manipulate their own articulators (tongue, lips, vocal folds) to produce more authentic pronunciations of the target language. For example, a perennial problem with languages which have the close front rounded vowel [y] is teaching English-speaking students to differentiate it from [u] (as in French 'tu' versus 'tout' or German 'drücken' versus 'drucken'). Sometimes the problem is an inability to pronounce the [y], but the rapidly spreading tendency for young British English speakers to front the vowel of words like 'goose' or 'too' (Torgersen 2002) means that students now frequently have a problem with producing an authentic [u] in French, German and other Modern Languages. The basic ability to characterize vowels in terms of frontness and backness (allowing parallels to be drawn between [y] and [u]) and the rounding or unrounding of the lips (allowing contrast between [y] and [i]) can be a great help to students in understanding exactly what it is they are doing wrong and rectifying the problem.

The benefits of a rudimentary understanding of the phonetic/phonological framework go beyond accuracy in the articulatory details; an understanding of simple phonological distributional effects can also be helpful. The characterization of sound systems in terms of phonemes (significant sounds) and allophones (their variant forms in different, predictable contexts) is no longer central to phonological theory, but is still a useful tool for both linguistics and language teaching. For example, /l/ in English has two allophonic variants, the 'clear' [l], which occurs in syllable onsets, that is at the beginnings of syllables, (e.g. *leap* [liːp]) and the 'dark' or 'velarized' [ɫ], which occurs at the ends of syllables, in syllable codas, (e.g. *pill* [pɪɫ]). It is well known that in (e.g.) French and German /l/ is never velarized, so students have to learn to produce a relatively clear [l] in all positions. Teaching students to understand that sounds such as [l] and [ɫ], which they think are the same in their L1 (mother tongue), are actually different allophones of the same phoneme (that is different versions of something that can be characterized in some more abstract sense as 'the same') can be very helpful in making them aware of the potentially problematic influence of their L1 on their L2 (or foreign language) production. Conversely, showing how sounds that are different in the L1 might, in other languages, belong to the same phoneme can help with apparent paradoxes such as the distribution of [b] and [v] or [β] in Spanish (i.e. why the letter 'b' represents [b] in 'baño' but [β] in 'haber').

Syntax

In the same way, insights from syntactic analysis such as constituent structure and movement can be invoked to help students understand grammatical

Figure 24.1

processes. For example, in the French sentence 'Il met le livre [près de la chaise]$_{PP}$', seeing the Preposition Phrase (PP) as a unit can help students grasp the parallels between replacing it with a pronoun and replacing a Noun Phrase (NP) (or Determiner Phrase in more recent syntactic theories) such as 'L'homme' or 'le livre', with 'il' or 'le': both the PP and the NPs are clearly identifiable units (cf. Figure 24.1).

Seeing the PP as having internal structure with constituent parts can also be a helpful aid to the knotty problem of how to represent it in a relative clause, again drawing parallels with NPs: the whole is moved, but the internal structure must be maintained, even when part is replaced by a pronoun. Figure 24.2 is a condensed version of how this could be put to students: to transform the sentence 'Il met le livre près de la chaise' into a relative clause, one unit, the NP, is replaced by a pronoun 'laquelle'; another, the PP, is moved as a whole to the beginning, with its internal structure (the relationship between its constituent parts) maintained.

Notions such as movement are, of course, metaphors, as are all linguistic constructs, and it should be stressed to students that this is the case, but they

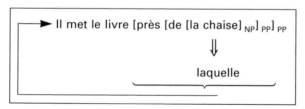

Figure 24.2

are nevertheless helpful metaphors. A different metaphor, that of valency (taken from chemistry and used in Dependency Grammar), is commonly used in the teaching of German to explain the relationship between the verb and what some linguists would call its arguments, that is its subject and other complements.[1] The valency of any given verb is, then, 'the type and number of complements required by a particular verb to construct a grammatical sentence' (Durrell 2002: 366). So, just as oxygen has a negative valency of two and thus requires a positive complement of two to form a complete molecule (e.g. in H_2O, where each hydrogen atom has a positive valency of only one), the verb 'kaufen' has a valency that requires it to be attached to both a subject and an accusative object to be complete, as in: 'Das Mädchen kauft das Buch.' *'Das Mädchen kauft dem Buch' does not form a complete sentence, just as *HO does not form a complete water molecule. See West (2001) for a further brief introduction and illustration.

Obviously the theory is no good without the practice, either for syntax or phonetics/phonology. One model that works well with students is an informal lecture-style class to explain the theory (with some input from the students, who are required to mimic the lecturer) backed up by intensive half-hour small-group practical sessions for phonetics or hour-long small-group classes for grammar. As for any aspect of language teaching, students will only learn if they are themselves prepared to perform. In teaching phonetics, both as a language-learning tool and for linguistics purposes, it is particularly important to get them to play with their own articulators so that they learn to introspect about how phonetic descriptions apply to them. This can be done in both lectures and tutorials. In the latter, lecturers have to be prepared at once to sacrifice their own dignity ('make 'em laugh'!) and to be strict in forcing students to vocalize and in enforcing classroom discipline: students have to be told repeatedly that they cannot do what is required by whispering or if their hands are over their mouths – this too can be implemented with humour. In the case of phonetics, alongside the less satisfactory internet resources, there are some very useful sites for students to listen to the sounds of languages and of the IPA; there is a list in the Sources of information section at the end of this chapter.

Sociolinguistics

The insights and debates of sociolinguistic studies of the past half-century are well known among modern linguists but their usefulness to the language teacher (and across the Languages, Linguistics and Area Studies curriculum) has perhaps shifted in recent years. One essential feature in any advanced language programme must be to teach students an awareness of how a given language varies from the textbook norm, not least to help prepare them for the leap from classroom to residence abroad placement. However, in these days when communicative approaches to language teaching are dominant and students arriving at university have relatively little expertise in using language formally, a basic understanding of language variation and the social value of norms can help them at the opposite end of the scale. Gone are the days when venerable colleagues would argue that a final-year student should be penalized in his/her oral examination for having a strong regional accent, and yet we do our students a disservice if we do not teach them that style and register matter in their use of a foreign language (cf. Milroy and Milroy 1991). To give a trivial example, appeals to such principles can depersonalize the otherwise hard-to-understand request to use polite forms of address (*vous*, *Sie*, *Usted* and so on) in a department where staff and students are on first-name terms (which is unlikely to be the case in France, Germany or Spain).

The rest of the iceberg

As already mentioned, phonetics/phonology, syntax and sociolinguistics are just some of the core areas of linguistics that can be applied to language teaching. Other areas of linguistics can also provide useful tools for Modern Language teaching. For example, the distinction made in semantics between the thematic roles of 'agent' (who does the action) and 'patient' (who receives the action) in relation to verbs can be useful in explaining the relationships between passive and active sentences. Teaching students about language change, including semantic change, can serve to warn them to be careful in interpreting texts from older sources, such as older literary texts. And there is a wealth of other areas, including those mentioned in the introduction to this chapter, which can be fruitful for the language teacher. A note of caution should, perhaps, be added here, though: a little knowledge can indeed be a dangerous thing; most areas of linguistics were not designed with language teaching in mind and it is wise for the teacher to consult a range of good, general texts on linguistics before introducing new notions into the classroom.

Linguistics in Modern Language degree programmes

The place of theory

Most linguists would agree with Adger (2002) that theory is essential to the study of linguistics: 'One important thing to get over to students about these kinds of data [corpus data, experimental data and intuition data] is that they are meaningless in the absence of a theory.' The great problem in teaching linguistics to undergraduates in Modern Languages is that there is very little time available to teach the theoretical basics; undergraduates may acquire an excellent descriptive knowledge of a language but cannot be expected to be sufficiently equipped with the up-to-date theoretical and analytic tools to engage in postgraduate research on that language. Conversely, undergraduates who have linguistics as a major part of their programme will have the opportunity to explore the application of theoretical and analytic concepts to a range of languages, but may have little time left to develop a thorough knowledge of the history and structure of a given language (with the obvious exception of English) from the point of view of linguistics. Neither of these problems is totally insurmountable, however.

Modern Languages undergraduates may have neither the time nor the inclination to acquire an in-depth knowledge of Minimalist syntax or Optimality Theory in phonology, but that is not to say that linguistic theory cannot, or should not, be brought into undergraduate courses. Books such as Ayres-Bennett and Carruthers (2001) explicitly set out to bridge the gap between theory and the 'meaningless' analysis of data:

> All too often students, even quite advanced students, cling to the belief that linguistics is somehow about 'facts'; we hope to show that the analysis of French is a much more challenging and demanding, but at the same time a much more rewarding, pursuit.
>
> (2001: xvii)

Books in a similar vein have been published on other languages (e.g. Boase-Beier and Lodge 2003, on German) as well as books aimed at the slightly less advanced student which, nevertheless, draw on linguistic theory (e.g. the Routledge series of introductions to the linguistics of particular languages: Battye *et al.* 2000, Lepschy and Lepschy 1988, Russ 1994, Stewart 1999).

Lodge (1993) takes a theoretical framework in macro-sociolinguistics (Haugen's model of standardization) and applies it to the history of French. The existence of a paper presenting a counter-argument to his analysis (Ayres-Bennett 1994) provides the teacher with an ideal opportunity to exercise students' skills in critical argumentation centred on a linguistic topic. These two examples will not make experts in French linguistics of our undergraduates, but they will make them think, and that, surely, is a primary aim of degree-level study.

The converse problem of incorporating knowledge about a Modern Language into a linguistics programme is, perhaps, less easy to remedy. There are very few departments of linguistics in the UK that are fortunate enough to have experts in more than one or two areas of the linguistics of a given language. There are, of course, others that stand alongside Modern Languages departments, but even in these happy situations there are constraints of space within the degree programme, lack of staff time and viability with small numbers of students, which severely limit the scope for a thorough grounding in linguistic theory as well as knowledge of the history and structures of the language they are interested in. We do best to aim to give our students a theoretically informed linguistic knowledge of the language(s) and encourage them to do one of the many good MA courses in general linguistics on offer. For some years it has been difficult to find good candidates for lecturing and research posts in the linguistics of Modern Languages, or even for PhD studentships, so we should be urging our good students to do just that.

Analysing data

The internet has made available huge amounts of linguistic data as well as many analytic tools. Students should be encouraged to take advantage of these and of materials available locally in their examinations of the theoretical and descriptive questions of interest in the language concerned. However, a strong caveat is needed: they must be carefully guided as to how to use both the data and the tools. For example, GoldVarb (Rand and Sankoff 1990, Robinson *et al.* 2001), the user-friendly statistical package widely used by researchers in variationist linguistics, is available freely in versions for Macintosh and PC, with comprehensive instruction manuals, but it is not advisable to recommend these to non-linguistics undergraduates because they need proper training in how to use the package and interpret the results. Nevertheless, some of the principles and terminology can be incorporated into modules on the variationist linguistics of a given language.

Variationist linguistics studies linguistic variables (e.g. variably voiced stop consonants /b, d, g/ in French; Temple 2001) and how their behaviour is conditioned by independent linguistic and extra-linguistic variables (e.g. the position of the variable in the word, the sex of the speaker). One model of teaching this which works well is to give students some background on the sociolinguistic situation of the language in question and explain the principles of linguistic variables as applied to small, closed sets of data, and then to take them step by step through the preparatory stages that are a prerequisite to statistical analysis. Figure 24.3 shows how tokens of the variable mentioned above (/b, d, g/) would be coded for analysis with GoldVarb to assess the effect on the variability of the position the sound appeared in within the word.

Students can be asked (at a relatively late stage) to identify the relevant independent variables that might affect the behaviour of the variable they have chosen to investigate and work out how to code them using a model such as that given in Figure 24.3. This can be an extremely useful way of ensuring that students understand what a linguistic variable actually is. The stages can

	Position in word	
I	word–initial	e.g. *barque*
M	word–medial	e.g. *tabac*
F	word–final	e.g. *crabe*
%	Problematic cases	

Figure 24.3
Illustration of table for the coding of a phonological variable for one independent variable

Figure 24.4 Sample essay guidelines for project on variationist analysis

The essay will consist of roughly the following parts:

- a presentation of treatments of the variable in the prescriptive literature (grammars, dictionaries, pronunciation manuals, etc.)

- an account of research already published on the variable

- your evaluation of the analyses you report

- an outline of a research project (hypotheses to test (or re-test), methodology, etc.), highlighting points of interest and research questions

- a brief pilot study on a small dataset which you collected yourself or taken from a source in the public domain or from data held in the Department.

be organized around lectures and student-led seminars and an essay derived from the whole could form the bulk of the assessment. An extract from the guidelines for a module structured in this way is given in Figure 24.4.

There are various points that must be stressed to students, and this course structure is a helpful way of achieving that. One very important point is that empirical work must be grounded in the literature; the first seminar tasks can be geared towards this aim, getting students to produce bibliographies and preliminary reports on accounts of the variable in the prescriptive and descriptive literature. A second, which applies to other types of linguistic studies too, is that it must be based on a clear hypothesis or hypotheses which can feasibly be tested within the framework; accordingly, a further seminar can profitably be devoted to the presentation and discussion of hypotheses. The relationship between these and the independent variables can be illustrated by the coding exercise illustrated above.

Note

1   Different traditions of linguistics define the notion of complement in different ways.

Sources of information

Association for French Language Studies. Online. Available at: www.north.london met.ac.uk/afls/index.shtml (accessed 13 May 2004).

Deutsche Phonetik (symbols for the transcription of German). Online. Available at: www.obib.de/Schriften/Phonetik/deutsch.html (accessed 13 May 2004).

fənɛtɪks (excellent site at the University of Iowa with explanations of articulatory terms and animated diagrams of production of English and Spanish speech sounds). Online. Available at: www.uiowa.edu/~acadtech/phonetics/about.html (accessed 13 May 2004).

The International Phonetic Association. Online. Available at: www.arts.gla.ac.uk/IPA/ipa.html (accessed 13 May 2004).

Linguistics Association of Great Britain homepage (lots of links to useful sites). Online. Available at: www.lagb.org (accessed 13 May 2004).

Linguistics Association of Great Britain factsheet on Language and Linguistics (by Dick Hudson). Online. Available at: www.phon.ucl.ac.uk/home/dick/ec/facts.htm (accessed 13 May 2004).

SIL International – free downloadable phonetic fonts; information on linguistics, language learning, sociolinguistics; glossaries of linguistic terms (including French–English glossary). Online. Available at: www.sil.org (accessed 13 May 2004).

Grammis: a site of the Institut für Deutsche Sprache devoted to German grammar. Contains a systematic grammar of German and dictionaries of grammatical terms and linguistic terminology. Online. Available at: www.hypermedia.ids-mannheim.de (accessed 13 May 2004).

Various links to German linguistics sites. Online. Available at: www.linguistik.net/cgi-bin/linguistik.pl/selection?u=u&tId0=0&konjunkt (accessed 13 May 2004).

25

Area Studies

Alison Phipps

Area *n.* 1. superficial extent; region; tract. 2. defined space for particular use; subject field. Branch of study; scope, range.

Oxford English Dictionary

What is 'Area Studies'?

Area Studies, like Modern Languages, is a relative newcomer as a disciplinary field. It is made up of an array of sub-fields and disciplines and, like Modern Languages, has recently developed out of administrative convenience as much as academic concerns. In the UK, at least, the managing of categories of academic teaching and learning through networks such as UCAS (Universities and Colleges Admissions Service), the nationwide admissions process for higher education, or through the establishment of subject centres, aimed at developing learning and teaching in so-called cognate areas, has served to bring certain fields of study to the fore.

In this respect, Area Studies and Modern Languages may both be seen to operate as meta-categories of academic study, subsuming vast domains of study such as Africa, America, the Atlantic, German, Chinese and Spanish. To tick the Area Studies box or to tick the Modern Languages box on a university application form will indeed mean entering a 'superficial extent' as our dictionary definition above suggests. However, as Benedict Anderson notes in his now seminal work on the nation state, *Imagined Communities* (Anderson 1991), the human responses to tick boxes on forms can have widespread cultural consequences.

Political expediency and material conditions are important shapers of scholarly lines of questioning. Knowledge of areas and of the languages spoken by those inhabiting the areas is important. Area Studies developed notably during the Cold War, with interest in the Soviet Bloc accompanying an increased study of Russian. However, knowledge, like area, does not remain static and Area Studies today encompasses both geographically imagined territory (see Table 25.1) and discipline-specific concerns.

Recent energy has come to the field of Area Studies through the linking together of those learning and teaching in disparate but related fields. Much of the exemplary and innovative teaching and learning in Area Studies at present arises from this fusion of the traditional, defined space of an academic subject *area* (as outlined in definition 2 from the *OED* above) and (definition 1) the superficial extent or geographical *region*. For instance, American Studies teachers, through discussions of teaching and learning with modern linguists or anthropologists, have come to understand language in new ways, and develop courses and teaching approaches that reflect this.

Perhaps unsurprisingly, in a globalizing world, where 'area' means post-Cold War constellations and subjects are fragmenting, learning and teaching Area Studies is a more fluid affair than it was even in the recent past, seeking definition in ways that mirror the uncertainties of the age. The focus in innovative programmes today is not so much on the study of geo-politics as on themes such as border and boundaries, mobility, transnational migrations, Americanization, the global versus the local, cultural authenticity, language loss, commodification and on questions of cultural and intercultural encounter, reception and representation.

Table 25.1 Area Studies (adapted from: www.lang.ltsn.ac.uk/index.aspx)

Geographic area	Subject area
African	Anthropology
American and Canadian	Art
Asian	Art and Design
Australian	Art History
Chinese	Business
European	Benchmark statement
Latin-American	Cultural Studies
Middle-Eastern	Economics
Russian and East European	Film Studies
South-East Asian	Geography
	History
	International Relations
	Literature
	Performing Arts
	Philosophy
	Politics
	Sociology

Where do we start?

Given this development we have an interesting paradox as teachers of Area Studies. How do we teach something as seemingly static as 'area' when the intellectual field is focused on fluidity, process and mobility? The answer comes in acknowledging the fundamental shifts in the field from knowing about an area or the content of a discipline – Germany's Economic Miracle, the Berlin Wall, the New German Cinema movement, German as spoken within Germany or Austria or Switzerland, German as encountered in Goethe, Schiller, Schlegel – to handling knowledge and responses to knowledge as part of the learning process. Germany, to continue our example, under such a view, is encountered through German migration to America, German is spoken in a host of international tourist sites, intercultural communication is a constant of everyday life in Germany, be it through international trade, music, food, literature or translation. To understand the area – German-speaking Europe, Germany, Austria, Switzerland, the Border Region of Lake Constance – the starting point is not the region itself but different thematic constellations, or meeting points, acting as lenses onto cultural behaviours.

Such an approach to teaching Area Studies does not require the teacher to deliver a host of facts and figures relating to knowledge of the area, but rather to develop the critical faculties and identities of students as explorers, wayfinders, translators, cultural critics and cultural producers. In short, traditional cognitive pedagogic techniques need to complement other experiential methods. Luckily, in an interdisciplinary field such as Area Studies there are plenty of related disciplines from which practical approaches to knowledge gathering and analysis may be learned. Anthropology, geography and ethnography are obvious places to start, given their long traditions of field work.

How could you start to apply such approaches to your own domain?

A place to start applying thematic, critical and interdisciplinary approaches to Area Studies is with everyday life and popular culture. A theme that excites both the teacher and the learner and can bear the weight of investigation; a theme where there is an attendant literature and scope for critical analysis drawing on different disciplinary perspectives. Rubbish is one such theme. Readings from the anthropologist Kay Milton (Milton 1996) and Mary Douglas (Douglas 1966), coupled with specific internet searches of topics such as recycling in Germany, the US, Africa, etc., can provide the basis for group discussion and learning. Critical texts are not always easy texts. Individual readings identifying concerns, questions and difficulties that students discuss in groups and then bring collectively into a plenary discussion can help build confidence and fluidity in discussing new concepts such as 'discourse', 'taboo', 'purity', 'risk' and 'civilization'. Internet searches, or interviews with students from the area under investigation, can also help students to see semi-structured or ethnographic interviews as methods for gathering knowledge and understanding. They also enable a discussion of ethical issues involved in the collection of useful data and of the discourse and language in practice. For students of languages this also provides a way of developing vocabulary in action.

Examples of pedagogic approaches

A key element in many undergraduate Area Studies programmes, from Modern Languages through to American or African Studies, is that of a period of residence abroad or of field work. This may be an intensively taught residential programme of work or a year-long student exchange. These are important, liminal learning times for students, outside of the formal classroom structures, enabling trial and error with the practice of gathering knowledge and analysing it. They are usually highly memorable aspects of undergraduate courses, seen by students and by staff as important formative experiences, where attitudes, values and behaviours are shaped and risks can be taken. There has been some debate (Coleman 2001b) about the actual outcomes of resi-dence abroad (see Chapter 15), and it has led to the development of more integrated and reflective study of such experience.

Ethnography, whether it involves keeping a reflective journal, participant observation, or various forms of interviewing, is a key element in the develop-ment of reflective, integrated programmes of Area Studies. A full discussion of the use of ethnography in the Modern Languages curriculum can be found in Roberts *et al.* (2001).

Using ethnographic approaches is not without difficulty, however. Students are not actually doing a full research project and being ethnographers but, rather, using ethnographic modes of research pragmatically, as a means of developing their own active identities as Americanists, Africanists or Germanists. To be an Americanist no longer necessarily means having a full knowledge of American literature or a grasp of American politics, it also involves knowing how to work within the culture, to critically evaluate what may be termed American behav-iours and, crucially, to understand one's own biases and one's own position in making evaluations.

To enable students to develop in such an experiential way can be risky. It involves inviting students to examine and question their own common-sense assumptions and their own relationship to a culture or an area. This is an inter-cultural process, and a critical one. It can be troubling. It also involves the teacher in devolving power for the learning process to the students, accepting that some of what students will discover will be outside of one's own area of expertise, that team teaching may be necessary. It does not make for neatly tickable boxes of aims and outcomes. Assessment is the subject of much debate (Byram 1997), and it is often a slow, messy process of developing ways of being intercultural. Higher education is not in the business of the quick and easy solution.

Ways forward: imaginative approaches

The active engagement of skilful Area Studies students is shaped through the development of a critical relationship between process and subject. Knowledge of an area is important. As the discipline responds to globalizing and localizing pressures, and derives energy from the attitudes of Cultural Studies, there are innovative opportunities for the subjects that are the focus of Area Studies. Table 25.1 above shows the relationship between Area Studies and subject disciplines. Table 25.2 charts some alternative, innovative starting points and constellations for the development of Area Studies knowledges.

Such approaches clearly require intercultural, comparative and interdisciplinary approaches. They highlight the shifting nature of knowledge and cultural construction, and draw on theoretical work ranging from post-colonial studies through anthropology and geography and into Modern Languages. They demonstrate the actuality of change in Area Studies as both practical and theoretical concerns come together to reshape research as pedagogy and break open the curriculum.

Table 25.2 Alternative constellations of themes and geography in Area Studies

Geographic area	Theme
Atlantic	Borders
Baltic	Translation
Pacific	Migration
Celtic	Material culture
Andean	Kinship and genealogy
Oil nations	Cultural approaches to rubbish
First nations	Bilingualism
Former colonies	Tourism

Two case studies

These are activities you might try out with your students to help develop their awareness of key issues in Area Studies.

Case study 1: **When is an area not an area?**

Search the websites of selected airports in your area. What common features do you find in each? What are the key differences? Are these really differences? What can a traveller do in the airports?

Now discuss your findings in small groups and present your consensus on key themes and differences orally to the rest of the class.

Reading: Non-Places: introduction to an anthropology of supermodernity by Marc Augé (Augé 1995).

Discuss the reading in groups and consider how the concept of 'non-places' might illuminate the findings of the search.

Case study 2: **Where is the area?**

Task: Map the geographical extent of the area today and then at key points in history. Now map the cultural reach of the area, noting clusters of diaspora, etc.

Discuss your findings in small groups and prepare a poster presentation of this mapping exercise.

Reading: Signifying Identities: anthropological perspectives on boundaries and contested values by Anthony Cohen (Cohen 2000).

How does the discussion of boundaries aid an understanding of the geographical, cultural and political extent of the area?

Sources of information

The Area Studies pages of the Subject Centre for Languages, Linguistics and Area Studies provide a portal and fund of information, events, workshops, newsletter items, etc., serving those teaching Area Studies. Online. Available at: www.lang.ltsn.ac.uk/index.aspx (accessed 29 April 2004).

See also ATLAS: The Area Studies Project Bulletin. Online. Available at: www.lang.ltsn. ac.uk/news/newsitem.aspx?resourceid=1635 (accessed 17 May 2004).

26

Literary Studies

Diana Holmes and David Platten

University teaching of Modern Languages (ML) was modelled, for most of the twentieth century, on that of classical languages: until at least the later 1970s, the majority of ML degree programmes were composed of language study, which involved a great deal of literary translation, and a set of largely period-based courses in literature that demanded extensive reading[1] (see also Chapter 1). Over the past two to three decades, things have changed. At the beginning of the twenty-first century, a typical ML degree – at least in the UK and the US – offers non- or only partially literature-based language courses, together with options in some or all of the following: politics, history, linguistics, specialized language, film, gender, popular culture – and literature, organized as often by theme, genre or the class/ethnicity/gender of authors as by period, and requiring students to read far fewer texts.

▶ Before reading any further, reflect for a moment on whether the widespread downgrading of literary studies has been necessary and inevitable.
▶ Do you believe it has had any positive effects on the study of Modern Languages and on language learning?
▶ What has been its most negative impact?

The demotion of literature from its central position in ML degrees lends itself to two different interpretations, both of which will be familiar to anyone involved in university ML teaching. The first is upbeat, a narrative of progress and positive change. According to this account of events, literature was never the most effective way to provide students with a high level of linguistic competence supported by a close understanding of another culture; rather, it was studied on the elitist, rarely articulated and erroneous assumption that 'high' culture represented the quintessence of national identity, and that exposure to this culture produced well-informed, properly educated graduates. A study of the history, political institutions, contemporary debates and conflicts, and popular culture of a nation provides a far better and more relevant education: we have moved on from the Dark Ages when the desire to become fully fluent in, for example, French led to tussling with sixteenth-century sonnets and translating Proust.

The opposing narrative is one of decline, cheap popularization and surrender to increasingly anti-intellectual and materialist generations of students. The study of literature demanded critical and analytical thought, sensitivity to language, engagement with the past rather than the reduction of all otherness to the familiar same. Extensive reading enriched students' language as well as their intellectual and emotional range: in effect, we have 'dumbed down' to more descriptive, spoon-fed, over-packaged modules that demand minimal intellectual effort. We are pandering to the prejudices of a generation that has been educationally encouraged and financially forced into a passively consumerist view of education, a generation that demands automatic high grades in exchange for investing the correct amount of time and effort, and rejects the reading of challenging texts as difficult and irrelevant.

Like most totalizing accounts of social change, both of these are a mixture of truth and misrepresentation: the chronology and the nature of change have been far more complex than either allow for. Literature-based degrees were not all alike, and not necessarily complacent in their assumptions: in the late 1960s French departments in the 'new' universities (such as Sussex) were team-teaching the intricate relationships between literature, history and competing senses of national identity, in ways that would seem progressive in many departments now. The demand-led move to a non-literary curriculum has only been partial: though the polytechnics (starting up around 1968 and becoming universities in 1992) pioneered new degrees that integrated language study with 'area' studies or business studies, many of them also continued to teach literature and to find an enthusiastic student audience for interdisciplinary courses on, for example, 'literature and ideology' or 'France and the 1914–18 war'. Meanwhile, most of the older universities were remarkably resistant to change, and have continued to provide a mainly literary curriculum up to – at least in the cases of Oxford and Cambridge – the present day. The employment-oriented student of the optimistic narrative is the same creature as the book-shy consumer of the pessimists; she or he undoubtedly exists, but the evidence does not support the view that student demand is leading inexorably to the demise of literary studies as a component of ML degrees. In their recent, extremely useful articles on the state of literature teaching in UK French departments, Gabriel Jacobs, Catherine Rodgers and Alan Watkins chart the reality of fewer literary options, reduction in the number, length and range of texts, and students' declining knowledge of French culture, but they also find counter-evidence in the fact that students display continuing enthusiasm for extra-curricular reading, a general belief in the relevance of literature to their lives, and a marked willingness to opt for precisely those departments where literature continues to form a compulsory component of the French Studies curriculum (Jacobs et al. 2002, and forthcoming).[2]

This latter point is worth exploring, because it introduces an important cluster of questions about the connection between teaching and research, and about which students, amid the national decline in the advanced study of languages, are continuing to opt for, and being given access to, ML study at university level. Jacobs et al. demonstrate the clear correlation between high Research Assessment Exercise scores in French, and a high degree of literariness in the undergraduate curriculum. The fact is that the most traditional, best-funded universities in the UK – those with a well-established research culture and what the French sociologist Bourdieu would call a high quota of 'cultural capital' to impart – have the most literary French (and no doubt other ML) departments, and that they also have the highest level of student demand for places. The class connotations of Oxbridge, Bristol, Durham, Nottingham – and even of Manchester or Leeds, as well as the facilities they offer, mean that they attract a high level of applications particularly from the private and selective grammar school sectors. Students are apparently undeterred by the prospect of some literary study, and they benefit from being taught by academics actively researching in the area they teach. Meanwhile, what were once highly innovative and thriving ex-polytechnic departments of languages are, at best, shrinking into beleaguered servicing departments and, at worst, have already closed down (see also Chapter 1). These departments, the most successful at 'widening participation' by attracting non-standard applicants, are least likely to offer any literature teaching, and least likely (particularly if the threat of even more selective research funding is realized) to be able to provide teachers who are also funded, active researchers. The reduction in student demand for languages has hit the 'vocational', 'relevant' departments hardest. If this is encouraging in the sense that it appears to undermine any belief in the inexorable decline of literary studies, it is also dispiriting in that it probably has a lot more to do with class than with curriculum. Languages are disciplines that produce highly employable graduates and culturally aware, adaptable people – and they are in danger of becoming disciplines mainly reserved for an upper middle-class elite. The argument against the separation of teaching from research goes well beyond the remit of this chapter; the argument for the continuing inclusion of literary studies in all departments of languages – and not just in the elite ones – is where we now want to turn, before offering some suggestions about learning and teaching strategies.

> ► Summarize – or, if you are new to a department, ask colleagues to summarize for you – the direction of recent curriculum changes. What factors drove them? What do colleagues feel about them? What has their impact been on student take-up of options?
> ► On the basis of experience, both as a student and as a teacher, what approaches to learning and teaching literature do you favour?

Why does it matter that we maintain literary studies as one central component of ML studies? First of all, though we might scoff now at the long unchallenged assumption that literature was the *only* route to advanced language study, it is the case that reading a variety of intelligent, imaginative, stylistically fluent writing familiarizes us with good practice, allows us to internalize modes of expression and even grammatical accuracy. The language of the literary text is, arguably, the one mode of discourse that is free of jargon. It may be plain or obscure, conventional or colloquial, literal or metaphorical. It is usually rich in lexical content and often exemplary in terms of grammar and syntax. The literary text will always be an inexhaustible resource for any student who seeks to deepen and broaden his or her knowledge of a foreign language. This is not to suggest that a literary training is a prerequisite for the production of successful linguists but, rather, that the successful linguist tends to be an avid reader. Second, one of the great advantages of language studies is surely that it broadens perspectives, allows us to inhabit an alternative linguistic and cultural construction of reality, enables an empathetic understanding of difference. The intensity of the one-to-one relationship between reader and text (novel, poem, essay, play) means, for example, that a male reader can get inside a female character's sense of the world, or a straight reader into the head of a gay character, or a white, middle-class English girl into the sense of self of a veiled, middle-aged Muslim woman. And a sensitive understanding of difference goes hand-in-hand with a recognition of sameness, of what people have in common across different cultures and different periods of history. In our own department, for example, the Level 1 course includes the study of Racine's *Phèdre*, and the lectures on the play emphasize the ways in which students, too, may well have experienced love, jealousy, conflict between duty and passion, or between family pressures and desire. Cultural and historical difference are not minimized, but the play provides the opportunity to demonstrate how students' concerns form part of a human continuum over space and time, not, as the colleague who lectures on *Phèdre* puts it, 'a continuum that is entirely the same, but one which has points of contact with the present and even more interestingly valuable areas of difference'.[3] And, finally, to return to the more practical and vocational concerns of students and institutions, a successful ML graduate needs to have acquired at least some of the cultural baggage of an educated native speaker of their second language. In most European countries, and certainly in France, this means a degree of familiarity with the literary past and present.

If we accept the desirability of continuing to teach foreign literatures, how can we best do this in the difficult climate of the new century? The constraints outlined above in the 'decline and fall' version of the story are very real:

- Students are more reluctant to read in an increasingly visual and computerized culture, and under the pressure of the need to combine study with paid work.
- Even those who have studied the language to advanced level before entering university begin degree studies ill-prepared for tackling literature, since the topic-based nature of language A levels encourages a view of the text as a functional source of information, diminishing the intellectual demands on the student and emphasizing the capacity for expression in the target language over the quality of what is expressed.
- Students are also understandably anxious about the immediate 'relevance' of what they choose to study (though the continuing high demand for degrees in English literature suggests that this is not an insuperable obstacle).

The authors of the 'Requiem for French Studies' article found that the near-universal response had been a massive reduction in the demands made on students, in terms of the amount of both primary and secondary reading. Adaptation to the real conditions of contemporary students' lives is clearly sensible, but in departments across the UK (and no doubt elsewhere) more proactive strategies are also being used to persuade students of the value of literary studies, and to make literature central to contemporary, 'relevant' languages degrees.

The French department at the University of Leeds will be our example here, not only because we work there and thus have detailed knowledge of its curriculum and teaching practices, but also because as one of the largest departments in the country, in a very popular university, it has retained more freedom to design, test and adapt its curriculum than have the many smaller departments that suffer from conflicting institutional imperatives to, on the one hand, attract students in a declining market and, on the other, impose strict economies that reduce the options on offer and, in many cases, lose language-specific options altogether. Therefore, we will be concentrating here on the case of degree programmes designed for well-qualified, post-A level students; the place of literature on non-specialist programmes raises a partially different set of questions.

Leeds has between 250 and 300 students in each year's cohort, about 50 of whom are Single Honours: Level 1 courses are compulsory for all students, Levels 2 and 3 make language modules compulsory, but otherwise offer a wide range of options in all areas of French Studies. As part of a Widening

Participation strategy, we have established links with local secondary schools and offer 'Master Classes' for A level students that include some literature – but like other departments in the UK, we can assume no prior experience of literary study in most of our students. We will pick out four aspects of the curriculum here to illustrate approaches that seem to be working:

- the interdisciplinary foundational course at level 1;
- the use of information technology (IT);
- the predominance of a 'cultural studies' approach;
- a new module in which experimental learning/teaching methods are currently being piloted.

All students of French follow a compulsory, year-long introductory course entitled *Resistance and Desire*, which brings together history, politics, literature and film in the study of French national and cultural identity. The texts are mainly canonical, range from the seventeenth to the late twentieth century, take in the genres of novel, political tract, essay, play and poetry, and include the category of non-metropolitan francophone literature. They are also (as the module title suggests) thematically linked, and chosen for their capacity to engage the heart as well as the brain. The reasons for studying literary texts (as set out above) are clearly articulated to students at the start of the module: the aim is to convince them both of the pleasure and relevance of literary study, and of their own ability to read closely and analyse effectively. Central to this aim are lectures free of obfuscatory jargon, and seminars in which students' views are both taken seriously, and widened out by reference to existing critical perspectives.

The thematic structure of the course precludes a chronological, century-by-century approach. And yet, as Jacobs *et al.* (2002) argue, students need some sense of the history both of nation and of national culture, in order to make informed choices about future options, and because such a framework is part of the knowledge a fully literate, advanced speaker of the target language should have. This is where IT first appears in a literary context: alongside the lecture and seminar programme, all students are required to read from a pre-scribed list of histories of France and French literature – some of these from web sources – and to complete two computerized multiple-choice question-naires that test this knowledge, and contribute to formal assessment of the mod-ule. This seems to be working as a relatively painless way to acquire a broad 'map' of both political and cultural history. In later options, IT is used in a number of ways: a dedicated computer-assisted language learning programme provides a working knowledge of Old French for the options in medieval lit-erature; some modules provide web pages containing supplementary materials and links, as well as notice-boards on which students may communicate with each other and the tutor.

Notwithstanding such initiatives, a majority of French students at Leeds University opt, wherever possible, for non-literary modules. Two lecturers have recently taken this perceived indifference to the study of literature as the starting-point in their development of a new module: The Twentieth-Century French Novel. They identified two key inhibiting factors. Many students find their initial contact with a literary work an unsettling experience, especially when the work in question may be perceived as a difficult novel written in a foreign language. Then, worried and disappointed at their inability to read the text fluently or productively, they find themselves listening to 'contextualizing' lectures that seem to have, at best, a tangential relationship to what they have just read. In an attempt to alleviate these problems, the twin modes of course delivery, lecture and seminar, have been revised. Lectures now target more precisely the set texts, elaborate original readings, and are intended to be more partisan, polemical even, in order to emphasize that there is no such thing as a 'right' or 'wrong' interpretation, rather that the literary text should be a site for conflicting readings. The historical context for each novel is provided in written form for the students, either electronically or in hard copy.

Second, the lecturers have carefully plotted a programme of seminars that addresses the needs of the students by helping to develop their reading and analytical skills. The seminars fall into three categories or types – 'student-led' seminars, 'bridging' seminars and 'tutor-led' seminars – all of which revolve around pre-prepared worksheets based on selected extracts from each set text. The first of these, the 'student-led' seminar, takes place in the absence of the tutor. Students are encouraged to share problems of comprehension with their peers in an unthreatening environment and, prompted by the questions on the worksheet, exchange their ideas on the passage. They are required to minute their discussion and subsequently forward copies of these minutes to members of the group and to the seminar tutor. In the next 'bridging' seminar, their previous discussion is reviewed in the light of the minutes, before they embark on a new discussion, centred on a different passage, in the presence this time of the tutor. In the final, 'tutor-led' seminar, the group tackles a more challenging passage, and the discussion, which is now orchestrated by the tutor, ideally broadens out so as to encompass other themes and aspects of the novel.

At the time of writing, this module is being delivered for the first time. Informal student responses have been positive. They find the more targeted, 'spiky' lectures useful and stimulating, and the system of graduated seminars has not only engendered a spirit of co-operation and trust within the groups but has also facilitated discussion and debate of a high quality. It is hoped that the value of this collaborative work will be borne out in forthcoming 'Group Presentations' that will form part of the formal assessment of the module.

The development of this module received support from an internal fund established to promote 'blue skies' thinking about learning and teaching. There is a presumption that the allocation of financial resources to teaching development requires the introduction of new technology. In this instance, the lecturers felt that obvious steps to 'sex up' the teaching of literature in a foreign language would be counterproductive, since the introduction of teaching gadgets would inevitably detract from the mission and seems at odds with the nature of the literary experience. Thus, in the preparation stages a concerted attempt was made to focus on pedagogy rather than cosmetic presentation. Likewise, any temptation to reshape the literary canon by drafting in examples of a more popular idiom were resisted; on the contrary, the lecturers did not fight shy of choosing supposedly difficult texts such as *Combray*, the first part of the first volume of Proust's *À la Recherche du Temps Perdu* despite much head-wagging on the part of some experienced colleagues. So far, so good.

In conclusion then, the reduction in numbers of students choosing to do languages, and the institutional difficulties this creates, is pushing us towards an increasingly cautious, apologetic stance on literature teaching that may actually represent a retreat from the practice of the more progressive departments in the 1960s and 1970s. Yet literary studies are a vital component of the practical/vocational as well as the academic/intellectual value of higher education language study, and our experience justifies a cautious optimism about students' willingness to be persuaded of this.

Notes

1   The starting point for this chapter was a talk given by Diana Holmes ('Critical questions: literature and French Studies in the 2000s') at a day conference organized by the Languages, Linguistics and Area Studies Subject Centre at CILT, London, in June 2003. The day was entitled 'Set texts? New approaches to the teaching of literature in languages and area/related studies', and the papers delivered, and the discussion among participants, also contributed to the arguments above.

2   We are grateful to the authors for allowing us to read an advance copy of the second article.

3   Thanks to colleagues in Leeds University's Department of French, and particularly to Russell Goulbourne, Ros Brown-Grant, Paul Rowe and Nigel Saint for their contributions, both to the case for literary studies and to the suggestions for teaching strategies. The comment on teaching *Phèdre* comes from Russell Goulbourne.

Sources of information

Entering 'Literature' in the 'Browse by Keyword' section of the website of the Subject Centre for Languages, Linguistics and Area Studies will produce a wealth of links on literary studies in a range of languages. Online. Available at: www.ltsn.ac.uk/resources (accessed 17 May 2004).

References

Adam, H., Atkinson, T., Butcher, C., Deepwell, F., Hall, K., Tidd, U. and Walker, L. (2001) 'Learning from experience: initial training in six universities' in J. Klapper (ed.) *Teaching Languages in Higher Education: issues in training and continuing professional development*, London: CILT.

Adamson, R., Coutin, M.-Th., Hare, G. E., Lang, M., Lodge, A., Mason, I., Taylor, S. S. B., Wakely, R. and Walker, A. L. (1980) *Le Français en Faculté*, London: Hodder and Stoughton.

Adger, D. (2002) 'Why theory is essential: the relationship between theory, analysis and data'. Online. Available at: www.lang.ltsn.ac.uk/resources/goodpractice.aspx?resource id=405 (accessed 12 May 2004).

Alderson, C. J. (2000) *Assessing Reading*, Cambridge: Cambridge University Press.

—— and Wall, D. (1993) 'Does washback exist?', *Applied Linguistics*, 14: 115–29.

——, Clapham, C. and Steel, D. (1997) 'Metalinguistic knowledge, language aptitude and language proficiency', *Language Teaching Research*, 1: 93–121.

Allen, C. and Graham, S. (1995) 'Enabling learner autonomy through independent learning at higher stages' in *Fifth National Institution-Wide Languages Programmes Conference Proceedings*, Nottingham: Nottingham Trent University.

ALTE (The Association of Language Testers in Europe) (2004) Online. Available at: www.alte.org (accessed 6 February 2004).

Anderson, B. (1991) *Imagined Communities: reflections on the origin and spread of nationalism*, London and New York: Verso.

Anderson, J. (1983) *The Architecture of Cognition*, Cambridge: Cambridge University Press.

Arnold, J. (1999) *Affect in Language Learning*, Cambridge: Cambridge University Press.

Arthur, L. and Hurd, S. (2001) *Supporting Lifelong Language Learning*, London: CILT, in association with The Open University.

Atkinson, R. and Raugh, M. (1975) 'An application of the mnemonic keyword method to the acquisition of Russian vocabulary', *Journal of Experimental Psychology: Human Learning and Memory*, 1: 126–33.

Augé, M. (1995) *Non-Places: introduction to an anthropology of supermodernity*, London and New York: Verso.

Ayres-Bennett, W. (1994) 'Elaboration and codification: standardization and attitudes towards the French language in the sixteenth and seventeenth centuries' in M. M. Parry, W. V. Davies and R. A. M. Temple (eds) *The Changing Voices of Europe*, Cardiff: University of Wales Press.

—— and Carruthers, J., with Temple, R. A. M. (2001) *Problems and Perspectives: studies in the modern French language*, Harlow: Longman.

Bailey, K. M. (1998) *Learning about Language Assessment: dilemmas, decisions and directions*, Boston: Heinle and Heinle.

Barthes, R. (1957) *Mythologies, Pierres vives*, Paris: Seuil.

—— (1973) *Mythologies*. Translated by A. Lavers, London: Paladin.

Bartlett, F. C. (1932) *Remembering: a study in experimental and social psychology*, Cambridge: Cambridge University Press.

Bassnett, S. (2000) 'Comment', *The Independent (Education)*, 23 November: 2.

Battye, A., Hintze, M.-A. and Rowlett, P. (2000) *The French Language Today*, 2nd edn, London: Routledge.

Baume, D. (2001) *A Briefing on Assessment of Portfolios*, LTSN Generic Centre Assessment Series, York: LTSN.

Beaton, A., Gruneberg, M. and Ellis, N. (1995) 'Retention of foreign vocabulary learned using the key-word method: a ten year follow-up', *Second Language Research*, 11: 112–20.

Beavan, C. (2000) 'Icons or iconoclasm? The case for multimedia technologies in language learning' in M. Fay and D. Ferney (eds) *Current Trends in Modern Languages Provision for Non-Specialist Linguists*, London: CILT/APU.

Benson, P. (1996) 'Concepts of autonomy in language learning' in R. Pemberton, E. Li, W. Or and H. Pierson (eds) *Taking Control: autonomy in language learning*, Hong Kong: Hong Kong University Press.

—— (2001) *Teaching and Researching Autonomy in Language Learning*, Harlow, Essex: Longman/Pearson Education.

—— and Voller, P. (1997) 'Introduction: autonomy and independence in language learning' in P. Benson and P. Voller (eds) *Autonomy and Independence in Language Learning*, London: Longman.

Bloomfield, L. (1933) *Language*, New York: Holt.

Boase-Beier, J. and Lodge, K. (2003) *The German Language. A Linguistic Introduction*, Oxford: Blackwell.

Borrás, I. and Lafayette, R. (1994) 'Effects of multimedia courseware subtitling on speaking performance of college students', *The Modern Language Journal*, 78: 61–75.

BP-BLTM (2004) Website of the project Best Practice – Best Language Teaching Methods. Online. Available at: www.languages.dk/methods (accessed 12 February 2004).

Brammerts, H. (1996) 'Tandem language learning via the internet and the International E-Mail Tandem Network' in D. Little and H. Brammerts (eds) *A Guide to Language Learning in Tandem via the Internet*, Dublin: Centre for Language and Communication Studies, Trinity College Dublin.

—— (2003) 'Autonomous language learning in tandem: the development of a concept' in T. Lewis and L. Walker (eds) *Autonomous Language Learning in Tandem*, Sheffield: Academy Electronic Publications.

Brennan, J., Williams, R. and Blaskó, Z. (2003) *The English Degree and Graduate Careers*, English Subject Centre. Online. Available at: www.english.ltsn.ac.uk/resources/general/publications/reports/gradcareers.pdf (accessed 7 June 2004).

Brett, P. (1994) 'Using text reconstruction software', *ELT Journal*, 48: 329–36.

British National Corpus (1997) Online. Available at: www.info.ox.ac.uk/bnc/what/index.html (accessed 21 May 2004).

Broady, E. (2000) 'Second language writing in a computer environment: A different kind of writing? A different kind of teaching?' in E. Broady (ed.) *Second Language Writing in a Computer Environment*, London: CILT/AFLS.

—— (2002) *Teaching Languages with Audio and Video*. Online (password required). Available at: www.delphi.bham.ac.uk/modules.htm (accessed 12 May 2004).

—— and Kenning, M.-M. (1996) 'Learner autonomy: an introduction to the issues' in E. Broady and M.-M. Kenning (eds) *Promoting Learner Autonomy in University Language Teaching*, London: AFLS/CILT.

—— and Meinhof, U. (1995) *Télé-textes*, Oxford: Oxford University Press.

—— and Shade, M. (1996) *Tele con textos*, Oxford: Oxford University Press.

Brown, G. (2001) *Assessment: a guide for lecturers*, LTSN Generic Centre Assessment Series No. 3, York: LTSN.

——, Anderson, A., Shillcock, R. and Yule, G. (1984) *Teaching Talk*, Cambridge: Cambridge University Press.

Brumfit, C. (1984) *Communicative Methodology in Language Teaching*, Cambridge: Cambridge University Press.

—— and Johnson, K. (eds) (1979) *The Communicative Approach to Language Teaching*, Oxford: Oxford University Press.

Buck, G. (1992) 'Translation as a testing procedure: does it work?', *Language Testing*, 9: 123–48.

—— (2001) *Assessing Listening*, Cambridge: Cambridge University Press.

Burns, R. (ed.) (1995) *German Cultural Studies: an introduction*, Oxford: Oxford University Press.

Business Education Support Team (2000) *Managing Better: UK business schools today and tomorrow: issues and challenges*, Milton Keynes: Learning and Teaching Support Network, Open University Business School.

Bygate, M. (2001) 'Effects of task repetition on the structure and control of oral language' in M. Bygate, P. Skehan and M. Swain (eds) *Researching Pedagogic Tasks: second language learning, teaching and testing*, Harlow: Longman.

Byram, M. (1997) *Teaching and Assessing Intercultural Communicative Competence*, Clevedon: Multilingual Matters.

—— (ed.) (2000) *Routledge Encyclopedia of Language Teaching and Learning*, London: Routledge.

—— and Zarate, G. (eds) (1997) *The Sociocultural and Intercultural Dimension of Language Learning and Teaching*, Strasbourg: Council of Europe.

Byrne, N. (2002) *Communitec, National Teaching Fellowship Project*. Online. Available at: www.lse.ac.uk/Depts/language/Communitec/HTML/frame.htm (accessed 5 February 2004).

Canale, M. and Swain, M. (1980) 'Theoretical bases of communicative approaches to second language teaching and testing', *Applied Linguistics*, 1: 1–47.

Candlin, C. and Murphy, D. (1987) *Language Learning Tasks*, Englewood Cliffs, NJ: Prentice Hall.

Carroll, J. B. (1979) 'Psychometric approaches to the study of language abilities' in C. J. Fillmore, D. Kempler and W. S.-Y. Wang (eds) *Individual Differences in Language Ability and Language Behaviour*, New York: Academic Press.

Carty, T. and O'Connell, F. (1998) 'But what is a preposition? Grammar learning in a comparative perspective' in *Proceedings of the Institution-Wide Languages Programmes' 7th National Conference*, Sheffield: Sheffield Hallam University.

Chomsky, N. (1957) *Syntactic Structures*, The Hague: Mouton.

—— (1965) *Aspects of the Theory of Syntax*, Cambridge, MA: MIT Press.

Chun, D. M. (1994) 'Using computer networking to facilitate the acquisition of interactive competence', *System*, 22: 17–31.

CIEL Language Support Network (2000) 'Assessment and independent language learning'. Online. Available at: www.lang.ltsn.ac.uk/resources/goodpractice.aspx?resourceid=14 07#toc_bib (accessed 6 February 2004).

CIEL Project (2000a) *CIEL Project Handbook 1, Integrating Independent Learning with the Curriculum* in the Subject Centre for Languages, Linguistics and Area Studies *Good Practice Guide*. Online. Available at: www.lang.ltsn.ac.uk/resources/guidecontents.aspx (accessed 20 June 2004).

—— (2000b) *CIEL Project Handbook 3, Resources for Independent Language Learning: design and use* in the Subject Centre for Languages, Linguistics and Area Studies *Good Practice Guide*. Online. Available at: www.lang.ltsn.ac.uk/resources/guidecontents.aspx (accessed 20 June 2004).

CILT, ALL and UCML (2003) *Language Trends 2003*. Online. Available at: www.cilt. org.uk/trends2003.htm (accessed 7 June 2004).

CILT/TES (2002) *Key Stage 4 Provision in MFL: outline results from CILT/TES survey – autumn 2002*. Online. Available at: www.cilt.org.uk/news/latest/ks4survey1.rtf (accessed 17 May 2004).

Clahsen, H., Meisel, J. and Pienemann, M. (1983) *Deutsch als Zweitsprache. Der Spracherwerb ausländischer Arbeiter*, Tübingen: Gunter Narr.

CML (2003) Web-based placement tests of the Centre for Modern Languages, University of Birmingham. Online. Available at: www.cml.bham.ac.uk/test/ (accessed 6 April 2004).

Cohen, A. D. (1998) *Strategies in Learning and Using a Second Language*, Harlow, Essex: Longman.

Cohen, A. P. (2000) *Signifying Identities: anthropological perspectives on boundaries and contested values*, London and New York: Routledge.

Coleman, J. A. (1996) *Studying Languages: a survey of British and European students. The proficiency, background, attitudes and motivations of students of foreign languages in the United Kingdom and Europe*, London: Centre for Information on Language Teaching and Research.

—— (1997) 'Residence abroad within language study', *Language Teaching*, 30: 1–20.

—— (2000) 'Video in university language teaching' in T. Lewis and A. Rouxeville (eds) *Technology and the Advanced Language Learner*, London: CILT/AFLS.

—— (2001a) 'Lessons for the future: evaluating FDTL languages' in J. A. Coleman, D. Ferney, D. Head and R. Rix (eds) *Language Learning Futures: issues and strategies for modern languages provision in higher education*, London: CILT.

—— (2001b) 'What is residence abroad for? Intercultural competence and the linguistic, cultural, academic, personal and professional objectives of student residence abroad' in R. Di Napoli, L. Polezzi and A. King (eds) *Fuzzy Boundaries? Reflections on modern languages and the humanities*, London: CILT.

—— (2004) 'Modern languages in British universities: past and present', *Arts and Humanities in Higher Education*, 3: 147–62.

—— and Parker, G. (1992) *French and the Enterprise Path: developing transferable and professional skills*, London: AFLS/CILT.

—— and Parker, L. (2001) 'Preparing for residence abroad: staff development implications' in J. Klapper (ed.) *Teaching Languages in Higher Education. Issues in training and continuing professional development*, London: CILT.

Connell, T. (2002) *Languages and Employability. A question of careers*. Online. Available at: www.cilt.org.uk/careers/pdf/reports/employability.pdf (accessed 7 June 2004).

—— (2004) *Longitudinal Surveys of Employment Among Language Graduates*. Online. Available at: www.cilt.org.uk/careers/research/connell04.rtf (accessed 7 June 2004).

Corder, S. P. (1967) 'Error analysis' in S. P. Corder and P. Allen (eds) *The Edinburgh Course in Applied Linguistics, Volume 3*, Oxford: Oxford University Press.

Council of Europe (2001) *A Common European Framework of Reference for Languages: learning, teaching, assessment*, Cambridge: Cambridge University Press. Online. Available at: www. coe.int/T/E/Cultural_Cooperation/education/Languages/Language_Policy/Common _Framework_of_Reference/default.asp (accessed 23 April 2004).

Council of Europe Committee of Ministers (1998) *Recommendation No. R (98) 6 of the Committee of Ministers to Member States Concerning Modern Languages*, 17 March 1998. Online. Available at: www.cm.coe.int/ta/rec/1998/98r6.htm (accessed 23 April 2004).

Crookes, G. and Schmidt, R. W. (1991) 'Motivation: reopening the research agenda', *Language Learning*, 41: 469–512.

Cummins, J. (1980) 'The cross-lingual dimensions of language proficiency: implications for bilingual education and the optimal age issue', *TESOL Quarterly*, 14: 175–87.

Dam, L. (2003) 'Developing learner autonomy: the teacher's responsibility' in D. Little, J. Ridley and E. Ushioda (eds) *Learner Autonomy in the Foreign Language Classroom: teacher, learner, curriculum and assessment*, Dublin: Authentik.

Danan, M. (1992) 'Reversed sub-titling and dual coding theory: new directions for foreign language instruction', *Language Learning*, 42: 497–527.

d'Anna, C., Zechmeister, E. and Hall, J. (1991) 'Towards a meaningful definition of vocabulary size', *Journal of Reading Behaviour: A Journal of Literacy*, 23: 109–22.

Davies, V. (2003) 'Tools of diplomacy: the language policy of the Foreign and Commonwealth Office and what it means for higher education' in D. Head, E. Jones, M. Kelly and T. Tinsley (eds) *Setting the Agenda for Languages in Higher Education*, London: CILT in association with the Subject Centre for Languages, Linguistics and Area Studies, UCML and SCHML.

—— and Jones, M. R. (2001) 'The European Language Portfolio: a major step on the road to learner autonomy' in J. A. Coleman, D. Ferney, D. Head and R. Rix (eds) *Language Learning Futures: issues and strategies for modern languages provision in higher education*, London: CILT/SCHML.

——, McKenzie, P. and Mozzon-McPherson, M. (2001) 'From learner training to learner development: an analysis of changes in the teacher–learner relationship' in J. Klapper (ed.) *Teaching Languages in Higher Education: issues in training and professional development*, London: CILT.

Decoo, W. (1994) 'In defence of drill and practice in CALL: a re-evaluation of fundamental strategies', Selected Papers from the EUROCALL 93 conference, *Computers and Education*, 23: 151–59.

DELPHI (2002) Website of the DELPHI National Teaching Fellowship project (Development of Language Professionals in Higher Education Institutions). Online. Available at: www.delphi.bham.ac.uk (accessed 14 May 2004).

Diack, H. (1975) *Standard Literacy Tests*, London: Hart-Davis Educational Ltd.

DIALANG (2002) Diagnostic tests. Online. Available at: www.dialang.org (accessed 6 April 2004).

Doble, L. (1999) 'Publishing on the Web', *CALL REVIEW*, March special issue: 3–7.

Dörnyei, Z. (2001) *Teaching and Researching Motivation*, Harlow, Essex: Longman.

—— (2003) 'Attitudes, orientations and motivations in language learning: advances in theory, research and applications', *Language Learning*, 53 SUPP/1: 3–32.

—— and Czisér, K. (1998) 'Ten commandments for motivating language learners: results of an empirical study', *Language Teaching Research*, 2: 203–29.

—— and Ottó, I. (1998) 'Motivation in action: a process model of L2 motivation', *Working Papers in Applied Linguistics* (London: Thames Valley University), 4: 43–69.

Doughty, C. and Williams, J. (eds) (1998) *Focus on Form in Classroom Second Language Acquisition*, Cambridge: Cambridge University Press.

Douglas, D. (2001) *Assessing Languages for Specific Purposes*, Cambridge: Cambridge University Press.

Douglas, M. (1966) *Purity and Danger: an analysis of the concepts of pollution and taboo*, London and New York: Routledge.

Dubin, F. and Olshtain, E. (1986) *Course Design: developing programs and materials for language learning*, Cambridge: Cambridge University Press.

During, S. (ed.) (1993) *The Cultural Studies Reader*, New York: Routledge.

Durrell, M. (2002) *Hammer's German Grammar*, 4th edn, London: Arnold.

Easthope, A. (1991) *Literary into Cultural Studies*, New York: Routledge.

—— and McGowan, K. (eds) (1992) *A Critical and Cultural Theory Reader*, Toronto: University of Toronto Press.

Elias, P. and Purcell, K. (2003) *Measuring Change in the Graduate Labour Market*, Research Paper 1 of the Researching Graduate Careers Seven Years On project. Online. Available at: www2.warwick.ac.uk/fac/soc/ier/research/current/7yrs2/rp1.pdf (accessed 7 June 2004).

Ellis, R. (1989) 'Are classroom and naturalistic acquisition the same? A study of the classroom acquisition of German word order rules', *Studies in Second Language Acquisition*, 11: 305–28.

—— (1990) *Instructed Second Language Acquisition*, Oxford: Blackwell.

—— (1994) *The Study of Second Language Acquisition*, Oxford: Oxford University Press.

—— (1997) *Second Language Acquisition Research and Language Teaching*, Oxford: Oxford University Press.

—— (2002a) 'The place of grammar instruction in the second/foreign language curriculum' in E. Hinkel and S. Fotos (eds) *New Perspectives on Grammar Teaching in Second Language Classrooms*, Mahwah, NJ: Lawrence Erlbaum Associates.

—— (2002b) 'Methodological options in grammar teaching materials' in E. Hinkel and S. Fotos (eds) *New Perspectives on Grammar Teaching in Second Language Classrooms*, Mahwah, NJ: Lawrence Erlbaum Associates.

—— (2003) *Task-based Language Learning and Teaching*, Oxford: Oxford University Press.

Engel, D. and Myles, F. (eds) (1996) *Teaching Grammar: perspectives in higher education*, London: AFLS/CILT.

Esch, E. and Zähner, C. (2000) 'The contribution of Information Communication Technology (ICT) to language learning environments or the mystery of the secret agent', *ReCALL*, 12: 5–18.

EUROCALL (2004) Online. Available at: www.eurocall-languages.org (accessed 12 February 2004).

Evans, C. (1988) *Language People*, Milton Keynes: Open University Press.

Fay, M. (1995) 'Articulating university credits with National Vocational Qualifications: work in progress' in *Proceedings of the 5th National Institution-Wide Languages Programmes Conference*, Nottingham: Nottingham Trent University.

—— (2003) *Learning from Languages*, TransLang Project, Preston: University of Central Lancashire.

—— and Ferney, D. (eds) (2000) *Current Trends in Modern Languages Provision for Non-Specialist Linguists*, London: CILT/APU.

Featherstone, M. (1995) *Undoing Culture: globalization, postmodernism and identity*, London: Sage.

Ferney, D. (2000) 'Introduction' in M. Fay and D. Ferney (eds) *Current Trends in Modern Languages for Non-Specialist Linguists*, London: CILT/APU.

Fisher, L. (2001) 'Modern foreign languages recruitment post-16: the pupils' perspective', *Language Learning Journal*, 23: 33–40.

Flower, L. and Hayes, J. R. (1980) 'The dynamics of composing: making plans and juggling constraints' in L. W. Gregg and E. R. Steinberg (eds) *Cognitive Processes in Writing*, Hillsdale: Lawrence Erlbaum Associates.

Forbes, J. and Kelly, M. (eds) (1995) *French Cultural Studies: an introduction*, Oxford: Oxford University Press.

Forshaw, M. (2000) 'Introduction' in CIEL Project Handbook 5, *Supporting Independent Language Learning: development for learners and teachers* in the Subject Centre for Languages, Linguistics and Area Studies *Good Practice Guide*. Online. Available at: www.lang.ltsn.ac.uk/resources/guidecontents.aspx (accessed 20 June 2004).

Freed, B. (1995) 'What makes us think that students who study abroad become fluent?' in B. Freed (ed.) *Second Language Acquisition in a Study Abroad Context*, Amsterdam: John Benjamins.

Fun With Texts (2004) Online. Available at: www.camsoftpartners.co.uk/fwt.htm (accessed 12 February 2004).

Gapkit (2004) Online. Available at: www.camsoftpartners.co.uk/gapkit.htm (accessed 12 February 2004).

Gardner, G. and Miller, L. (1999) *Establishing Self-Access: from theory to practice*, Cambridge: Cambridge University Press.

Gardner, R. C. (1985) *Social Psychology and Second Language Learning. The role of attitudes and motivation*, London: Edward Arnold.

—— and Lambert, W. E. (1972) *Attitudes and Motivation in Second Language Learning*, Rowley, MA: Newbury House.

—— and MacIntyre, P. D. (1993) 'On the measurement of affective variables in second language learning', *Language Learning*, 43: 157–94.

Garrett, N. (1991) 'CARLA comes to CALL', *Computer-Assisted Language Learning*, 4: 41–45.

Garza, T. (1991) 'Evaluating the use of captioned video materials in advanced language learning', *Foreign Language Annals*, 24: 239–58.

Gauthier, V. (2002) 'The ELP: useful references for teachers', *CercleS Bulletin*, 15: 5–6.

Gilligan, C. (1998) 'The development of learner autonomy in Japanese and other minority languages: the internet and the social nature of learning' in *Proceedings of the Institution-Wide Languages Programmes' 7th National Conference*, Sheffield: Sheffield Hallam University.

Goethals, M. (1992) 'COBUILD, BNC, LET, LCL, Marzano and others. Forging an instrument for vocabulary learning/teaching from word frequency counts, word clusters and other types of vocabulary lists', *ITL Review of Applied Linguistics*, 97–98: 121–58.

Gougenheim, G., Michéa, R., Rivenc, P. and Sauvageot, A. (1964) *L'Élaboration du Français Fondamental*, 2nd edn, Paris: Didier.

GramEx (2002) Online. Available at: www.hull.ac.uk/cti/tell/gramxeng.htm (accessed 12 February 2004).

Gravestock P., Gray, C., Klapper, J. and McCulloch, R. (eds) (2000) *DOPLA Teacher Training Materials*, Birmingham: University of Birmingham.

Gray, C. (2001) 'Training postgraduates and foreign language assistants: the DOPLA approach' in J. Klapper (ed.) *Teaching Languages in Higher Education: issues in training and continuing professional development*, London: CILT.

Grossberg, L., Nelson, C. and Treichler, P. A. (eds) (1992) *Cultural Studies*, New York: Routledge.

Gruneberg, M. (1993) *French Linkword Language System*, London: Corgi.

Hampden-Turner, C. and Trompenaars, F. (2000) *Building Cross-Cultural Competence: how to create wealth from conflicting values*, Chichester: John Wiley and Sons.

Hampel, R. and Hauck, M. (2004) 'Towards an effective use of audio conferencing in distance language courses', *Language Learning and Technology*, 8: 66–82.

Hardisty, D. and Windeatt, S. (1989) *CALL*, Oxford: Oxford University Press.

Hartley, P. D. (1992) 'Language provision for the non-mainstream linguist: the development of institution-wide languages programmes' in J. A. Coleman and G. Parker (eds) *French and the Enterprise Path*, London: CILT.

—— (1994) 'The institution-wide languages programme as preparation for study and work abroad' in D. Ferney (ed.) *Institution-Wide Languages Programmes. Proceedings of the Second National Conference*, Cambridge: Anglia Polytechnic University.

Harvey, L., Moon, S. and Geall, V. (1997) *Graduates' Work: organisational change and students' attributes*, Birmingham: Centre for Research into Quality, University of Central England.

Hatim, B. and Mason, I. (1990) *Discourse and the Translator*, London: Longman.

—— (1997) *The Translator as Communicator*, London and New York: Routledge.

HEA (2004) Website of the Higher Education Academy. Online. Available at: www. heacademy.ac.uk (accessed 5 February 2004).

Hedge, T. (1988) *Writing*, Resource Books for Teachers, Oxford: Oxford University Press.

Hémard, D. and Cushion, S. (2001) 'Evaluation of a web-based language learning environment: the importance of a user-centred design approach for CALL', *ReCALL*, 13: 15–31.

Hinkel, E. and Fotos, S. (eds) (2002) *New Perspectives on Grammar Teaching in Second Language Classrooms*, Mahwah, NJ: Lawrence Erlbaum Associates.

Hofstede, G. (1991) *Cultures and Organisations: software of the mind: intercultural cooperation and its importance for survival*, London: HarperCollins Business.

Horwitz, E. K., Horwitz, M. B. and Cope, J. (1986) 'Foreign language classroom anxiety', *Modern Language Journal*, 70: 125–32.

Howarth, M. (1995) 'The development of EUROQUALIFICATION: aspects of a European-wide language programme' in *Proceedings of the 5th National Institution-Wide Languages Programmes Conference*, Nottingham: Nottingham Trent University.

Howatt, A. P. R. (1984) *A History of English Language Teaching*, Oxford: Oxford University Press.

Hughes, A. (2003) *Testing for Language Teachers*, 2nd edn, Cambridge: Cambridge University Press.

Hunt, M. (2001) 'Principles and theoretical approaches in assessment' in L. Arthur and S. Hurd (eds) *Supporting Lifelong Language Learning*, London: CILT in association with The Open University.

Hurd, S. (2000) 'Helping learners to help themselves: the role of metacognitive skills and strategies in independent language learning' in M. Fay and D. Ferney (eds) *Current Trends in Modern Languages Provision for Non-Specialist Linguists*, London: CILT/APU.

—— (2001) 'Managing and supporting language learners in open and distance learning environments' in M. Mozzon-McPherson and R. Vismans (eds) *Beyond Language Teaching Towards Language Advising*, London: CILT.

——, Beaven, T. and Ortega, A. (2001) 'Developing autonomy in a distance language learning context: issues and dilemmas for course writers', *System*, 3: 341–55.

Huss, M.-M. (1994) 'Building the IWLP team' in D. Ferney (ed.) *Institution-Wide Languages Programmes. Proceedings of the Second National Conference*, Cambridge: Anglia Polytechnic University.

ICT4LT (2000) Information and Communications Technology for Language Teachers. Online. Available at: www.ict4lt.org (accessed 12 February 2004).

Ife, A. (1994) 'Graded language acquisition and the institution-wide languages programme' in D. Ferney (ed.) *Institution-Wide Languages Programmes. Proceedings of the Second National Conference*, Cambridge: Anglia Polytechnic University.

—— and Peña-Calvo, A. (2000) 'Supporting and sustaining language growth during periods of residence abroad' in M. Fay and D. Ferney (eds) *Current Trends in Modern Languages Provision for Non-Specialist Linguists*, London: CILT/APU.

International Phonetic Association (1999) *Handbook of the International Phonetic Association*, Cambridge: Cambridge University Press. Online. Available at: www.arts.gla.ac.uk/IPA/ipa.html (accessed 12 May 2004).

Ioannou-Georgiou, S. (2000) 'Synchronous computer-mediated communication and its potential benefits for language learning'. Talk given at the conference 'Steering the English classroom to the new Millennium', Intercollege, Cyprus.

—— and Michaelides, P. (2001) 'MOOtivating English language learners in pastures new'. Talk given at the 2001 TESOL conference 'Gateway to the Future', St Louis, USA.

Jacobs, G., Rodgers, C. and Watkins, A. (2002) 'Requiem for French literary studies', *Australian Modern Languages Association (AUMLA)*, 98: 1–27.

—— (forthcoming) 'Students and French literature: a case-study', *AUMLA*.

Jahr, V. and Teichler, U. (2002) 'Employment and work of former mobile students' in U. Teichler (ed.) *The ERASMUS Experience. Major findings of the ERASMUS evaluation research*, Luxembourg: Office for Official Publications of the European Community.

James, P. (2000) 'The assessment of transferable skills' in M. Fay and D. Ferney (eds) *Current Trends in Modern Languages Provision for Non-Specialist Linguists*, London: CILT/APU.

Johns, T. and King, P. (eds) (1991) *Classroom Concordancing*, Special issue of *ELR Journal*, 4, University of Birmingham: Centre for English Language Studies.

Johnson, K. (1982) *Communicative Syllabus Design and Methodology*, Oxford: Pergamon.

—— (1996) *Language Teaching and Skill Learning*, Oxford: Blackwell.

Kellerman, E. (1979) 'Transfer and non-transfer: where are we now?', *Studies in Second Language Acquisition*, 2: 37–57.

Kelly, M. and Jones, D. (2003) *A New Landscape for Languages*, London: Nuffield Foundation. Also online. Available at: www.nuffieldfoundation.org/filelibrary/pdf/languages_report_48pp_hires.pdf (accessed 17 May 2004).

Kenning, M.-M. (2000a) 'Corpus-informed syllabus development: parallel concordances and pedagogical grammars' in A. Rouxeville and T. Lewis (eds) *Technology and Language Learning*, London: AFLS/CILT.

—— (2000b) 'Concordancing and comprehension: preliminary observations on using concordance output to predict pitfalls', *ReCALL*, 12: 157–69.

Kern, R. G. (1995) 'Restructuring classroom interaction with networked computers: effects on quality and characteristics of language production', *The Modern Language Journal*, 79: 457–76.

King, A. and Honeybone, A. (2000) 'The language of graduate skills' in A. King (ed.) *Languages and the Transfer of Skills*, London: CILT.

Kingston, B. (2003) 'Top ten retain poll positions', *Times Higher Education Supplement*, 10 October 2003.

Klapper, J. (2001a) (ed.) *Teaching Languages in Higher Education: issues in training and continuing professional development*, London: CILT.

—— (2001b) 'Introduction: professional development in modern languages' in J. Klapper (ed.) *Teaching Languages in Higher Education: issues in training and continuing professional development*, London: CILT.

—— (2002) *DELPHI (Developing Language Professionals in Higher Education Institutions) National Teaching Fellowship Project*. Online (password required). Available at: www.delphi.bham.ac.uk/ (accessed 14 June 2004).

—— (2003a) *Approaches to Assessment*. Online (password required). Available at: www.bham.ac.uk/delphi/private/Module%2015/index13.htm (accessed 14 June 2004).

—— (2003b) *Varieties of Language Testing*. Online (password required). Available at: www.bham.ac.uk/delphi/private/Module%2015/index14.htm (accessed 14 June 2004).

—— (2003c) 'Taking communication to task? A critical review of recent trends in language teaching', *Language Learning Journal*, 27: 4–13.

Klippel, F. (1985) *Keep Talking: communicative fluency activities for language teaching*, Cambridge: Cambridge University Press.

Knight, P. (2001) *A Briefing on Key Concepts*, LTSN Generic Centre Assessment Series No. 7, York: LTSN.

Kolb, D. (1976) *Learning Styles Inventory*, Boston, MA: McBer and Company.

Krashen, S. (1981) *Second Language Acquisition and Second Language Learning*, Oxford: Pergamon.

—— (1982) *Principles and Practice in Second Language Acquisition*, Oxford: Pergamon.

—— (1985) *The Input Hypothesis: issues and implications*, London: Longman.

—— (1989) 'We acquire vocabulary and spelling by reading: additional evidence for the input hypothesis', *Modern Language Journal*, 73: 440–64.

—— and Terrell, T. (1983) *The Natural Approach*, Oxford: Pergamon.

Kreeft, P. J. and French, M. (1996) 'Teaching with text (TWT): computer networks to develop deaf students' English literacy' in M. Warschauer (ed.) *Virtual Connections*, University of Hawaii at Manoa: Second Language Teaching and Curriculum Center.

Lado, R. (1964) *Language Teaching: a scientific approach*, New York: McGraw Hill.

Lamy, M.-N. and Klarskov Mortensen, H. J. (2002) *Using Concordance Programs in the Modern Foreign Languages Classroom*. Online. Available at: www.ict4lt.org/en/en_mod2-4.htm (accessed 21 May 2004).

Languages Subject Centre (2003a) Website of the Subject Centre for Languages, Linguistics and Area Studies. Online. Available at: www.lang.ltsn.ac.uk (accessed 5 February 2004).

—— (2003b) Subject Centre for Languages, Linguistics and Area Studies, *Good Practice Guide*. Online. Available at: www.lang.ltsn.ac.uk/resources/guidecontents.aspx (accessed 5 February 2004).

—— (2003c) Subject Centre for Languages, Linguistics and Area Studies, *The Materials Bank*. Online. Available at: www.lang.ltsn.ac.uk/resources/bankcontents.aspx (accessed 5 February 2004).

Larsen-Freeman, D. (2000) *Techniques and Principles in Language Teaching*, 2nd edn, Oxford: Oxford University Press.

Leconte, M.-O. (1995) 'Staff development and the training of part-time tutors' in *Proceedings of the 5th National Institution-Wide Languages Programmes Conference*, Nottingham: Nottingham Trent University.

Lenneberg, E. (1967) *Biological Foundations of Language*, New York: Wiley.

Lepschy, A.-L. and Lepschy, G. (1988) *The Italian Language Today*, London: Routledge.

Levy, M. (1997) *Computer-assisted Language Learning: context and conceptualization*, Oxford: Oxford University Press.

Lewis, T., Walker, L. and Stickler, U. (2000) 'Do it yourself: the role of autonomy in the preparation of non-specialist language learners for residence abroad' in M. Fay and D. Ferney (eds) *Current Trends in Modern Languages Provision for Non-Specialist Linguists*, London: CILT/APU.

Little, D. (1991) *Learner Autonomy 1: Definitions, Issues and Problems*, Dublin: Authentik.

—— (2000) 'Learner autonomy and human interdependence: some theoretical and practical consequences of a social-interactive view of cognition, learning and language' in B. Sinclair, I. Mcgrath and T. Lamb (eds) *Learner Autonomy, Teacher Autonomy: new directions*, Harlow: Longman.

—— (2001) 'How independent can independent language learning really be?' in J. A. Coleman, D. Ferney, D. Head and R. Rix (eds) *Language Learning Futures: issues and strategies for modern languages provision in higher education*, London: CILT/SCHML.

—— (2003a) 'Learner autonomy and second/foreign language learning' in the Subject Centre for Languages, Linguistics and Area Studies *Good Practice Guide*. Online. Available at: www.lang.ltsn.ac.uk/resources/goodpractice.aspx?resourceid=1409 (accessed 20 June 2004).

—— (2003b) 'Tandem language learning and learner autonomy' in T. Lewis and L. Walker (eds) *Autonomous Language Learning in Tandem*, Sheffield: Academy Electronic Publications.

—— and Perclová, R. (2001) *European Language Portfolio Guide for Teachers and Teacher Trainers*, Strasbourg: Council of Europe.

—— and Ushioda, E. (1998) *Institution-wide Language Programmes: a research-and-development approach to their design, implementation and evaluation*, London: CILT, in association with The Centre for Language and Communication Studies, Trinity College Dublin.

Littlejohn, A. (1998) 'The analysis of language teaching materials: inside the Trojan horse' in B. Tomlinson (ed.) *Materials Development in Language Teaching*, Cambridge: Cambridge University Press.

Littlewood, W. T. (1984) *Foreign and Second Language Learning*, Cambridge: Cambridge University Press.

Lodge, R. A. (1993) *French. From Dialect to Standard*, London: Routledge.

Loftus, G. and Loftus, G. (1992) *TV und Texte*, Oxford: Oxford University Press.

Long, D. R. (1990) 'What you don't know can't help you: an exploratory study of background knowledge and second language listening comprehension', *Studies in Second Language Acquisition*, 12: 65–80.

Long, M. (1991) 'Focus on form: a design feature in language teaching methodology' in K. de Bot, R. Ginsberg, and C. Kramsch (eds) *Foreign Language Research in Cross-cultural Perspective*, Cambridge: Cambridge University Press.

Luoma, S. (2004) *Assessing Speaking*, Cambridge: Cambridge University Press.

Lyne, C. (1995) 'Incorporating peer-teaching observation into a staff development programme' in *Proceedings of the 5th National Institution-wide Languages Programmes Conference*, Nottingham: Nottingham Trent University.

McBride, N. (2000) 'Studying culture in language degrees in the UK: target culture – target language? A survey' in N. McBride and K. Seago (eds) *Target Culture – Target Language?*, London: AFLS/CILT.

McCarthy, B. (1996) 'Fully integrated CALL: mission accomplished', *ReCALL*, 8: 17–34.

McDonough, J. and Shaw, C. (1993) *Materials and Methods in ELT*, London: Blackwell.

MacIntyre, P. D., Baker, S. C., Clément, R. and Donovan, L. A. (2003) 'Talking in order to learn: willingness to communicate and intensive language programs', *Canadian Modern Language Review*, 59: 589–607.

——, Clément, R., Dörnyei, Z. and Noels, K. A. (1998) 'Conceptualizing willingness to communicate in a L2: a situational model of L2 confidence and affiliation', *Modern Language Journal*, 82: 545–62.

McLaughlin, B. (1987) *Theories of Second Language Acquisition*, London: Edward Arnold.

—— (1990) 'Restructuring', *Applied Linguistics*, 11: 113–28.

Malmkjaer, K. (ed.) (1998) *Translation and Language Teaching*, Manchester: St Jerome.

Marshall, K. (2001) *Survey of Less Specialist Language Learning in UK Universities*. Online. Available at: www.lang.ltsn.ac.uk/resources/resourcesitem.aspx?resourceid=614 (accessed 7 June 2004).

Meara, P. (1994) 'What should language graduates be able to do?', *Language Learning Journal*, 9: 36–40.

Millan, C. (2002) *Using Translation in the Language Classroom*. Online (password required). Available at: www.bham.ac.uk/delphi/private/Module%203/index3.htm (accessed 29 April 2004).

Milroy, J. and Milroy, L. (1991) *Authority in Language*, 2nd edn, London: Routledge and Kegan Paul.

Milton, J. and Meara, P. (1995) 'How periods abroad affect vocabulary growth in a foreign language', *ITL Review of Applied Linguistics*, 107/108: 17–34.

Milton, K. (1996) *Environmentalism and Cultural Theory: exploring the role of anthropology in environmental discourse*, London and New York: Routledge.

Mitchell, R. (2003) 'Rationales for foreign language education in the 21st century' in S. Sarangi and T. van Leeuwen (eds) *Applied Linguistics and Communities of Practice*, London: Continuum.

—— and Myles, F. (1998) *Second Language Learning Theories*, London: Arnold.

Morley, J. and Truscott, S. (2001) 'The quantity and quality of corrective feedback on a tandem learning module' in J. A. Coleman, D. Ferney, D. Head and R. Rix (eds) *Language Learning Futures: issues and strategies for modern languages provision in higher education*, London: CILT/SCHML.

Moys, A. (ed.) (1998) *Where Are We Going with Languages?*, London: Nuffield Foundation.

Mozzon-McPherson, M. (2002) 'Language advising' in the Subject Centre for Languages, Linguistics and Area Studies *Good Practice Guide*. Online. Available at: www.lang.ltsn. ac.uk/resources/goodpractice.aspx?resourceid=93 (accessed 20 June 2004).

Nagy, W. and Anderson, R. (1984) 'How many words are there in printed school English?', *Reading Research Quarterly*, 19: 304–30.

——, Anderson, R. and Herman, P. (1989) 'Learning word meanings from context during normal reading', *American Educational Research Journal*, 24: 237–70.

Naiman, N., Frohlich, M., Stern, H. and Tedesco, H. (1975) *The Good Language Learner*, Toronto: Ontario Institute for Studies in Education.

NALA (1999) *Effective Teaching in Modern Foreign Languages*, London: NALA.

Nation, P. (ed.) (1994) *New Ways in Teaching Vocabulary*, Alexandria, Virginia: TESOL Inc.
—— (2001) *Learning Vocabulary in Another Language*, Cambridge: Cambridge University Press.
Neu, H. and Reeser, T. W. (1997) *Parle-moi un peu!: Information Gap Activities for Beginning French Classes*, Boston, MA: Heinle and Heinle.
Newson, D. (1998) 'Translation and foreign language learning' in K. Malmjkær (ed.) *Translation and Language Teaching*, Manchester: St Jerome.
Nolasco, R. and Arthur, L. (1987) *Conversation*, Resource Books for Teachers, Oxford: Oxford University Press.
Nott, D. (2002) 'Translation from and into the foreign language' in the Subject Centre for Languages, Linguistics and Area Studies *Good Practice Guide*. Online. Available at: www.lang.ltsn.ac.uk/resources/goodpractice.aspx?resourceid=427 (accessed 19 June 2004).
Nuffield Languages Inquiry (2000) *Languages: the next generation. The final report and recommendations of the Nuffield Languages Inquiry*, London: The Nuffield Foundation.
Nunan, D. (1989) *Designing Tasks for the Communicative Classroom*, Cambridge: Cambridge University Press.
—— (1996) 'Towards autonomous learning: some theoretical, empirical and practical issues' in R. Pemberton, E. Li, W. Or and H. Pierson (eds) *Taking Control: autonomy in language learning*, Hong Kong: Hong Kong University Press.
—— (1999) *Second Language Teaching and Learning*, Boston, MA: Newbury House.
Nuttall, C. (1996) *Teaching Reading Skills in a Foreign Language*, 2nd edn, London: Macmillan Heinemann.
O'Leary, C. (1998) 'Developing a specialist lexis and register in the higher stages of an IWLP: a student's perspective' in *Proceedings of the Institution-Wide Languages Programmes' 7th National Conference*, Sheffield: Sheffield Hallam University.
—— (2000) 'Developing a specialist lexis and register in the higher stages of an IWLP: a teacher's perspective' in M. Fay and D. Ferney (eds) *Current Trends in Modern Languages Provision for Non-Specialist Linguists*, London: CILT/APU.
—— and Drew, F. (1995) 'Developing a specialist lexis and register in the higher stages of an IWLP' in *Proceedings of the 5th National Institution-wide Languages Programmes Conference*, Nottingham: Nottingham Trent University.
Olk, H. (2001) 'Language Students and the Translation of Culture: a psycho-linguistic investigation into the translation of culture-specific lexis by degree-level language students of English and German', unpublished PhD, Canterbury: Christ Church University College.
O'Malley, J. M. and Chamot, A. U. (1990) *Learning Strategies in Second Language Acquisition*, Cambridge: Cambridge University Press.
——, —— and Kupper, L. (1989) 'Listening comprehension strategies in second language acquisition', *Applied Linguistics*, 10: 418–37.
Open University (1998) *Supporting Language Learning: a handbook for associate lecturers*, Milton Keynes: The Open University.
—— (2002) *Learning with the OU: your guide to OU study*. Online. Available at: www.open.ac.uk/learning/induction/undergraduate/index.htm (accessed 22 February 2004).
—— (2003) *A Learner's Guide to the OU*. Online. Available at: www.open.ac.uk/learners-guide (accessed 22 February 2004).
—— (ongoing) *Open Teaching Toolkits*, Milton Keynes: The Open University.
Open University Institute of Educational Technology (1999) *H851 Teaching in Higher Education Practice Guide: teaching foreign/second languages*, Milton Keynes: The Open University.

Oxford, R. (1990) *Language Learning Strategies: what every teacher should know*, New York: Newbury House.

—— (1999) 'Anxiety and the language learner: new insights' in J. Arnold (ed.) *Affect in Language Learning*, Cambridge: Cambridge University Press.

—— and Shearin, J. (1994) 'Language learning motivation: expanding the theoretical framework', *Modern Language Journal*, 78: 12–28.

Pachler, N. (1999) (ed.) *Teaching Modern Foreign Languages at Advanced Level*, London: Routledge.

—— (2000) 'Secondary education' in M. Byram (ed.) *Encyclopedia of Language Teaching and Learning*, London: RoutledgeFalmer.

—— (2001) 'Those who can, teach? Issues and challenges in the recruitment, training and retention of teachers of German in the United Kingdom', *German as a Foreign Language*, 2: 60–92. Online. Available at: www.gfl-journal.de/downloads/2-2001/pachler.pdf (accessed 17 May 2004).

—— (2002) 'Foreign language learning in England in the 21st century', *Language Learning Journal*, 25: 4–7.

——, Norman, N. and Field, K. (1999) 'A "new" approach to language study', *Studies in Modern Languages Education*, 7: 1–33.

Parkes, G. (1992) 'Intégration horizontale ou profession: enseignant. Comment être généraliste', in J. A. Coleman and A. Rouxeville (eds) *Integrating New Approaches. The teaching of French in higher education*, London: AFLS/CILT.

Partington, J. (1998) *The Induction of Foreign Language Assistants to Universities and Colleges in the UK: a training manual*, Sheffield: UCoSDA.

Pattison, P. (1987) *Developing Communication Skills: a practical handbook for language teachers, with examples in English, French and German*, Cambridge: Cambridge University Press.

Pemberton, R. (1996) 'Introduction' in R. Pemberton, E. Li, W. Or and H. Pierson (eds) *Taking Control: autonomy in language learning*, Hong Kong: Hong Kong University Press.

Perez, I. (2002) 'Interpreting' in the Subject Centre for Languages, Linguistics and Area Studies *Good Practice Guide*. Online. Available at: www.lang.ltsn.ac.uk/resources/good practice.aspx?resourceid=316 (accessed 19 June 2004).

Phillips, H. (2000) 'Consolidation of non-specialist courses with provision for specialist language students: moving towards one language provision' in M. Fay and D. Ferney (eds) *Current Trends in Modern Languages Provision for Non-Specialist Linguists*, London: CILT/APU.

Phillips-Kerr, B. (1991) *Survey of Career Destinations: 1985 modern language graduates of the Universities of Bradford, Hull, Newcastle upon Tyne, Sheffield and the Polytechnic of Newcastle upon Tyne*, University of Newcastle upon Tyne, Careers Advisory Service.

Phipps, A. and Gonzalez, M. (2004) *Modern Languages: learning and teaching in an intercultural field*, London: Sage.

Pienemann, M. (1984) 'Psychological constraints on the teachability of languages', *Studies in Second Language Acquisition*, 6: 186–214.

Pilkington, R. (1997) *Survey of Non-Specialist Language Provision in Further and Higher Education Institutions in the United Kingdom*, FDTL TransLang Project, Preston: University of Central Lancashire. Summary online. Available at: www.uclan.ac.uk/facs/class/languages/translang/tlweb.htm (accessed 19 June 2004).

—— (ed.) (2000) *The Translang Guide to Transferable Skills in Non-Specialist Language Learning: a guide for practitioners*, FDTL TransLang Project, Preston: University of Central Lancashire.

Pressley, M., Levin, J., Hall, J., Miller, G. and Berry, J. (1980) 'The keyword method and foreign language acquisition', *Journal of Experimental Psychology: Human Learning and Memory*, 6: 163–73.

Prospects (2002) Online. Available at: www.prospects.ac.uk/cms/ShowPage/Home_page/ What_do_graduates_do__2004/charts_and_tables_pages/p!edXLFe?subject_id=20 (accessed 19 June 2004).

Purpura, J. (2004) *Assessing Grammar*, Cambridge: Cambridge University Press.

QAA (2002) *Subject Benchmark Statement: Languages and related studies*, Quality Assurance Agency for Higher Education. Online. Available at: www.qaa.ac.uk/crntwork/bench mark/phase2/languages.pdf (accessed 7 June 2004).

QCA (2000) *GCSE Criteria for Modern Foreign Languages*, London: QCA. Online. Available at: www.qca.org.uk/nq/framework/modern_foreign_lang.pdf (accessed 17 May 2004).

——, ACCAC and CCEA (1999) *GCE Advanced Subsidiary and Advanced Level Specifications Subject Criteria for Modern Foreign Languages*, London: QCA. Online. Available at: www. qca.org.uk/nq/subjects/mfl.asp (accessed 17 May 2004).

Race, P. (2001a) *The Lecturer's Toolkit: a practical guide to learning, teaching and assessment*, 2nd edn, London: Kogan Page.

—— (2001b) *A Briefing on Self-, Peer and Group Assessment*, LTSN Generic Centre Assessment Series No 9, York: LTSN.

Rand, D. and Sankoff, D. (1990) 'GoldVarb. A Variable Rule Application for the Macintosh'. Online. Available at: www.crm.umontreal.ca/~sankoff/GoldVarb_Eng.html (accessed 12 May 2004).

Read, J. (2000) *Assessing Vocabulary*, Cambridge: Cambridge University Press.

Reid, J. (1997) 'The learning style preferences of ESL students', *TESOL Quarterly*, 21: 87–111.

Reimann, N. (2001) 'Dropping out, opting out or staying in: reasons for continuation and non-continuation of German on an institution-wide languages programme' in J. A. Coleman, D. Ferney, D. Head and R. Rix (eds) *Language Learning Futures: issues and strategies for modern languages provision in higher education*, London: CILT/SCHML.

Rézeau, J. (2004) 'Data-driven learning page'. Online. Available at: www.uhb.fr/campus/ joseph.rezeau/concord.htm (accessed 21 May 2004).

Rinvolucri, M. (1984) *Grammar Games*, Cambridge: Cambridge University Press.

Roberts, A. and Shaw, J. (1998) 'Autonomous learners or automatons: learning for life on the IWLP' in *Proceedings of the Institution-Wide Languages Programmes' 7th National Conference*, Sheffield: Sheffield Hallam University.

Roberts, C., Byram, M., Barro, A., Jordan, S. and Street, B. (2001) *Language Learners as Ethnographers*, Clevedon: Multilingual Matters.

Roberts, J. (1998) *Language Teacher Education*, London: Arnold.

Robinson, J. S., Lawrence, H. R. and Tagliamonte, S. A. (2001) 'GOLDVARB 2001: A multivariate analysis application for Windows'. Online. Available at: www.york.ac. uk/depts/lang/webstuff/goldvarb (accessed 12 May 2004).

Rodgers, C., Jacobs, G. and Watkins, A. (2002) 'Requiem for French literary studies', *AUMLA*, 98: 1–27.

Rodríguez, M. and Sadoski M. (2000) 'Effects of rote, context, keyword and context/ keyword methods on retention of vocabulary in EFL classrooms', *Language Learning*, 50: 385–412.

Rothwell, L. (1995) 'Improving the effectiveness and efficiency of the management of part-time tutors' in *Proceedings of the 5th National Institution-wide Languages Programmes Conference*, Nottingham: Nottingham Trent University.

Rowntree, D. (1990) *Teaching through Self-Instruction: how to develop open learning materials*, London: Kogan Page.

Rubin, J. (1975) 'What the "good language learner" can teach us', *TESOL Quarterly*, 9: 41–51.

Russ, C. V. J. (1994) *The German Language Today*, London: Routledge.

Rutherford, W. (1987) *Second Language Grammar: learning and teaching*, London: Longman.

Sage, J. and Stanbridge, P. (2000) 'Language – a critical business in the internet age', *European Business Forum*, 2 (Summer): 71–73.

Saskatchewan Education (1988) *Understanding the Common Essential Learnings: a handbook for teachers*, Regina, SK: Saskatchewan Education. Online. Available at: www.sasked.gov.sk.ca/docs/policy/cels (accessed 20 June 2004).

Savignon, S. (1991) 'Communicative language teaching: state of the art', *TESOL Quarterly*, 25: 261–77.

Schmidt, R. (1990) 'The role of consciousness in second language learning', *Applied Linguistics*, 11: 17–46.

Scott, M. (1996) *Wordsmith Tools 3.0*, Oxford: Oxford University Press.

Selinker, L. (1972) 'Interlanguage', *International Review of Applied Linguistics*, 10: 209–31.

Sewell, P. (2002) 'Hidden merits of the translation class' in Languages Subject Centre *Good Practice Guide*. Online. Available at: www.lang.ltsn.ac.uk/resources/goodpractice.aspx?resourceid=1433 (accessed 19 June 2004).

—— and Higgins, I. (1996) *Teaching Translation in Universities*, London: AFLS/CILT.

Sheerin, S. (1989) *Self-Access*, Oxford: Oxford University Press.

Sinclair, B. (2000) 'Learner autonomy: the next phase?' in B. Sinclair, I. Mcgrath and T. Lamb (eds) *Learner Autonomy, Teacher Autonomy: new directions*, Harlow: Longman.

Singleton, D. (1999) *Exploring the Second Language Mental Lexicon*, Cambridge: Cambridge University Press.

Skehan, P. (1989) *Individual Differences in Second-Language Learning*, London: Edward Arnold.

—— (1996) 'A framework for the implementation of task based instruction', *Applied Linguistics*, 17: 38–62.

—— (1998) *A Cognitive Approach to Language Learning*, Oxford: Oxford University Press.

Skinner, B. F. (1957) *Verbal Behaviour*, New York: Appleton Crofts.

Spada, N. (1997) 'Form-focussed instruction and second language acquisition: a review of classroom and laboratory research', *Language Teaching*, 30: 73–87.

Stern, H. H. (1983) *Fundamental Concepts of Language Teaching*, Oxford: Oxford University Press.

—— (1990) 'Analysis and experience as variables in second language pedagogy' in B. Harley, P. Allen, J. Cummins and M. Swain (eds) *The Development of Second Language Proficiency*, Cambridge: Cambridge University Press.

Stewart, E. (1995) 'The IWLP: bureaucratic nightmare, technocratic paradise or curricular necessity?' in *Proceedings of the 5th National Institution-wide Languages Programmes Conference*, Nottingham: Nottingham Trent University.

Stewart, M. (1999) *The Spanish Language Today*, London: Routledge.

Stickler, U. (2001) 'Using counselling skills for language advising' in M. Mozzon-McPherson and R. Vismans (eds) *Beyond Language Teaching: towards language advising*, London: Centre for Information on Language Teaching and Research.

—— (in press) '". . . and furthermore I will correct your mistakes": kulturelle Unterschiede bei der Fehlerkorrektur im Tandem', *Theorie und Praxis: Österreichische Beiträge zu Deutsch als Fremdsprache*, Innsbruck.

——, Lewis, T. and Speight, R. (1999) 'Taking students seriously: the use of self-assessment and peer-assessment on a university-wide language programme' in D. Bickerton and M. Gotti (eds) *Language Centres: integration through innovation*, Plymouth: Cercles.

Sturtridge, G. (1997) 'Teaching and language learning in self-access centres: changing roles?' in P. Benson and P. Voller (eds) *Autonomy and Independence in Language Learning*, London: Longman.

Swain, M. (1995) 'Three functions of output in second language learning' in G. Cook and B. Seidlhofer (eds) *Principle and Practice in Applied Linguistics*, Oxford: Oxford University Press.

Tarone, E. (1988) *Variation in Interlanguage*, London: Edward Arnold.

Teichler, U. (1997) *The ERASMUS Experience. Major findings of the ERASMUS evaluation research*, Luxembourg: Office for Official Publications of the European Community.

—— (ed.) (2002) *ERASMUS in the SOCRATES Programme. Findings of an evaluation study*, Bonn: Lemmens.

Temple, R. A. M. (2001) 'The interaction between speaker sex and changes in regional patterns of voicing in metropolitan French: a case of over-levelling?' in M.-A. Hintze, A. Judge and T. Pooley (eds) *French Accents: phonological and sociolinguistic perspectives*, London: CILT/AFLS.

Thomas, G. (1993) *Survey of European Languages in the United Kingdom 1992*, London: CNAA.

Thomas, R. (2001) 'Interview', *The Independent (Business Review)*, 25 April: 4.

Thornberry, S. (1996) 'Teachers research teacher talk', *ELT Journal*, 50: 279–89.

Tomlinson, B. (2000) 'Access-self materials' in B. Tomlinson (ed.) *Materials Development in Language Teaching*, Cambridge: Cambridge University Press.

Torgersen, E. N. (2002) 'Phonological distribution of the FOOT vowel, /U/, in young people's speech in south-eastern British English', *Reading Working Papers in Linguistics*, 6: 25–38.

Towell, R. and Hawkins, R. (1994) *Approaches to Second Language Acquisition*, Clevedon: Multilingual Matters.

Tudor, I. (1996) *Learner-centredness as Language Education*, Cambridge: Cambridge University Press.

Underhill, N. (1987) *Testing Spoken Language: a handbook of oral testing techniques*, Cambridge: Cambridge University Press.

University of Hull (2003) Postgraduate Certificate in Advising for Language Learning. Online. Available at: www.hull.ac.uk/languages/prospective/courses/pg/langlearn/index.html (accessed 5 February 2004).

University of Manchester (2002) *Policy on Independent Language Learning*. Online. Available at: www.langcent.man.ac.uk/ill/illpolicy.doc (accessed 20 June 2004).

Ur, P. (1981) *Discussions that Work*, Cambridge: Cambridge University Press.

—— (1998) *Grammar Practice Activities*, Cambridge: Cambridge University Press.

—— and Wright, A. (1992) *Five Minute Activities: a resource book of short activities*, Cambridge: Cambridge University Press.

Vanderplank, R. (1988) 'The value of teletext subtitles in language learning', *ELT Journal*, 42: 272–81.

Van Lier, L. (1996) *Interaction in the Language Curriculum: awareness, autonomy and authenticity*, London and New York: Longman.

Victori, R. M. (1992) 'Investigating the Metacognitive Knowledge of Students of English as a Second Language', unpublished Masters thesis, University of California.

Vilmi, R. (2000) *Collaborative Writing Projects on the Internet*. Online. Available at: www. ruthvilmi.net/hut/Project (accessed 8 August 2003).

Virtual Language Centre of Hong Kong (2004) *Web Concordancer*. Online. Available at: www.edict.com.hk/concordance/default.htm (accessed 21 May 2004).

Vygotsky, L. S. (1978) *Mind in Society: the development of higher psychological processes*, Cambridge, MA: Harvard University Press.

Wajnryb, R. (1990) *Grammar Dictation*, Oxford: Oxford University Press.

Walker, L. (2001) 'Collaboration and the role of learner strategies in promoting second language acquisition in tandem learning partnerships' in J. A. Coleman, D. Ferney, D. Head and R. Rix (eds) *Language Learning Futures: issues and strategies for modern languages provision in higher education*, London: CILT/SCHML.

—— (2003) 'The role of the tandem learner diary in supporting and developing learner autonomy' in T. Lewis and L. Walker (eds) *Autonomous Language Learning in Tandem*, Sheffield: Academy Electronic Publications.

Warschauer, M. (1995) *E-mail for English Teaching*, Alexandria, VA: TESOL Inc.

—— (1996) 'Comparing face-to-face and electronic discussion in the second language classroom', *CALICO Journal*, 13: 7–26.

——, Shetzer, H. and Meloni, C. (2000) *Internet for English Teaching*, Alexandria, VA: TESOL Inc.

Weigle, S. C. (2002) *Assessing Writing*, Cambridge: Cambridge University Press.

Weinmann, S. (1996) 'Know before you go! Using internet resources in a pre-departure orientation for study or work abroad' in M. Warschauer (ed.) *Virtual Connections*, University of Hawaii at Manoa: Second Language Teaching and Curriculum Center.

Wenden, A. (1991) *Learner Strategies for Learner Autonomy*, Hemel Hempstead: Prentice Hall.

West, J. (2001) 'German grammar pages'. Online. Available at: www.staff.ncl.ac.uk/jon. west/nhggr/nhggr_valency_data.htm (accessed 31 May 2004).

White, C. (1994) 'Language learning strategy research in distance education: the yoked subject technique', *Research in Distance Education*, 3: 10–20.

—— (2003) *Language Learning in Distance Education*, Cambridge: Cambridge University Press.

White, G. (1998) *Listening*, Resource Books for Teachers, Oxford: Oxford University Press.

White, R. and Arndt, V. (1991) *Process Writing*, London: Longman.

Wida Authoring Suite (2004). Online. Available at: www.wida.co.uk/noframes/auth.htm (accessed 12 February 2004).

Willis, D. (1996) 'Introduction' in J. Willis and D. Willis (eds) *Challenge and Change in Language Teaching*, Oxford: Macmillan Heinemann.

Willis, J. (1996) *A Framework for Task-based Learning*, Harlow: Longman.

Willis, J. and Willis, D. (eds) (1996) *Challenge and Change in Language Teaching*, Oxford: Macmillan Heinemann.

Woodin, J. and Lewis, T. (1995) 'Staff development on an institution-wide languages programme' in *Proceedings of the 5th National Institution-wide Languages Programmes Conference*, Nottingham: Nottingham Trent University.

Wyburd, J. (2002) *PORTAL, National Teaching Fellowship Project*. Online. Available at: www.langcent.man.ac.uk/staff/portal.htm (accessed 5 February 2004).

Zechmeister, E., d'Anna, C., Hall, J., Paus, C. and Smith, J. (1993) 'Metacognitive and other knowledge about the mental lexicon: do we know how many words we know?', *Applied Linguistics*, 14: 188–206.

Zeichner, K. M. and Liston, D. P. (1996) *Reflective Teaching: an introduction*, Mahwah, NJ: Lawrence Erlbaum Associates.

Index

eBooks – at www.eBookstore.tandf.co.uk

A library at your fingertips!

eBooks are electronic versions of printed books. You can store them on your PC/laptop or browse them online.

They have advantages for anyone needing rapid access to a wide variety of published, copyright information.

eBooks can help your research by enabling you to bookmark chapters, annotate text and use instant searches to find specific words or phrases. Several eBook files would fit on even a small laptop or PDA.

NEW: Save money by eSubscribing: cheap, online access to any eBook for as long as you need it.

Annual subscription packages

We now offer special low-cost bulk subscriptions to packages of eBooks in certain subject areas. These are available to libraries or to individuals.

For more information please contact webmaster.ebooks@tandf.co.uk

We're continually developing the eBook concept, so keep up to date by visiting the website.

www.eBookstore.tandf.co.uk